SOUND BARRIER

SOUND BARRIER

The Rocky Road to Mach 1.0+

Peter Caygill

Pen & Sword
AVIATION

First published in Great Britain in 2006 by
Pen & Sword Aviation
an imprint of
Pen & Sword Books Ltd
47 Church Street
Barnsley
South Yorkshire
S70 2AS

Copyright © Peter Caygill, 2006

ISBN 1 84415 456 4
978 1 84415 456 2

The right of Peter Caygill to be identified as Author of this Work has
been asserted by him in accordance with the Copyright, Designs and
Patents Act 1988.

A CIP catalogue record for this book is
available from the British Library

Printed and bound in England by
Biddles, King's Lynn

Pen & Sword Books Ltd incorporates the imprints of Pen & Sword Aviation,
Pen & Sword Maritime, Pen & Sword Military, Wharncliffe Local History,
Pen & Sword Select, Pen & Sword Military Classics and Leo Cooper.

For a complete list of Pen & Sword titles please contact
PEN & SWORD BOOKS LIMITED
47 Church Street, Barnsley, South Yorkshire, S70 2AS, England
E-mail: enquiries@pen-and-sword.co.uk
Website: www.pen-and-sword.co.uk

Contents

Introduction vii

1   The Pioneers 1

2   A Quest for Speed 11

3   Trouble Ahead 20

4   Problems with Compressibility 29

5   Early Allied Jets 45

6   Jet and Rocket Engine Development 56

7   Germany Shows the Way 64

8   Meteoric Records 79

8   The Miles M.52 Fiasco 89

10 The Barrier is Broken 103

11 Flying the DH.108 115

12 Fighter Development in the USSR and France 126

13 The USA Forges Ahead 145

14 Britain Lags Behind 159

15 Better Late Than Never 189

Glossary 202

Bibliography 204

Index 206

Introduction

On 11 August 1954 English Electric P.1 WG760 was being flown on its third flight out of Boscombe Down by Roland Beamont, chief test pilot of the Warton-based company. Having levelled off at 30,000 feet over the English Channel near Poole, Beamont opened the throttles and watched as the pointer on the Machmeter showed a steady increase in speed before coming to a halt at 0.98M. With no apparent increase in speed after nearly two minutes the throttles were closed and a return was made to base. As Beamont headed back to Boscombe Down he was completely unaware that he had become the first pilot to fly supersonically in level flight in a British-built aircraft; significant position error having accounted for the non-appearance of the magic figure of 1.0 on the cockpit display. During the period of acceleration no buffeting had been experienced, neither had there been any undesirable trim changes to worry the pilot. In fact, breaking the so-called 'sound barrier' had proved to be a complete non-event.

This was all in marked contrast to what had gone before. The spectre of compressibility began to have a significant effect on the progress of aviation in the mid 1930s when the new stressed-skin monoplanes, featuring retractable undercarriages, variable pitch propellers and piston engines of increased power, first began to suffer from violent buffeting, control problems and a lack of controllability as localised airflows reached the speed of sound. The advent of the jet engine, which offered even greater levels of power, had the effect of raising the stakes a good deal higher and the myth of an impenetrable barrier began to take hold. Of course this did not stop extremely brave pilots from attempting to fly at sonic speeds but if they tried too hard the only thing they were going to achieve was to rearrange part of the earth's scenery as they dived straight into the ground. What was needed was a radical rethink on the form an aircraft was to take if it was to fly faster than sound.

The swept wing, which was to play a big part in delaying the effects of compressibility, had been put forward as a means of allowing aircraft to fly faster even before the Second World War had begun. Under the stimulus of a country fighting for its very survival, the basic theory was turned into practice by the various research institutions in Germany so that by the end of the war the German aircraft industry was far in advance of any other. With the cessation of hostilities, however, all this secret work was then plundered by the advancing Allied forces with research data, together with anyone who had been involved in advanced weapons projects, being spread between east and west. This led to an explosion of activity in all the leading aeronautical nations, with the notable exception of Britain who thought it was much better to forget about manned supersonic flight and concentrate on radio controlled models instead.

Within two and a half years of the end of the war Chuck Yeager had flown supersonically in the rocket-powered Bell XS-1 and the first swept-wing fighter for the USAF, the F-86 Sabre, which was supersonic in a dive, had been flown in prototype form. In the Soviet Union the forerunner of the MiG-15 was flown for the first time in December 1947 and this aircraft led to a family of interceptors, all of which extended the boundaries of performance with each succeeding generation. By the time that Roland Beamont took the P.1 above Mach 1.0 in August 1954 the USAF already had the Mach 1.3 capable F-100 Super Sabre in service and the equivalent MiG-19 was almost ready for its introduction with the Soviet Air Force. Even France, which had had to start from scratch in 1945, was catching up fast with the Super Mystere II and the delta-winged Mirage nearing their first flights. By the mid-1950s the perils involved in flying faster than the speed of sound were a thing of the past and designers were already looking to Mach 2.0 and beyond.

This book looks at the period leading up to that time and highlights the difficulties for designers and test pilots alike. From the very first occasions when compressibility was encountered during terminal velocity dives in piston-engined fighters, to the eventual goal of achieving supersonic flight in rocket and jet-powered aircraft, the quest for the holy grail of aviation is recorded in graphic detail. Along the way many pilots were to die in their endeavour to be the first through the 'sound barrier' and there were also to be a number of missed opportunities which, if they had been taken, may have rewritten the history books.

Although the prime reason for all this feverish activity was to achieve some measure of dominance over rival air forces, there was to be a spin-off in commercial aviation with the development of the incomparable Anglo-French Concorde. It is to be hoped that the untimely demise of this aircraft does not mean the end of supersonic passenger flight and that when a new generation of SST eventually takes to the air, the pioneers who gave their lives to the cause of aeronautical progress will be remembered.

CHAPTER ONE

The Pioneers

W hen Orville Wright made the first powered flight by a heavier-than-air machine at Kill Devil Hills, Kitty Hawk, North Carolina on 17 December 1903 he set in motion a train of events that would lead to the aeroplane achieving dominance both as a weapon of war and as a means of transport. This order of things was anything but clear cut, however, so that even the most informed observers at the time can be forgiven if they considered that the seemingly frail-looking contraption created by the Wright brothers would be anything more than just a curiosity. For the aeroplane to be accepted it had to be able to carry out useful work which meant that it had to fly faster, further and carry a worthwhile payload, or perform a duty that no other machine could do. With the exception of the Wrights who made excellent progress with their developments of the original Flyer, the vast majority of the pioneers who followed their example were fortunate if their machines actually made it into the air at all.

It was the invention of the internal combustion engine that provided the means by which sustained flight could be contemplated; previously, much experimenting had been carried out with gliders. Initially, Europe led the way following the inspired work of Sir George Cayley who was the first to establish aeronautics as a science and was to discard the flapping wing in favour of fixed wings. The culmination of Cayley's research was his man-carrying glider of 1853 which successfully carried his coachman aloft at Brompton Hall near Scarborough. Unfortunately the coachman was less than impressed by the experience and immediately resigned his job as he deemed that flying was not part of his job description.

Although he maintained an interest in developing a workable ornithopter until his death in 1896, Otto Lilienthal was one of the most gifted of the early pioneers. A trained engineer, he built and flew a series of fixed-wing hang gliders with control being effected by movements of the pilot's body, although shortly before he died he was experimenting with different forms of control and was working towards rudder and

1

elevator control with a form of wing warping for lateral control. His work was not to be completed as he lost his life when his glider stalled and crashed from a height of about 50 feet.

A similar fate befell the Scot, Percy Pilcher whose gliders were closely related to those of Lilienthal who he had met on a number of occasions and whose ideas he adopted. His most successful glider was the Hawk which he was flying on 30 September 1899 when a section of the tailplane snapped and it suddenly pitched nose down. Pilcher was severely injured in the accident and died two days later without having regained consciousness. At the time of his death he was developing a glider powered by a lightweight engine that he had designed himself. Had he lived there is a possibility that he may have become the first to achieve powered flight, although compared to the Wright brothers he gave very little thought to the question of stability and control.

On the other side of the Atlantic the French-born Octave Chanute was experimenting with multiplane gliders and was to have a big influence on the Wright brothers. His most successful design was a biplane with a cruciform tail unit that was flown around the turn of the century. Chanute was then contacted by the Wrights and a close relationship blossomed with information being freely passed back and forth. The Wrights had been carrying out their own experiments for some time and although their later gliders showed a distinct resemblance to Chanute's design, their work was much more advanced. Many of the early aviators were obsessed with inherent stability and as a result gave little thought as to how their creations could be controlled in the air. The Wrights deliberately adopted an unstable configuration that did not feature wing dihedral with the aircraft's lateral attitude instead being controlled by wing warping. An indication of how far the Wrights were ahead of everyone else was their identification of adverse yaw. This occurred in a turn when the upgoing wing, the trailing edge of which had been warped downwards, created more drag and led to yaw against the direction of the turn. This could easily lead to a stall, but the problem was eventually cured by the use of a rear-mounted rudder which was interconnected with the wing warping system. Having built a suitably strong biplane structure which generated sufficient lift and was controllable, all that was needed was a suitable power source.

By the turn of the century the first internal combustion engines were offering power-to-weight ratios that held the prospect of an application in heavier-than-air craft. The most advanced was that designed by the American, Charles Manley: a five-cylinder radial that developed around 50 hp and incorporated a carburettor, spark ignition and water cooling. Unfortunately, it was used to power S.P. Langley's *Aerodrome* which succeeded only in plunging into the river Potomac on two occasions in

1903 from its catapult above a houseboat. The Wright brothers had their own petrol engine designed and built by their mechanic Charles Taylor and although this was far less advanced than Manley's radial, the 12 hp that it developed from its four in-line cylinders was just sufficient to power the Flyer. By 1904 the engine had been improved so that it developed 16 hp and this process was continued so that by 1906 it was capable of producing 25 hp. The basic Flyer was also developed, the 1905 machine having flat wings with no trace of anhedral and a pilot-controlled rudder. This aircraft was a truly practical machine and during a demonstration in October 1905 it flew a distance of 24 miles in 38 minutes and 4 seconds during circuits of the Wrights testing ground at Huffman Prairie near Dayton (now part of Wright-Patterson Air Force Base).

Europe in the meantime had fallen well behind despite possessing the most advanced engine of the day in Leon Levavasseur's Antoinette. By 1905 this water-cooled vee-8 was developing around 50 hp for a weight of only 265 lb but its use of evaporative (steam) cooling and fuel injection meant that reliability was poor. Nevertheless, it was used to power the extraordinary tail-first 14-*bis* of Alberto Santos-Dumont who achieved the first sustained flight in Europe by travelling 722 feet in 21.2 seconds at Bagatelle, Paris. Although the European pioneers were not lacking in endeavour, their adherence to the theories of inherent stability rather than the development of adequate means of control meant that only faltering progress was made. It was not until 9 November 1907 that Henry Farman managed to exceed the duration of 59 seconds that Wilbur Wright had achieved in December 1903 when he flew the Voisin-Farman I for a distance of 3,380 feet in 1 minute 14 seconds.

The arrival of Wilbur Wright in France in 1908 to demonstrate the Flyer A was to come as something of a shock to those early aviators who were suddenly made aware of how inadequate their own machines were. From 21 August until the end of the year he flew from Camp d'Auvours, a military field near Le Mans and in the course of 104 flights set several records, including those for distance and duration during a flight on 21 September when he covered 41 miles in 1 hour 31 minutes. Although European experimenters were no match for the Wrights at this time, there were at least sufficient numbers to form the basis of a new industry and the demonstrations by Wilbur Wright acted as a catalyst for this nascent technology to grow. Within a year Louis Bleriot had flown his Anzani-powered No.XI monoplane across the English Channel and the first aviation meeting had been held at Rheims. The distance prize of £2,000 was won by Henry Farman with a flight of 112 miles and the £400 for the competitor that achieved the highest speed went to Glenn Curtiss of the USA with his *Golden Flyer* which attained 46.6 mph. The spectacle of heavier-than-air craft being flown by daring pilots racing around pylons captured the public's imagination, but the question remained as to whether the aeroplane could be developed into anything more than mere entertainment.

In Britain the rate of progress had been even slower than in France and the first to fly a distance of more than 1 mile was the American S.F. Cody who flew his British Army Aeroplane No.1 at Laffans Plain near Aldershot in Hampshire on 14 May 1909. The first Briton successfully to fly in a British machine was Alliott Verdon Roe in his Roe 1 triplane at Lea Marshes in Essex, however, his work was hampered by lack of funds and his triplane looked distinctly frail compared to the sturdy Bleriot. This lack of progress did not stop Britain from getting in on the act and in October 1909 the first flying meeting was held at Doncaster Town Moor, home of the classic St Leger race. Top billing went to Cody but many of the other pioneer aviators were also in attendance including Henry Farman, Leon Delagrange, Roger Sommer and Hubert Leblon. The Bleriot of Delagrange was notable in that it was powered by a seven-cylinder Gnome rotary engine that had been developed by the Seguin brothers. This type of engine was to have a major impact on the development of aviation in its formative years as it offered, for the day, a very high power-to-weight ratio and excellent reliability. Using the Gnome-powered Bleriot, Delagrange won the Tradesman's Cup for the highest speed achieved during the meeting at 49.9 mph.

Although the Wrights had moved to secure their position by offering licence deals to European manufacturers, their pusher biplane design did not lend itself to a significant increase in performance and it was rapidly overhauled by the tractor monoplane. In a little over two years the newly established World Absolute Speed Record for aircraft was doubled from around 50 mph to the magic figure of 100 mph. It was at this time that certain enlightened individuals really began to sit up and take notice of the aeroplane as with speeds of this order, it was beginning to challenge the more traditional view that the air was the preserve of balloons and airships. As already mentioned the Gnome engine provided much of the impetus as its ingenious design kept weight to a minimum (around 3.8 lb/hp) and also provided a novel form of cooling as the crankshaft was fixed and the cylinders revolved together with the propeller. This allowed the cooling fins that surrounded each cylinder to be reduced to the bare minimum as the rotation of the engine meant that sufficient cooling air was always available, even when the aircraft was stationary. As inadequate cooling was the major cause of engine failures at this time, this was of great importance. The spinning mass of the engine also acted like a huge flywheel so that the installation was well balanced with the minimum of vibration.

The problem of lubrication was solved by employing a one-way system which used castor oil. Once it had done its job the burnt oil poured out of the exhaust ports to cover everything in its wake, including the unfortunate pilot. It can thus be concluded with a fair degree of certainty that any pilot who flew aircraft powered by rotary-type engines never suffered from constipation. The rotary revolution, as it has often been called, spawned the rival Le Rhone engine which differed from the original Gnome in having more traditional inlet valves with distinctive copper pipes to take the mixture to the valve at the top of the cylinder [the Gnome employed a system in which the mixture was admitted to the cylinder via a valve in the crown of the piston]. Rotary engines were also produced by Clerget in France, Bentley in Britain and Oberursal in Germany and were to power many types of aircraft during the First World War.

The prospect of lighter and more powerful rotaries inspired several designers to produce equally radical aircraft to get the best out of the new type of engine. These included the Deperdussin racers designed by Louis Bechereau which raised the World Speed Record no less than ten times in a little under two years. The Deperdussin was the first real attempt to maximise speed potential by employing a high power engine, while at the same time making sure that aerodynamic drag was reduced by streamlining. The method of construction on the definitive racer was also extremely advanced as it introduced a fuselage monocoque which was built up in two halves and was formed with overlaying strips of tulip wood laid over a mould, the finished structure being fabric covered. The aircraft was a wire-braced, mid-wing monoplane with quite a low wing-area so that landing speeds were relatively high for the period. Engines of 70 and 140 hp were used initially with the later aircraft being powered by a two-row, 14-cylinder Gnome of 160 hp. The attention to detail could be seen in the use of a large propeller spinner to reduce the drag potential of the rotary engine behind it.

Although an open cockpit was retained, the pilot sat lower in the fuse-lage than had hitherto been the case where he had a control wheel to work the elevators and the wing warping system with a rudder bar for directional control. The Deperdussin was flown by two of the top racing pilots of the day in Jules Vedrines and Maurice Prevost who competed with the aircraft in Europe and the USA. The speed record was first taken by Vedrines on 13 January 1912 at Pau in France at 90.18 mph and was progressively raised to 126.64 mph, a figure set by Prevost at Rheims on 29 September 1913. The Deperdussin racers also took part in the Gordon Bennett races in Chicago in 1912 and 1913 where they were way ahead of any other competitor, Maurice Prevost winning the latter event at an average speed of 124.5 mph.

Despite a slow start as regards aircraft production Britain had caught up with the rest of Europe by this time and had its own speed contender in the S.E.4 (or Scout Experimental No.4) produced by the Royal Aircraft Factory at Farnborough. The process of evolution of this machine can be traced back to the B.S.1 (Bleriot Scout No.1) which was designed by Geoffrey de Havilland with the assistance of Henry Folland and S.J. Waters. The B.S.1 was a very clean looking single-bay biplane with a circular cross-section fuselage, the aft section of which was of monocoque construction. It was powered by a two-row 100 hp Gnome engine and was first flown on 13 March 1913, its top speed being measured at over 90 mph. Unfortunately the B.S.1 was written off in a crash following a spin shortly afterwards, but it was decided to rebuild it, by which time it had been re-designated S.E.2. During its reconstruction the S.E.2 was fitted with a single-row Gnome of only 80 hp but when it was flown in October 1913 it was found that it was nearly as fast as in its original guise due to reduced all-up weight. It was later modified once again with the rear monocoque being replaced by a conventional fuselage structure and the incorporation of streamlined 'Rafwire' bracing, before being delivered to the Royal Flying Corps (RFC) where it was flown by No.3 Squadron.

The same basic layout was adopted by Henry Folland for the S.E.4 (the S.E.3 was to have been powered by a 9-cylinder Gnome of 100 hp but was not proceeded with). The prime requirement for this aircraft was that it should have a very high top speed and with this in mind it was fitted with a 14-cylinder, two-row Gnome of 160 hp which was entirely enclosed by a tight fitting cowling with a spinner for the four-blade propeller. The fuselage was less advanced that the S.E.2 as the basic structure comprised four cross-braced longerons with formers and stringers to produce a circular cross-section. Wing bracing, with a single I-strut on each side was reduced to the absolute minimum to reduce drag, the bases of the struts being widened for fixing to both wing spars. Wire bracing was again the newly developed 'Rafwire' which also led to a significant reduction in drag. An unprecedented feature for the day was a moulded celluloid cockpit canopy but this was never tested in the air as it was considered by pilots to be a safety hazard.

The control surfaces of the S.E.4 were extremely advanced as all four wings were fitted with full-span ailerons which could also be lowered to act as landing flaps or raised slightly when flying at high speeds to reduce drag. The gap between the horizontal stabiliser and the elevator was also covered so that drag was kept to a minimum. The S.E.4 was first flown in June 1914 and it immediately became apparent that it was capable of very high speeds. Although no attempt was ever made at the World Speed Record, there is little doubt that the S.E.4 would have set a new bench-

mark as its top speed was around 135 mph. Its engine installation was, however, found to be extremely temperamental, initially as a result of overheating (which was cured) but continued unreliability led to it being replaced with a 100 hp Gnome Monosoupape (single-valve) which cut maximum speed down to a mere 92 mph. Despite the fact that at 52 mph its landing speed was considered to be too high, the S.E.4 was about to enter RFC service when it was wrecked in a landing accident on 12 August 1914. It was not repaired and the top speed that it had attained with its original engine was not to be surpassed for another five years.

In the meantime the interest in air racing which had led to the development of high speed landplanes had also extended to seaplanes thanks to the foresight and patronage of Jacques Schneider. Having been inspired by the sight of Wilbur Wright's demonstrations of flight at Le Mans in 1908, Schneider was determined to aid the development of seaplanes, or hydro-aeroplanes as they were known at first, as he was convinced that the future for air travel lay with this type of craft due to the fact that they were able to take advantage of the unlimited space offered by the sea for taking off and landing. The first race for La Coupe d'Aviation Maritime Jacques Schneider, known in the English speaking world as the Schneider Trophy, took place in Monaco in April 1913 and was contested by France and the USA, although even Charles Weymann, the American competitor, was flying a French Nieuport powered by a Gnome engine.

The race was eventually won by Maurice Prevost in a seaplane version of the Deperdussin racer at an average speed of 45 mph, although this was not a true reflection of his race pace as he forgot to fly over the finishing line and taxied over it instead. This led to a disqualification but when Weymann was forced to drop out with engine trouble, Prevost took off again to complete the race legally, the clock having been ticking in the meantime. Of the two aircraft the Nieuport was the faster, lapping at around 70 mph, compared with the 60 mph of the Deperdussin, even though the former was powered by a Gnome rotary of only 100 hp. The speed of all machines was considerably reduced from their landplane equivalents as a result of the drag created by the floats and their support structures. Also, the nature of the course, with a particularly sharp 165 degree bend, meant that pilots lost much time in making their turns.

Following the success of the first contest, the second race took place at Monaco the following year. Considering the level of domination achieved by France in all forms of air racing, few were willing to bet against another victory for the French monoplanes, especially as the only real opposition was a tiny low-powered biplane produced by the fledgling Sopwith company in Britain. This was the Tabloid whose design philosophy was similar to that of the B.S.1/S.E.2., and in its original form was powered by an 80 hp Gnome. For the Schneider race it was re-engined with a 100 hp

Gnome Monosoupape but still appeared to have no chance against the Deperdussin, which had now been fitted with an 18-cylinder Gnome of double the power of the little Tabloid, and the 160 hp Nieuport. The performance gap, however, was not as big as some imagined because the monoplanes of the day still required large amounts of external bracing which created excessive drag. They were also less manoeuvrable and lost out heavily to the much nimbler biplane in closed circuit races. In the event Howard Pixton flew the Tabloid with metronomic precision to complete the course at an average speed of 86.78 mph, the various French competitors all suffering from engine problems as they pushed too hard in an attempt to keep in touch with the Sopwith.

The 1914 Schneider contest was the last major air race before the First World War and it marked the end of the pioneer age of flight. It also pointed the way to the future of aircraft development as with the exception of a few notable designs, such as the Fokker Eindecker, Morane-Saulnier Scout and the Bristol M.1C, the monoplane was to be discarded in favour of the biplane for a considerable period. The golden age of flying had seen a dramatic increase in the top speed of aircraft from the 48.20 mph set by Hubert Latham in an Antoinette in 1910 to the 126.64 mph as recorded by Prevost in the Deperdussin in 1913. During this period the emphasis had been on pushing back the boundaries of flight with wealthy benefactors sponsoring speed and distance events with large cash prizes underpinning the world's first aircraft manufacturers. The descent into war changed everything so that the plane makers suddenly became entirely dependent on government contracts to design and build aircraft to fulfil a specific military need for which the requirements were diverse.

The move away from the monoplane had begun in France with a number of fatal crashes in 1911/12 resulting in all military monoplanes being grounded for a time. Similar accidents in Britain led the War Office to ban the flying of monoplanes in September 1912 until improvements were made. The safety issue was just one aspect in the monoplane's decline as biplanes invariably had a lower wing-loading and were thus much easier to fly with a lower stalling speed which suited the small landing grounds of the day. As the aeroplane was about to be flown by large numbers of trained airmen rather than experienced company pilots, if accident levels were to be kept to reasonable levels the new breed of aircraft had to be a long way removed from the specialised monoplane racers that had been developed for outright speed. Biplanes also tended to be more manoeuvrable and as far as most pilots were concerned, this quality was more important than the ability to outpace a rival. Due to their greater wing area they were more capable of lifting heavy military loads and throughout the war fighting aeroplanes were festooned with

more and more equipment. Given that they were needed in large numbers, ease of manufacture was another important factor so the technical innovation which had characterised the brief period from 1910 fell into rapid decline. The net result was that at the end of the war the principal fighters of 1918 were little faster than the racers of the pre-war era.

One area in which aviation did make great strides was in the development of a new range of liquid-cooled aero engines which offered a much improved power-to-weight ratio compared with those of the pre-war period. Although the rotary engine was to remain in service for the duration of the war (the Sopwith Snipe powered by a Bentley B.R.2 rotary of 230 hp was to remain in service with the RAF until 1926) its dominance was gradually eroded. The trend away from the rotary was effectively begun in Germany by the Daimler motor company which produced a 6-cylinder aero engine in 1912 under the name Mercedes. Developments of this engine gave up to 300 hp and powered a number of German aircraft in the First World War including the Albatros D.V. In Britain Sunbeam entered the aero-engine market in 1914 but the dominant player was to become Rolls-Royce which produced the 6-cylinder Hawk, the vee-12 Eagle, together with the smaller Falcon of the same layout. An engine of vee-8 configuration was designed by Swiss-born Marc Birkigt of Hispano-Suiza and this was to be produced in France. It was to power fighters designed by Louis Bechereau of the Societe Provisoire des Avions Deperdussin (SPAD), the successors to Armand Deperdussin's enterprise which had collapsed when its founder was arrested on charges of fraud, and was also to be built under licence by Wolseley to power the S.E.5/S.E.5a.

In contrast to the amount of progress made with aero-engines, airframe development hardly moved forward at all during the period 1914–18 and at the end of the war the wire-braced biplane still reigned supreme. The top speed of the latest British fighters, the Sopwith Snipe and the S.E.5a, was 121 mph and 132 mph respectively, despite the fact that they were powered by engines of around 220/230 hp. These figures can be compared with the monoplane Bristol M.1A of 1916 which was able to match the speed of the S.E.5a even though its Clerget rotary engine developed only 110 hp. Despite its outstanding performance, a paltry 125 production examples of the M.1C were ordered but even these did not see any service on the Western Front and their only operational use was in the Middle East. This emphasised the bias that had rapidly built up in favour of the biplane based on its rapid rate of climb, manoeuvrability and low landing speed.

After the First World War the chief exponents of the biplane were then promoted to become the decision makers in the post-war period so that the antipathy against the monoplane was carried on far longer than was really necessary. As a result the air forces of the world descended into a state of reactionary stagnation which saw only marginal improvements in performance levels over the next 10–15 years. It has to be admitted that this situation was not exactly helped by the severe budget restraints that were imposed. However, the lack of development cannot be put down to this factor alone and was more to do with the conservative attitudes of the military hierarchy. There was, however, one area that did offer hope for the future of aviation and that was the resurgence of interest in air racing. Despite a paucity of funds the air arms of Britain, France, Italy and the USA did manage to find sufficient cash to compete in the major air races, although the increasingly specialised nature of the aircraft that were developed meant that their value in a military sense was extremely limited. The main benefit to be derived from competing in air racing was prestige, and in an increasingly air minded age the glory that came from success in the Pulitzer race or the Schneider Trophy was considerable. The next chapter looks at the golden age of air racing which played an important part in the development of the monoplane fighters of the mid 1930s, aircraft that were the first to be troubled by compressibility.

CHAPTER TWO

A Quest for Speed

During the First World War the aeroplane had come of age and by 1918 its capabilities, both as a weapon of war and as a future means of long distance transport were there for all to see, however, the prospect of being able to extend the boundaries in terms of speed was the most exciting of all. One of the most successful aircraft in the immediate post-war years in this respect was the Nieuport-Delage 29 which was the first aircraft to extend the world speed record (the name Delage was that of chief engineer, Gustave Delage). During the war Nieuport had produced fighters for all the Allies culminating in the elegant Type 28. The Type 29 was a development of the earlier machine and was powered by a Hispano-Suiza engine, the fuselage being exceptionally slim and formed from strips of tulip wood attached to spruce longerons and plywood bulkheads. Without its military load the Nieuport-Delage 29 was exceptionally fast and on 7 February 1920 it was flown by Sadi Leconte at a speed of 171.01 mph, the first notable achievement in an illustrious career which included winning the Gordon Bennett race. Nieuport followed this with a 'sesquiplane' design which was, effectively, a monoplane with an axle fairing of aerofoil section, the wing being strut-braced. This aircraft became the first to exceed 200 mph when Leconte recorded a speed of 205.20 mph on 20 September 1922. It was progressively developed to include flush underwing radiators and went on to achieve a speed of 233 mph on 15 February 1923.

In Britain in the early 1920s, while RAF fighter squadrons had to put up with the Sopwith Snipe, similar progress in speed was being made and the Gloucestershire Aircraft Company began to embrace air racing as a means of attracting publicity for its wares. This resulted in the Mars I racer (nicknamed 'Bamel') which was designed by Henry Folland who had been responsible for the pre-war S.E.4. As was to be expected from his previous attempt at high speed flight, the Mars I was an extremely clean design with a tight-fitting cowling around the 450 hp Napier Lion 12-cylinder engine, and single-bay wings. It was of all-wooden construction and featured a single-I strut between the wings. The first flight took

11

place on 20 June 1921 and it was entered for the Aerial Derby at Hendon the following month which it won at a speed of 163.34 mph. After this encouraging debut the Mars I was flown with reduced wing area in the Coupe Deutsch at Villasauvage in France but had to drop out of the race. It was, however, flown in this form at Boscombe Down in December 1921 where it established a new British speed record at 196.4 mph. To minimise drag the wing area was reduced even further for an attempt on the World Speed Record but the 212 mph attained was not sufficiently more than that achieved by the French Nieuport. The Mars I was eventually renamed as the Gloster I and its last use was as a floatplane trainer for the RAF's attempt on the Schneider Trophy in 1925 and 1927.

The greatest progress as regards high speed flight in the early post-war period came from the USA, in particular the aircraft produced by Curtiss. During the First World War Curtiss had built up a profitable business and had latterly produced the model 18 triplane powered by a 400 hp K-12 engine designed by Charles Kirkham. For the first time Curtiss used a three-ply monocoque for the construction of the fuselage and with a top speed of 163 mph it could well have been the fastest warplane of its day. With the cessation of hostilities no production orders were received but it was to have a successful, albeit short, career in air racing. The Model 18 was to be followed by a pure racing machine that was designed for the Texas oil millionaire S.E.J. Cox whose ambition was to achieve fame by winning the Gordon Bennett race.

With the whole project being funded by Cox who was prepared to pay virtually anything to achieve his goal, the design emerged as a monoplane that had a similar overall layout to the Nieuport sesquiplane, except that the pilot sat further back in the fuselage just ahead of the raked fin. The fuselage was once again of monocoque construction and the wings were also veneered but were not load bearing. The design aim was to achieve a speed of 200 mph and the engine used was a geared C-12 offering 430 hp. The clean lines of the Curtiss racer were spoilt only by the use of side-mounted radiators (flush wing-mounted radiators were considered but could not be made to work in the time available). As a result of the positioning of the radiators the aircraft made a distinctive shriek when in the air and could be heard several miles away. Known as the Texas Wildcat, the racer was first flown by Roland Rohlfs on 2 August 1920 with a high-lift wing. After initial testing the intention was to fit a smaller race wing of bi-convex design but this resulted in a landing speed of around 100 mph which was much too fast for the airfield in use (Roosevelt Field, Long Island). The first flight of the aircraft in full race configuration was thus carried out in France shortly before the Gordon Bennett Trophy but unfortunately it needed half a county to take off and proved to be so unstable longitudinally as to be completely unacceptable for the race. In a matter of days the racer was converted into a biplane but was wrecked in a landing accident and so was unable to compete. A second aircraft, known as the Cactus Kitten, had been transported all the way to Europe but was not even removed from its crate.

Having failed as a monoplane and as a biplane, the Cactus Kitten sprouted yet another set of wings on its arrival back in the USA so that it then emerged as a triplane. In fact the wing layout was adapted from the S-3 Scout of 1918 and with it the racer was rather more successful, achieving a speed of 193 mph. It was entered for the 1921 Pulitzer Trophy (a race series that had been set up to commemorate the publisher Joseph W. Pulitzer) and was placed second behind a Curtiss CR-1. Although it appeared to have much better straight line speed, the tricky handling characteristics of the triplane meant that it was difficult to manoeuvre. It was entered for the same race the following year but did not compete and was not flown again.

Although the Curtiss Gordon-Bennett racers had not been particularly successful, a lot had been learnt and this was put to good use with the development of the CR racers. These were funded by the US Navy and were designed to be much more pilot-friendly. Wooden construction was again used for ease of manufacture and to provide a smooth external surface and the engine was the direct drive CD-12 in place of the geared C-12 which had been less than reliable. As the CD-12 had to be run at reduced rpm, power was initially down to 368 hp, however, continued development produced a gradual increase in compression ratios, which, together with the use of improved fuels, brought power levels back up to a little over 400 hp. The CR-1 was entered for the 1921 Pulitzer which it won at a speed of 176.75 mph, beating the Cactus Kitten triplane into second place.

For the 1922 Pulitzer contest the CR-1 was re-designated CR-2 and featured flush wing radiators and the latest version of the 12-cylinder Curtiss engine, the D-12. This unit was to have a profound effect on the development of liquid-cooled engines, particularly in Britain where it was built under licence for the Fairey Fox light-bomber and was to provide the inspiration for Rolls-Royce to commence its own work on V-12 aero engines. With more power and reduced drag there was a substantial improvement in performance so that Curtiss finally achieved its aim of producing an aircraft capable of 200 mph. In the race the CR-2s finished third and fourth but such was the pace of development at this time that the aircraft that finished ahead of them in the Pulitzer were two more racers from the Curtiss stable, the R-6 which had been designed for the US Army Air Service.

As the basic CR design had been relatively conservative, there was plenty of scope for increasing speed even further. Wing span was reduced by 4 feet and the R-6 was also lighter by 215 lb. To reduce drag its frontal area was reduced by around 25 per cent and I-type wing struts were used in place of the N-type struts used on the CR. The undercarriage was also made simpler and the horizontal stabiliser was a cantilever with no external bracing. On its very first flight the R-6 exceeded 200 mph and was soon taken to 220 mph which was 15 mph faster than the world speed record. The R-6 captured the record officially on 18 October 1922 when General Billy Mitchell posted a speed of 222.93 mph and this was raised to 236.54 mph in March 1923 by Russell Maughan. The R-6 was not without controversy as Burt Skeel was killed in the 1924 Pulitzer event when his aircraft broke up as he was diving at full speed to begin the race. It was thought that the disintegration might have been caused by the wooden propeller de-laminating at full throttle but a more than capable alternative was available in the metal propeller devised by Dr S.A. Reed. This was much thinner at the tip than a comparable wooden propeller with less drag and was ideally suited to the direct-drive engines of the Curtiss racers. With this new type of propeller Curtiss was able to utilise the increased power of the D-12A engine in the R2C which was flown for the first time on 9 September 1923.

The R2C was the US Navy's response to the Army R-6 of the previous year and did away with the cabane struts of the latter as the upper wing was attached directly to the top of the fuselage. By increasing the cylinder bore slightly and increasing compression ratio to 5.8 the D-12A engine produced 507 hp at 2,300 rpm. A wooden propeller was fitted at first but this was soon replaced by one of the new Reed metal propellers which immediately produced a 10 mph increase in top speed. The wings were also improved in that a stronger ply covering allowed weight savings on the internal structure and a revised aerofoil section led to greater overall efficiency. Fuselage construction was virtually identical to that of the R-6 with the forward section being built of high-tensile steel tube. Soon after its first flight the R2C was taken to 244 mph which was the speed that Al Williams averaged to win the 1923 Pulitzer air race. Such was the performance of the racers that pilots were experiencing a new phenomenon, a high-g blackout during the turns which had first been noted the previous year. By now aircraft were pulling around 7g during the steeply banked turns around the pylons so that a high 'g' tolerance on the part of the pilot was as important as extracting every bit of performance from the machine itself. After the Pulitzer race a concerted effort was made to extend the speed record with Al Williams finally recording a speed of 267.16 mph on 3 November 1923.

The last Curtiss racer was the R3C which was closely related to the R2C and was funded jointly by the Army and Navy. It was fitted with a further adaptation of the D-12 engine which was of increased bore and stroke so that capacity was raised to 1,400 cubic inches and was known as the V-1400. The V-1400 had a power-to-weight ratio of only 1.12 lb per hp, which was virtually the same as that of the Rolls-Royce Merlin engine. The latest Reed model 'R' propeller was fitted which was drop-forged rather than being twisted and was said to have had an efficiency of nearly 89 per cent. The first R3C was flown in September 1925 and took part in the Pulitzer the following month, the race being won by Lieutenant Cyrus Bettis at a speed of 248.975 mph which was something of a disappointment as unofficial testing had shown that the R3C was capable of much more with speeds of 300 mph being recorded with a slight following wind.

Curtiss was also heavily involved for a brief but glorious period in the Schneider Trophy races with several of its landplane racers being converted as seaplanes. The event had restarted in 1919 and until the arrival of the Curtiss racers in 1923 had been won by Italy and Britain with various flying-boats which owed everything to brute power and nothing to aerodynamic efficiency. In 1923 the race was held at Cowes and marked the arrival of the USA with the CR racers which had been modified to take part in the competition and were re-designated CR-3. The only chance for the Supermarine Sea Lion which had won the previous year was that the Curtiss seaplanes would not be seaworthy, but once they had successfully passed the navigability tests there was little doubt as to the eventual outcome. The CR-3s duly came in first and second with Lieutenant David Rittenhouse winning outright with a speed of 177.38 mph.

One of the rules of the Schneider contest was that the winning country would host the next race and this was due to have taken place at Baltimore in October 1924, but the withdrawal of the Italians, together with an accident to the British Gloster II, left the USA with no challengers for its R2C-2 racers. Rather than claim a walk-over, the Americans sportingly chose to cancel the race and the next event was at Baltimore in 1925. The US Navy entered three Curtiss R3C-2 seaplanes but these were up against formidable opposition in the extremely advanced cantilever-wing Supermarine S.4 monoplane which was powered by a 700 hp Napier Lion. In the event the S.4 crashed as a result of wing flutter which left Lieutenant James H. Doolittle to win the race easily at a speed of 232.57 mph. Afterwards the same pilot set a new seaplane record with a speed of 246 mph.

The final Curtiss participation in the Schneider Trophy was the 1926 race at Hampton Roads in which an R3C-3 powered by a 700 hp geared Packard 2A-1500, and an R3C-4 with the latest D-12 derivative, the V-1550, were to participate. For the Americans the race was an inauspicious one as team pilot Hersey Conant was killed in a flying accident before the event and during the navigability tests the R3C-3 crashed on landing. With the R3C-4 of Lieutenant George Cuddihy having to retire on the last lap due to fuel pick-up problems, this left the Macchi M.39 of Major Mario de Bernardi as the winner at a speed of 246.50 mph, with an R3C-2 flown by Lieutenant Frank Schilt in second place. The 1926 Schneider race marked the end of official US participation and from now on it would be a straight fight between the British and the Italians. The Curtiss racers had set new standards in aerodynamic refinement, and in terms of frontal area and drag coefficient the R3C was only marginally inferior to the later racing monoplanes developed by Supermarine. The area in which the later Schneider racers stood out was in their use of engines of extremely high power which allowed the seaplane to overtake its land based counterpart to become, for a brief period, the fastest aircraft in the world.

Following the Italian win in 1926, the next race was held in Venice in 1927. The British team consisted of three different designs, the Gloster IV biplane, Short Crusader and the Supermarine S.5 of which the latter was the most advanced. After the loss of the mid-wing S.4 due to flutter, designer R.J. Mitchell went for a low-wing configuration with wire bracing for the S.5 which reduced structure weight. Great emphasis was placed on streamlining and by better contouring of the 875 hp Napier Lion engine the frontal area was reduced by 35 per cent. The biggest gain, however, was the adoption of wing-surface radiators in place of the Lamblin radiators as used on the S.4 which led to a speed increase of approximately 24 mph. The contender for Italy was the Macchi M.52 which was powered by a Fiat AS.3 of 1,000 hp and had been developed from the M.39 that had won the previous contest. Of similar configuration to the S.5, the M.39 was lacking in development, in particular its Fiat engine which in the quest to achieve the magical 1,000 hp had had its compression ratio raised, together with an increase in rpm. Alloys were also used extensively to reduce weight. The AS.3 suffered repeated failures during bench tests and in the race both the AS.3-powered aircraft were forced to retire with engine problems. A third M.52 was flown with the earlier 800 hp AS.2 but even this was forced out with a fractured fuel line. All this drama left the S.5 of Flight Lieutenant S.N. Webster to win the race at an average speed of 281.65 mph which was 3 mph faster than the world speed record.

As the Napier Lion was reaching the end of its development, if Britain was to mount a serious challenge to win the next race in 1929 it would need to find a new engine. This ultimately led to the Rolls-Royce 'R' engine which, in the Supermarine S.6 and S.6B, would win the Schneider Trophy outright. The S.6 was the first aircraft to exceed 400 mph and the technology that went into it would lead to the immortal Spitfire. The 'R' engine was based on the 950 hp Rolls-Royce Buzzard which had a capacity of 36.7 litres compared with the 24 litres of the Napier Lion. The need for a high power-to-weight ratio together with low frontal area to reduce drag meant that the 'R' would have to have an extremely efficient supercharger. This was designed by Jimmy Ellor who had recently joined Rolls-Royce from the RAE, the impellor being of double entry type with vanes on both sides which reduced the overall dimensions of the supercharger, whilst still ensuring that the required fuel/air mixture was delivered to the cylinders.

The engine was fed via a forward facing air intake which was positioned so that it was able to take full advantage of the ram effect, the internal ducting then changing from convergent to divergent type so that the velocity of the air was reduced and converted into pressure energy. A new crankcase was designed by A.J. Rowledge to cater for the increased stresses of the racing engine and the rest of the engine was strengthened with the external accessories being tidied up so that close-fitting cowlings could be used. The first test runs of the 'R' engine were carried out in May 1929 which showed that it was developing 1,545 hp at 2,750 rpm. By September 1,900 hp had been achieved, largely thanks to the work of F.R. 'Rod' Banks who came up with a suitable fuel cocktail that comprised 78 per cent benzole, 22 per cent naphthalene-based gasoline with a small amount of lead as an additive. With a weight of only 1,530 lb, the 'R' produced 1.24 hp/lb, which was better than any other comparable engine of the day.

The S.6 airframe bore a distinct similarity to the earlier S.5 but was scaled up to accept the heavier 'R' engine, the empty weight being 4,471 lb compared with 2,680 lb for the S.5. One of the biggest problems facing R.J. Mitchell was the dissipation of heat generated by the engine and his solution was to lead to the S.6 being dubbed 'the flying radiator'. The entire upper and lower surfaces of the wings, with the exception of the ailerons and the tips, incorporated radiators, but unlike the copper strips of the S.5, the S.6 used 24-gauge duralumin sheet with spacers of $\frac{1}{16}$ inch thick to provide the space for the coolant to flow. Oil cooling was also a problem and this was solved by positioning the oil tank in the fin. The oil thus had to travel virtually the full length of the aircraft and back, in the process of which it was cooled by admitting it to the interior of the fin before it was collected once again and pumped back to the engine. Fuel was contained in the centre portions of both floats.

For the 1929 Schneider contest the Italians had three Macchi M.67 floatplanes powered by 18-cylinder Isotta-Fraschini engines of 1,800 hp, however, one of these was lost in an accident during pre-race training which claimed the life of Captain Guiseppe Motta. The race was held at Calshot on 7 September and resulted in a straightforward victory for

Britain as the two remaining M.67s had to retire with excessive fumes in the cockpit. The winner was Flight Lieutenant H.R. Waghorn at an average speed of 328.63 mph, a second S.6 flown by Flying Officer R.L.R. Atcherley being disqualified for cutting a pylon. By now the fastest float-planes as represented by the Schneider racers were comfortably faster than their landplane equivalents and this fact was reinforced on 12 September 1929 when Squadron Leader A.H. Orlebar recorded a speed of 357.67 mph in an S.6, although this was not ratified as a new world speed record.

With outright victory of the Schneider Trophy within its grasp, Britain did its best to throw it all away when it was decided that the RAF would not be entering a team for the next contest in 1931. Although it was conceded that participation had provided much useful information as regards high-speed flight, it was felt that little further benefit would be achieved by a continued RAF presence. To the embarrassment of the government the £100,000 that was needed to provide a challenge was put forward by Lady Houston in early 1931 which allowed very little time to come up with an aircraft that was capable of beating the likely Italian opposition. The only possibility was a minimal update of the S.6 and Rolls-Royce worked wonders to increase the amount of power generated by the 'R' engine to 2,300 hp. Modifications included utilising a higher supercharger gear ratio, increasing rpm and using sodium-cooled exhaust valves which had recently been developed in the USA. Due to the high torque levels of the 'R' engine more fuel was carried in the star-board float than in the port float in an attempt to improve the handling characteristics on take-off.

In the event the Italians were unable to send a team due to develop-ment problems and the RAF was left to claim the trophy outright with a walkover, Flight Lieutenant John Boothman taking victory at Calshot at an average speed of 340.08 mph. With its additional power the S.6B was capable of much more and on 29 September 1931 Flight Lieutenant G.H. Stainforth achieved 406.94 mph to set a new world speed record at Ryde in the Isle of Wight. Having won three Schneider contests in the required five years the trophy was claimed outright by Britain but this did not stop development of the Italian Macchi MC.72 which was to have been its contender for the 1931 event. The MC.72 was the most ambitious of all Schneider racers as it was powered by a Fiat AS.6 which comprised two 1,500 hp V-12 engines mounted in tandem, each crankshaft being connected via reduction gear to two airscrew shafts that drove contra-rotating propellers. This produced a vast improvement during take-off as torque effects were eliminated. The aircraft's development was trou-bled and there was a fatal crash involving Lieutenant Giovanni Monti. Having run out of time to compete in the Schneider Trophy the only avenue open to the Italians was an assault on the world speed record and in this they were assisted by Rod Banks who was able to give advice on how to overcome a persistent backfire problem which had been severe enough to crack the induction system and the supercharger casing. On 10 April 1933 Warrant Officer Agello set a new record of 423.76 mph which he raised to 440.60 mph the following year, a speed that remains as the fastest ever achieved by a propeller-driven seaplane.

Even though the airforces of the 1920s and early 1930s were still equipped with some extremely outdated designs, the use of air racing as a proving ground for new technology was to have a dramatic effect on the development of fighter aircraft when the political situation in Europe began to deteriorate following Adolf Hitler's rise to power in Germany. Although there were a number of high ranking officers in the RAF who thought participation in air racing to be worthless, including Lord Trenchard who thought that there was 'nothing of value in it', there can be little doubt that the pace of development was accelerated significantly. It may have been true that the racing seaplanes that competed in the Schneider Trophy were the freaks of the aviation world, but the experience gained by Supermarine and the like was to pave the way towards the stressed-skin monoplane fighters that were to produce a quantum leap in performance over the antiquated biplanes they replaced.

This process was repeated with the engine manufacturers as in the last few Schneider races power took over from aerodynamic efficiency as the most important factor in raising speeds. After Britain had won the Schneider Trophy outright in 1931 Mr A.F. Sidgreaves, the Managing Director of Rolls-Royce, was of the opinion that the research that his company had carried out over the 1929–31 period would otherwise have taken between six and ten years. He also expressed the view that, rather than the contest being unnecessarily expensive for the public purse, this contraction in the amount of time required to develop a high-powered aero engine actually produced economies over the likely cost for a more normal gestation. Although very few people realised it at the time, the rapid progress made in outright speed performance also hastened the biggest challenge of all, that of designing an aircraft to perform at transonic speeds and ultimately to exceed the speed of sound.

CHAPTER THREE

Trouble Ahead

By the mid-1930s aviation stood on the threshold of a period of remarkable expansion with new designs entering service that were capable of pushing back the barriers in terms of speed, operating altitude and range. The era was a curious mixture of the old and the new with biplane fighters that were very little faster than their First World War counterparts and often being out-paced by some of the newer commercial aircraft of the time. In Britain the fastest RAF fighter was the Hawker Fury which, on a good day, could just make it over 200 mph, but the standard bomber type was still the venerable Vickers Virginia which had a top speed of 108 mph and had even been known to fly backwards when faced with a stiff headwind at altitude. Pride of the Imperial Airways fleet was the Handley Page HP.42 four-engined biplane airliner. Imperial had little choice but to offer an opulent service on its routes as it took a long time to get anywhere when the cruising speed of its airliners could not quite make it into three figures. The spectre of compressibility, which at the time was known only to a few theoretical aerodynamicists, was just around the corner, but at the same time it seemed to be a world away.

Many of the advances in design and construction techniques entered mainstream service in the USA under the impetus of the airlines who were continually looking for new aircraft of increased performance to reduce journey times. The first transport aeroplane to feature a retractable undercarriage was the single-engine, low-wing Lockheed Orion which first flew in early 1931 and had a top speed of 220 mph. Within two years the Boeing 247 and Douglas DC-1 airliners had flown in prototype form, each aircraft being of monoplane design with all-metal, stressed-skin construction, a retractable undercarriage and very soon, variable pitch propellers. The new technology could, of course, easily be applied to bomber aircraft which in turn meant that fighters of much greater performance would then be needed as defence against the threat that these new bombers posed. This led to the development of the Curtiss P-36 and Brewster F2A in the USA, the Hawker Hurricane and

Supermarine Spitfire in Britain and the Messerschmitt Bf 109 in Germany. It was this type of aircraft that first began to be troubled by compressibility and even the Brewster F2A, which had the least impressive performance of the new breed of fighters, could be badly affected in a dive to its terminal velocity.

Although the study of airflows and how they behaved when confronted with an aircraft moving at high speed was still in its infancy, enough was known to give a good idea of what could be expected. The speed of sound at sea level had long been determined as it was easy for the length of time that it took for sound waves to travel from one point to another to be measured. One of the most obvious occurrences that could be measured was the time that it took for an observer to hear a clap of thunder having seen a flash of lightning. Any discharge of electricity would lead to a sudden compression of the air which would produce a pressure wave that would radiate out and eventually be heard, the time taken depending on the distance between the observer and the source. Calculations showed that sound travelled at around 1,100 ft/sec so that it took around 5 seconds for sound to travel 1 mile. When this was converted into speed it worked out at 760 mph. This figure is not constant, however, and varies with height. As air temperature drops as height is gained, so does the local speed of sound, so that at an altitude of 36,000 feet, where the outside air temperature is likely to be around -56 degrees C, the speed of sound is around 660 mph.

For pilots this was a potential dilemma as they would not be able to look at their airspeed indicators and know how close they were to the speed of sound at any particular time. Luckily the principles of supersonics had already been established by Ernst Mach who was a professor of experimental physics at the Charles University at Prague in the late 1800s. Between 1873 and 1893 he developed optical and photographic techniques for the measurement of sound waves and wave propagation, and gave the world the Mach number which was the ratio of the velocity of an object to the velocity of sound. In other words, if an aircraft was flying at a speed that was equivalent to 80 per cent of the local speed of sound it would be flying at a Mach number of 0.80.

Although it might not be quite on the scale of a thunder clap, an aircraft is nonetheless a large noise emitter but the length of time that it takes for any person to hear it depends not only on its distance away, but on the aircraft's motion relative to the observer. To move forward, briefly, to the present day, the culmination of most fast-jet displays is a high speed flypast at a speed just under that of sound, but spectators only hear the sound of the aircraft a fraction of a second before it actually arrives. This is because the aircraft is travelling nearly as fast as the noise it is emitting. Should that aircraft be flying at a speed greater than that of sound, it would only be heard after it had gone. This is born out by the old soldier's maxim – 'you never hear the one that gets you', because bullets and shells were flying supersonically long before aircraft were able to do so.

For an aircraft flying at low speed there is no problem as the pressure wave is able to spread out ahead of the machine effectively to warn the body of air in front of an aircraft that a disturbance is on the way. Wind tunnel experiments have shown that this air begins to prepare for the passage of an aircraft quite some distance ahead, the greatest movement occurring as the air sweeps upwards to pass over the upper surface of the wing above which is an area of low pressure (air has a natural tendency to flow from an area of high pressure to a corresponding area of low pressure). When an aircraft is flying at the speed of sound, however, this process cannot occur as the aircraft is flying as fast as the pressure wave is travelling. As a result the waves tend to pile up, or compress, ahead of the aircraft to form a reinforced pressure wave, or shock wave, which is perpendicular to the direction of travel of the aircraft. Unfortunately, on most fighter aircraft of the late 1930s and early 1940s shock waves began to form when the aircraft was flying well below the local speed of sound. This was due to the fact that there was a marked variation in the speed of different airflows over various parts of the aircraft. For instance the airflow over the cambered upper surface of the wing, would be travelling much faster than that flowing along the relatively flat underside. The speed at which the first shock waves began to occur represented the aircraft's critical Mach number (M_{crit}) which is defined as the lowest free stream Mach number at which a local Mach number of 1.0 will occur at any point on the aircraft.

The point at which the first shock wave begins to form is normally on the upper surface of the wing where the camber is at its greatest and the airflow is thus travelling at its fastest. On a wing of conventional section this is usually at around 20 per cent chord or one fifth of the way back from the wing's leading edge. The shock wave attaches to the wing surface, extending upwards and marks a sudden drop in the speed of the airflow over the wing. It also marks a division in a further sense as there is a rapid increase in pressure and density. As has already been stated, air would rather flow from high to low pressure, but the rise in pressure after the shock wave results in an adverse pressure gradient, the result of which is that the air is violently disturbed and the turbulent flow leads to a significant loss of lift and increase in drag. This separation of the air is similar to that experienced during a normal stall and as it is caused by the formation of a shock wave, it is known as a shock stall. The drag produced by the turbulent flow aft of the shock wave is normally referred to as wave drag and is at its greatest at M_{crit}.

If an aircraft was to fly faster than its critical Mach number the next stage would see a smaller shock wave form on the under surface of the wing. With further increase in speed (assuming that an aircraft was actually capable of doing this) both shock waves would tend to move rearwards so that when the aircraft was flying at Mach 1.0, they would be attached to the trailing edge. This gradual movement would result in a progressive reduction in wave drag and an increase in lift. At the same time a bow wave would be apparent ahead of the wing leading edge and with further increase in speed this would become attached to the wing itself, forming into a pronounced V-shape by the time that Mach 2.0 had been reached.

For piston-engined fighters of the Second World War, however, the prospect of flight at the speed of sound was a long way off as any increase in speed above M_{crit} very soon brought the aircraft to its limiting Mach number which was the Mach number at which compressibility effects caused serious handling problems that were likely to lead to a complete loss of control. The sequence of events would normally be the onset of buffet which gradually became heavier and more persistent with increase in speed, followed by sudden changes in trim in a nose-down sense. The controls would become increasingly heavy to the point where they were virtually immovable and the pilot would find himself diving with no control whatsoever in an aircraft that was making a horrendous racket due to the forces that it was being subjected to. This situation would continue until the aircraft entered the denser air at low level where the local speed of sound would be greater and the Mach number correspondingly lower. Although the aircraft might still be diving at the same indicated airspeed, the reduction in Mach number would lead to the controls gradually becoming effective once again so that a recovery could be made.

The process of research into compressibility effects in the 1930s was not helped by the fact that the wind tunnels of the day tended to 'choke' in the transonic region so that meaningful data was hard to come by. They worked well enough at subsonic speeds and a Swiss, Jacob Ackeret, had built a successful supersonic wind tunnel, however, the all-important region from Mach 0.70 to just in excess of Mach 1.0 was a big problem area. It was, however, known that a relatively thick conventional aerofoil, in which most of the lift was created over the forward part of the wing by employing pronounced camber, was not helpful in increasing an aircraft's penetration of the Mach scale. On the other hand, laminar flow wings where maximum lift occurred further aft due to re-profiling of the upper surface, and most especially wings of low thickness/chord ratio (even when of conventional section), performed much better at high speed and delayed the formation of shock waves which were in any case weaker as the adverse pressure gradient was kept to a minimum.

One of the most dangerous aspects of the first attempts at flight in the transonic region was that aircraft tended to be subject to a strong nose-down pitching moment. This was due to the fact that the centre of pressure moved aft and so the lift/weight couple was strengthened which resulted in the nose being pulled downwards, a situation that was made worse by the shock waves affecting airflow over the tailplane which increased lift at the rear. This made the aircraft speed unstable in that if no corrective action was taken (or was found to be impossible) the nose-down pitch would cause speed to increase which would then lead to the same cycle being repeated.

In the early 1930s the study of how air behaved when confronted with an aircraft flying at high speed was not an easy task as there were no aircraft capable of providing actual flight data and the wind tunnels of the time, as has already been stated, were only of limited use. Despite this, some advanced theories were put forward, usually accompanied by complex mathematical equations. Unfortunately these tended to be filed away and forgotten as the theory was still some way ahead of what was actually possible from a design point of view, given that the gas turbine engine, the method of propulsion that would allow a proper investigation of high speed flight, was still at the inception stage. Although a valid means of delaying the drag rise at compressibility speeds was postulated as early as 1935 it was to take another ten years before the idea was to see the light of day.

In 1935 the Volta Congress met in Rome, an event that was attended by Adolf Busemann who used the opportunity to expound his theory that the drag rise which occurred at high speed could be delayed by employing swept instead of straight wings. Busemann had grown up in the German town of Lubeck on the Baltic coast and, as a child, had been fascinated by the ships making their way through the harbour, in particular the V-shaped wave that spread back from the bow. As an aeronautical engineer he began to consider that a wing might operate more efficiently at high speed if it was swept back which would result in it being kept well away from the bow wave that started to form at the front of the aircraft. Many aviation luminaries heard the theory including Eastman Jacobs who was representing the National Advisory Committee for Aeronautics (NACA) of the USA, but outside Germany Busemann's work failed to make much of an impression.

With the start of the Second World War the free spread of new ideas throughout Europe and the rest of the world came to an end but there were others who were slowly coming to the same conclusion as Busemann. In the USA, Michael Gluhareff, a former graduate of the

Russian Imperial Military Engineering College who later joined Sikorsky Aircraft, was working on the design of a tailless aircraft with low aspect ratio wings. In 1941 he proposed a pursuit-interceptor which for the time was extremely radical as its wing was of delta configuration with leading edge sweep of 56 degrees. His reason for using this particular planform was to bring about 'a considerable delay in the action of the compressibility effect'. He went on 'the general shape and form of the aircraft is, therefore, outstandingly adaptable for extremely high speeds.' Despite favourable results from wind tunnel testing, the USAAF did not take the project any further although the wing shape was used in the design of an air launched glide bomb later in the war. It was a model of this weapon that came to the attention of Robert T. Jones, an aerodynamicist with the NACA at Langley, who quickly ascertained that Gluhareff was onto something.

Although some of the wing's attributes had been worked out using incorrect data, the revised figures that Jones compiled were still impressive and in early 1945 he felt it was time for his findings to be disseminated within NACA. On 5 March 1945 he wrote a memo to George W. Lewis, the director of research, part of which included the following – 'I have recently made a theoretical analysis which indicates that a V-shaped wing travelling point foremost would be less affected by compressibility than other planforms. In fact, if the angle of the V is kept small relative to the Mach angle, the lift and Centre of Pressure remain the same at speeds both above and below the speed of sound.'

The theory seemed promising enough but it could only be proved by testing. This was carried out in the supersonic wind tunnel at Langley and also by fixing small delta wing shapes to the upper surface of the wing of a P-51 Mustang. The aircraft was then dived to high speed to obtain the required data. At the same time as these tests were being carried out the first research material obtained from Germany began to arrive in the USA together with German scientists and technicians who had been involved in advanced weapons projects. Their testimony, together with the results of experimental testing and actual hardware brought back from Germany, backed up what Jones had been saying. However, the vast amount of information that was acquired showed that Germany was way ahead of both the USA and Britain when it came to advanced aerodynamics.

What the Germans had discovered at an early stage was that Busemann's theory was completely valid and that by sweeping the wings compressibility drag rise was delayed by an amount that was dependent on the sweep angle used (the greater the angle of sweep, the greater the benefit obtained). The primary factor when considering compressibility effects is the wing's thickness/chord (t/c) ratio. For example a straight wing with a maximum thickness of 1 foot and a chord of 10 feet (the distance from the leading edge to the trailing edge of a wing) has a t/c ratio of 10 per cent. Should that same wing be swept, although the actual chord remains the same, the effective 'aerodynamic chord' is increased as the airflow over the wing, which normally runs parallel to the direction of flight, ends up travelling obliquely over the swept wing surface. A measurement of the aerodynamic chord on a swept-wing (the distance that the air actually travels over the wing from

Straight Wing

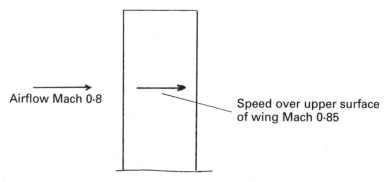

Airflow Mach 0·8

Speed over upper surface
of wing Mach 0·85

Fig 1

Swept Wing – 30°

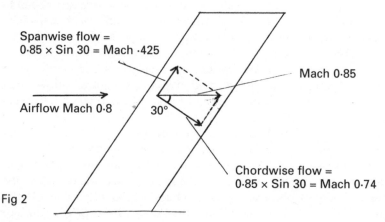

Spanwise flow =
0·85 × Sin 30 = Mach ·425

Mach 0·85

Airflow Mach 0·8

30°

Chordwise flow =
0·85 × Sin 30 = Mach 0·74

Fig 2

leading to trailing edge) shows a greater distance than the actual chord and so the effective t/c ratio is reduced.

This can also be explained in a slightly more mathematical way and is shown in Fig.1. On an aircraft with a straight wing flying at a speed of Mach 0.80, the airflow proceeds over the wing at right angles to its axis and it can be assumed that the air passing over the upper surface will be accelerated to around Mach 0.85. However, if the exact same wing was to be swept by an angle of 30 degrees and the aircraft was flown to the same speed, the end result would be somewhat different. The airflow over the wing would still be accelerated to Mach 0.85, but as far as critical Mach number is concerned, the component that matters is the vector speed along the actual chord of the wing and not the aerodynamic chord. As shown in Fig.2, the oblique passage of the air over a swept wing creates two vectors, one spanwise and one chordwise. It also reveals that the chordwise element of the airflow in this example is only Mach 0.74 which is 0.06M below the true speed of the aircraft and 0.11M below the airflow over a straight wing. The main benefit as far as the pilot is concerned is that a swept wing allows him to fly around 70 mph faster than in a straight-winged aircraft before anything nasty starts to happen in the way of buffeting, heavy controls and uncommanded trim changes.

Unfortunately in aviation, as in most other aspects of life, you do not get anything for nothing. As the chordwise flow of air passes over the wing at a reduced velocity, this also means that a swept wing will not generate as much lift as a straight wing of the same area. To allow for this the angle of attack has to be increased and on a swept wing aircraft this is most noticeable at low speed, especially during landing when the pilot has to adopt a nose-high attitude to compensate for the loss of lift.

Swept wings also cause problems due to the fact that the tip tends to stall before the inboard section of the wing. Whereas the chordwise flow of air as shown occurring over a swept wing is beneficial in delaying the onset of drag at compressibility speeds, the spanwise element of the airflow induces movement towards the tip which leads to a thickening of the boundary layer over the outer section of the wing. The boundary layer is one of the prime factors when it comes to the wing stalling as it tends to slow up the layers of air above it. With the spanwise flow of air on a swept wing leading to the boundary layer being at its thickest at the tip, there is a very real danger that the tip will stall before the root, especially at the high angles of attack that have to be adopted to counter the loss of lift mentioned above. Tip stall leads to loss of aileron control and an inward movement of the Centre of Pressure which, because of wing sweep, will also move forwards, thereby increasing the possibility of pitch up. Various fixes have been tried in an attempt to alleviate these problems, one of the first being the wing fence which was a physical barrier to the spanwise flow of air. Later attempts were rather more subtle and included extending the chord of the outer section of the wing so as to create a 'sawtooth' effect or incorporating a notch in the wing leading edge. Both of these methods produced a strong vortex which performed the same function as a wing fence.

The pitch-up tendency due to tip stall is exacerbated during tight turns as a swept wing, as well as bending in the normal fashion, also twists so that the wing tips are presented to the airflow at a reduced angle of attack. This means that they create less lift so that the overall Centre of Pressure again moves inwards and forwards with the result that the nose tends to lift and the aircraft tightens into the turn. This was to be a particular problem for a number of fighters of the 1950s such as the Supermarine Swift and to a lesser extent the Hawker Hunter.

Despite all the drawbacks the one big advantage in having swept wings, the fact that they allowed aircraft to fly much closer to the speed of sound before they encountered any undesirable effects caused by compressibility, was overriding. In the event the first swept wings as seen on the Messerschmitt Me 163 and Me 262 came about as a result of other factors, as they were included to maintain stability on the former and an acceptable CG range on the latter. By the end of the war, however, the 40-degree swept wing Messerschmitt P.1101 was nearing completion and Junkers were flying the Ju 287 jet bomber with wings swept forwards by 25 degrees.

Having expounded the advantages of swept wings, it was, of course, still possible to explore the transonic region of flight with a straight wing if, and it was a big if, it could be built thin enough. As the critical factor is thickness/chord ratio, there is no reason why a straight wing with a lower t/c value than a swept wing should not perform as well in terms of its ability to delay the drag rise at high Mach numbers. This distinction was unfortunately lost on some of the decision makers at the end of the Second World War who looked upon swept wings almost in awe. Anyone suggesting that a straight-winged aircraft could fly supersonically was suddenly looked at askance and this was one of the reasons why the Miles M.52 was cancelled in 1946. This particular affliction took hold mainly in Britain as Bell Aircraft in the USA happily continued with its similarly straight-winged, but rocket-powered XS-1 which ultimately was the first aircraft to fly in excess of Mach 1.0 on 14 October 1947.

CHAPTER FOUR

Problems with Compressibility

B y the late 1930s the rapid progress that was being made in the design
of fighter aircraft, in particular the adoption of the streamlined
monoplane and the use of stressed skin construction, together with
the availability of engines of vastly increased power, meant that there was
a significant improvement in top speed over a very short timescale. Not
only was the level speed of these aircraft vastly better than the machines
they were due to replace, but their terminal velocity in a dive was way in
excess of the speeds that had been possible with the biplanes that had
been produced in the years after the First World War. Although the
phenomenon of compressibility had been predicted by a number of aerodynamicists in various theoretical papers, nothing could prepare the test
pilots of the major fighter manufacturers for what they were about to
experience. Some of the first pilots to enter this new region of flight were
those associated with testing the Lockheed YP-38 which represented a
radical departure from its immediate forebears.

The YP-38 had been developed from the original XP-38 which had
been Lockheed's response to a USAAC Specification for a high-altitude
fighter capable of a top speed of at least 360 mph and the ability to reach
a height of 20,000 feet in 6 minutes. As long range and a heavy armament
were also specified, the requirements could only be met by a twin-
engined aircraft and Lockheed Chief Designer Hall Hibbard and his
assistant Clarence L. 'Kelly' Johnson eventually settled on a twin-boom
layout with a central nacelle for the pilot and the guns. The choice of
engine was the Allison V-1710 liquid-cooled in-line engine with turbo-
supercharging; the twin booms providing a convenient location for the
impeller and the exhaust wastegate, together with the lengthy ducting
that took the compressed air via an intercooler to the carburettor. The
XP-38 was flown for the first time on 27 January 1939 but was badly
damaged on 11 February when it crash-landed on a golf course just short

of Mitchel Field, New York as a result of carburettor icing. The first YP-38 did not fly until 17 September 1940 but dive tests were soon to show that the type was particularly prone to problems as a result of compressibility.

During 1941 an ever-growing number of test pilots carried out compressibility dives in the YP-38, their reports showing that the aircraft was prone to extreme buffeting and that it was extremely easy to lose control. One of these pilots was Major Signa Gilkey who had been allocated to Lockheed by USAAC. On one particular occasion he took a YP-38 up to 35,000 feet and put the aircraft into a dive, quickly reaching 320 mph IAS. At this point the aircraft became violently nose heavy and the complete tail unit began to shake as though flutter had set in. This caused the control wheel to move through a large amplitude so that it could not be held. Fortunately, the airframe held together and Gilkey was able to recover at a lower altitude by using the elevator trimmer which appeared to be the only means by which the aircraft could be pulled out of the dive.

Incidents such as this led to a thorough investigation of the dive characteristics of the YP-38 which ultimately led to a report being issued in February 1942 which discounted a number of theories as to what might be causing the condition. One possibility was the effect of propeller rotation as the aircraft flown by Gilkey had been equipped with two right-hand rotation engines. The test aircraft (c/n 2218) had opposite rotation engines but there was no change in its behaviour in the dive and the only method of recovery was by means of the elevator tab. During the pull out an acceleration of 5g was recorded as the effectiveness of the tab on the elevator developed suddenly as speed was reduced. If elevator flutter was occurring, this would most likely be caused by the elevator balance weights and so various elevator balance weight arrangements were tried without any noticeable difference in the buffeting characteristics or the airspeed when it took hold. Although this appeared to have ruled out flutter, elevator cable tension was varied and a horizontal stabiliser was built with thicker skinning of 0.051 inch duralumin in place of the standard 0.032 inch. Neither of the above modifications had any effect on the vibration that was occurring, and so flutter was discounted completely.

During the tests it was noted that the nose-wheel door was opening in flight at speeds above 300 mph and it was thought that this might be causing fuselage stalling which, in turn, was bringing about the tail buffeting. Revised locks were fitted to the nose-wheel door but there was no appreciable difference in the vibration. Other theories which were quickly given short shrift were the opening of the coolant air flaps and the effect of turbo-exhaust disturbances. Finally it was suspected that the cause of the high diving moment and the buffeting might be the development of shock waves due to compressibility phenomena on the wing and fuselage. Wind tunnel tests were being run concurrently with the flight tests and these suggested that a fuselage 'extension' might alleviate the problem. This was tried on aircraft 2218 but, again, without success. Continuing wind tunnel investigations, however, began to show that there was a problem occurring at the fuselage/wing and boom/wing intersections. Pressure patterns were plotted and these showed that a very high flow-velocity was being obtained at the fuselage/wing junction. The presence of the boom and fuselage caused a very high acceleration of the air over the wing amounting to 40 per cent of the flight speed. This meant that when the aircraft was flying at 500 mph TAS at 25,000 feet (345 mph IAS), the airflow speed over the wing close to the fuselage was up to the speed of sound.

In order to reduce the flow velocity over the wing, fifteen fuselage/wing fillets were developed and tested by means of pressure distribution and drag tests. Even a small leading edge fillet produced a substantial change in velocity and this had the effect of reducing not only the velocity near the fuselage, but also the velocity over the entire region between the fuselage and the boom. A leading edge extension was also proposed to reduce the speed of the airflow even further but it was found that this affected CG and fillets for the boom/wing were abandoned as the advantage gained was insufficient. Flight testing of the fuselage/wing fillet showed a marked reduction in the amount of tail buffeting that was experienced. Whereas previously the controls had oscillated some 4–8 inches during the period of violent buffeting, with the fillet in place the movement was reduced to around 1 inch. Although the dive tendency was practically unchanged, buffeting would not develop in steady dives at speeds up to 360 mph at 26,000 feet until the pull out was made. From the flight testing carried out it was thought that the most practical way to overcome the diving tendency was to provide the pilot with an automatic tab to aid him in pulling out of the dive.

The aircraft elevator was revised so that two additional servo tabs, one on each end of the elevator, would come into play when the stick forces exceeded a 30 lb pull on the control wheel. The amount of servo increased proportionally as the stick force increased until 13 degrees of tab was obtained with a stick force of 80 lb. Diving tests were extremely encouraging, the aircraft handling easily and smoothly in all conditions and it appeared as though a major improvement had been made, but in test flying nothing can be taken for granted. On 5 November 1941 Lockheed test pilot Ralph Virden took off to carry out dive tests to 350 mph IAS at 23,000 feet with the trim tab set to be in-trim at 300 mph IAS. He was to make one dive and, if no undue problems were apparent, this was to be followed by two further dives. Although the aircraft could not be seen, it was heard to make three dives before it reappeared flying straight and level at around 3,000 feet. It was then seen to pull up sharply and the empennage began to disintegrate. A loud shrieking noise was also heard and the aircraft entered an inverted spin before it dived into the ground, demolishing a house at 1147 Elm Street, Glendale, near Los Angeles. Virden was killed instantly, however, the occupant of the house, Jack Jenson, had a remarkable escape and was found by fire crews still in his bed sound asleep! Examination of the wreckage showed that catastrophic flutter had caused the disintegration of the empennage; however, the accident was witnessed by a large number of people and it was established with certainty that the aircraft was not undertaking a dive test when the flutter occurred.

During an investigation of the crash by Kelly Johnson of Lockheed, a failure of the left auxiliary tab control arm just outside the weld to its torque tube was noted. A visual inspection of this weld appeared to indicate that a crack of considerable magnitude had existed for some time in this arm. It was concluded that the control arm had broken apart during the time that Virden was returning to the airfield. A failure of this nature would have released the left-hand auxiliary tab so that destructive flutter would almost certainly have been the result. As a result of this accident wind tunnel testing was carried out by the NACA at Langley Field, Virginia, which confirmed that there was an appreciable rise in drag on the P-38 at the relatively low Mach number of 0.65 and that the limiting Mach number of the aircraft was 0.68.

A further modification intended to improve the P-38's characteristics at compressibility speeds was the use of under-wing dive-recovery flaps. These were approximately 4 feet long with a chord of around 8 inches and were fitted outboard of the engine nacelles with their hinged leading edge at the 35 per cent chord point of the wing. There was no slot between the flap leading edge and the wing surface and they were capable of being lowered to an angle of 30 degrees. When retracted they formed part of the under surface of the wing. They were hydraulically operated by a knob on the right-hand side of the pilot's seat. The purpose of the flaps was to overcome the tendency for the P-38 to dive at high Mach numbers by applying a nose-up pitch. These were tested on a P-38G on 9 April 1943 by Colonel Benjamin S. Kelsey but despite the system having been proved on several previous occasions, this flight would show that despite all the modifications the P-38 could still bite if it was pushed too far.

Ben Kelsey had been involved with the P-38 programme from the very beginning as in the mid 1930s he had been placed in charge of the Fighter Projects Office at Wright Field, Ohio. He had also taken the XP-38 on its first flight and a month later had stepped out of it unhurt following an undershoot when on the approach to Mitchel Field. Although the purpose of Kelsey's flight in the P-38G was to test the dive brakes, the sortie was to have been one of familiarisation and the intention was to stay well clear of any critical conditions during the dives. The first dive was entered from a height of 35,000 feet and an indicated airspeed of 155 mph and the dive angle was maintained at 45 degrees. As he passed 31,200 feet Kelsey noted that speed had risen to 290 mph IAS as noted by the pitot mounted on the wing tip, although the nose-mounted pitot produced an indication of only 260 mph. As it transpired, these were the last instrument readings that he was able to make.

With the aircraft approaching its limiting speed, Kelsey attempted to operate the lever to activate the dive recovery flaps, but it refused to move. During the brief period when he was occupied with the flap lever, the aircraft exceeded its critical speed and the dive angle increased to the point where it was descending vertically. An attempt was made at recovery using the controls and the trim tab, but without success. Kelsey then tried to raise the nose by yawing the aircraft with rudder. This resulted in a small nose-up pitch but when he applied aileron the aircraft snapped back into a dive which was even steeper than before and was estimated to be 10–20 degrees over the vertical. It was at this point that the controls began to oscillate violently fore-and-aft over 5–10 cycles and the aircraft went into an inverted spiral that quickly became an inverted spin. On taking spin recovery action Kelsey found the controls to be light or non existent and he later came to the conclusion that the tail surfaces had failed during the period when the controls had been oscillating.

As he had no apparent control over the aircraft and appeared to be getting dangerously close to a layer of cloud at 5,000 feet Kelsey decided to abandon his aircraft and after experiencing some difficulty releasing the canopy, he was able to leave his stricken machine. When his parachute opened he found that he was still at about 20,000 feet, far higher than expected. As he began a slow descent he became aware of the starboard outer-wing panel, with the aileron apparently intact, gliding slowly past him inverted, but in stable flight. Further up he noticed another large piece of P-38 that he could not identify for certain, but which he thought was some part of the horizontal tailplane. The main body of the aircraft at this time was below him, still spinning inverted. During his debrief Kelsey had no recollections of any severe buffeting at any point during the dive and also could not remember being subjected to any excessive g-loadings in any direction. If true, this was most unusual as an examination of the wreckage showed that the starboard outer wing had failed under down load, and the fact that Kelsey had encountered it during his parachute descent proved that this failure had occurred before he left the aircraft. Although careful contouring at the centre section and the use of dive flaps were ultimately successful in easing some of the P-38's compressibility problems during high speed dives, pilots still had to be wary of entering dives from heights above 30,000 feet as the aircraft's limiting Mach number could easily be exceeded. This tended to limit its effectiveness and the full potential of the aircraft could only be used below 25,000 feet where the Mach number was lower for a given indicated airspeed.

At the same time as compressibility was severely affecting the P-38 and other advanced fighter designs in the USA (notably the Republic P-47 Thunderbolt) it was also being experienced in Europe. In Britain the Supermarine Spitfire, which entered service with RAF Fighter Command in August 1938, was to have been replaced in the interceptor role by the Hawker Typhoon which was powered by a 24-cylinder Napier Sabre engine of 2,000 hp. Weighing in at around seven tons, the Typhoon's rugged appearance left no-one in any doubt that it was an extremely powerful machine but its lack of aerodynamic refinement, in particular its thick wing, meant that it was to be a dismal failure as a high altitude fighter due to lower than expected performance above 25,000 feet and a basic lack of manoeuvrability. The weight of the Typhoon at least allowed it to accelerate rapidly in a dive but when this was carried out from high level, the aircraft very soon ran into compressibility.

Throughout its troubled service career, one that was also plagued by severe engine problems and the ingress of carbon monoxide gases into the cockpit, a total of twenty-six Typhoon's were lost as a result of structural failures. The first recorded accident occurred on 29 July 1942 when a Typhoon of 257 Squadron dived into the ground near High Ercall in Shropshire. On 11 August Ken Seth-Smith, a Hawker test pilot, was killed in virtually identical circumstances when flying R7692. The investigation into the accident discovered that the rear fuselage had failed at the transport joint just forward of the tail assembly. A programme was initiated to reinforce the joint which led to the incorporation of 'Mod 286' whereby fishplates were fitted around each stringer but although the accident rate began to diminish, failures of the rear fuselage continued to occur. There was a long list of potential suspects of which compressibility effects were just one. Other culprits included excessive levels of engine-generated vibration, sudden changes of trim due to power alterations and elevator flutter. Particular attention was paid to the elevator mass balance but Typhoons continued to lose their tails right to the very end. As part of the investigations into the structural break-ups a major test programme was launched in which Hawker test pilots made full power dives to push the Typhoon to its limits. One pilot involved in these trials was Roland Beamont who described a compressibility dive in *Typhoon and Tempest at War* (Ian Allan, 1974) which he co-wrote with Arthur Reed:

Charlie Dunn, the flight-test engineer, briefed me that from a maximum power level at 30,000 feet, a push over into a near-vertical dive should enable us to reach about 450 mph indicated at 20,000 feet. At 28,000 feet there was no clear space in sight for the required dive, but I levelled at 31,000 feet on top of a cirrus deck and pushed up the power to maximum boost and the phenomenal Sabre rpm limit of 3,750. As speed built up, a break occurred in the clouds to port, and at the bottom of a quite well-defined cloud shaft, a bend in the Thames near Eton could be seen.

With instrumentation switches set for strain gauge recording, and initial flight conditions noted on the test pad, we peeled off to port, bringing the rpm back slightly as a margin against loss of propeller constant speed control in the dive, and rolling out into a near-vertical dive, trimmed with a slight residual push force, again as a safety margin, this time against the anticipated nose-down effects of compressibility. At 27,000 feet the general noise and fuss were becoming impressive, with buffet vibration building up through the controls, seat and cockpit sides. Even the motor-car side windows were away at their natural frequency, and it was while observing this with interest that the situation developed suddenly. I was conscious of the controls stiffening up quite rapidly, of the port wing trying to drop, and of the aircraft becoming nose-heavy to the accompaniment of violent buffeting and a general feeling of insecurity. When beginning to bear back on the stick, to hold the dive angle from getting too steep, and holding off starboard aileron to maintain wings level, it was markedly apparent that these actions were ineffective.

A full two-handed pull failed to reduce the dive angle at all, and we were now going downhill, and rolling to port, with maximum noise, buffet and general commotion, and with no conventional control of the situation. Here was the thing called compressibility about which Philip Lucas had said : 'Whatever you do, don't trim it out of the dive', as the consequent trim reversal would probably overstress something severely. So I didn't and, with throttle right back, continued to ride the bucking and uncontrolled device down through 20,000 feet until we passed 15,000 feet where, as the Mach number dropped, the shock waves were supposed to subside, and the elevator recover effectiveness. This indeed occurred and, with subsiding buffet, aileron effectiveness recovered first. Then the nose began to rise under my still heavy pull-force, until I was able at last to ease off the pressure and recover to a level attitude, still with the throttles closed, the indicated airspeed dropping back from 500 mph and, impressively, the altimeter steadying at only 8,500 feet!

Due to its failings as a high-altitude interceptor the Typhoon was eventually used, with great success, as a ground attack fighter where it could be fitted with two bombs of either 500-lb or 1,000-lb capacity, or eight 60-lb rocket projectiles, in addition to its standard armament of four 20 mm Hispano cannons. As it was very rarely flown above 10,000 feet in this role, compressibility effects did not come in to play during its later service life. Even though it was regularly flown at speeds up to 500 mph IAS during its attacking dives, the fact that this was only carried out at low level meant that the Typhoon's limiting Mach number was not exceeded. Three aircraft that did regularly come into contact with Mach effects, however, were the Spitfire, P-51 Mustang and P-47 Thunderbolt.

By the mid-war period experimental work in high speed wind-tunnels had delivered large amounts of data but very few flight trials had been carried out to enable the results to be checked. There was a good deal of qualitative information on high speed effects from the debrief reports of pilots who had encountered compressibility in dives, however, very little actual research had been conducted to measure the overall drag levels and pressure distribution over the wing section, together with longitudinal trim changes at high Mach numbers. A series of high speed dives were commenced at RAE Farnborough in May 1943 using a Spitfire XI (EN409) and a Mustang I (AG393). The tests were made at high altitude to obtain the greatest possible Mach number while keeping indicated airspeed and structural loads down to the lowest values for safety. As the Mustang used in the trial was an early Allison-engined example with a rated altitude of only 10,000 feet the aircraft had to be stripped of guns and radio to save weight but even so the dives could only be commenced from 28,000 feet. In contrast the Spitfire XI with its two-speed, two-stage supercharged Merlin 61 could easily be climbed to 40,000 feet so that the dives could be maintained for a longer period before recovery action had to be taken.

With both aircraft the dives were started by accelerating to maximum level speed at the highest altitude that could be attained before putting the nose down and setting the engine controls to a position which would give maximum permissible continuous boost at the end of the dive (in the case of the Spitfire this was the Moderately Supercharged or MS setting). The dive angle was usually around 45 degrees, the procedure being to maintain the dive until maximum Mach number had been reached (this took about 11,000 feet in all cases) then to continue for a few more seconds before starting a gentle (2-3g) pull out. A Mach meter was fitted to both aircraft but as it was only calibrated to 0.80 it was only of benefit to the Mustang as with the Spitfire it was off the scale. The pilot throughout the test was Squadron Leader J.R. Tobin AFC.

Before commencing the dive the pilot was warned of the possibility of large trim changes in the nose-down direction and of the possible ineffectiveness of the elevator trimming tab. He therefore trimmed into the dive at the beginning, but when the nose-down change appeared near maximum Mach, he made no attempt to correct on the trimmer, but held the aircraft by stick force alone, assuming that this was physically possible. During the trial it was discovered that the drag coefficient rose only gradually in the region of 0.60-0.70M with the formation of small shock waves on excrescences such as the windscreen and radiator. With further increase in speed, however, there was a rapid rise in drag as the shock-stall occurred over the main wing. The most interesting aspect of the trial was the discovery that this steep drag rise set in much later with the Spitfire despite the fact that the Mustang had an advanced laminar flow wing. The latter had been designed so that its maximum thickness was further aft than on a conventional aerofoil at around 40 per cent chord. The intention was to reduce drag by maintaining smooth, laminar flow over a greater proportion of the wing but at high Mach numbers this effect was only minor and was eclipsed by the fact that the Spitfire's wing, although of conventional section with maximum thickness further forward, was much thinner. The Spitfire's thickness/chord ratio was 13 per cent at the root and 7 per cent at the tip which compared with 16 per cent and 11 per cent respectively for the Mustang.

The P-47 Thunderbolt had a wing of conventional section of 16 per cent t/c ratio at the root and 9 per cent at the tip and its capabilities at high Mach numbers were further degraded by its large air-cooled radial engine. Although the Thunderbolt was not tested at Farnborough, information was available from the USA which showed that the steep drag rise commenced at a very low Mach number. It was also more liable to go out of control as at the maximum drag coefficient, the greatest elevator angle that the pilot could apply was 7 degrees which was insufficient to hold the aircraft. A rough comparison was made with the Spitfire which required a pull force of 50–60 lb to maintain control at 0.89M at 30,000 feet. In similar circumstances a pull of 200 lb, even if a pilot was able to exert such a force, would still be inadequate to hold a Thunderbolt at 20,000 feet.

The trim changes experienced by all three aircraft were very similar as all developed a nose-down moment near to maximum Mach number which had to be countered by applying negative or up elevator. The sequence of events as experienced by the pilot was generally as follows. For the initial part of the dive a push force was required to maintain a steady dive angle. After a few thousand feet this push force had to be gradually relaxed until finally the control column had to be pulled back to prevent the dive angle from becoming steeper. The pull reached a maximum upon or just after reaching the aircraft's maximum Mach number and subsequently diminished. Should the pilot not apply the correction quickly enough, either because of inattention or because he was physically unable to apply the necessary force, the dive angle became steeper and the Mach number increased more rapidly to the point where it was likely that the pilot would be unable to regain control until reaching lower levels.

In many cases the most dangerous part of the compressibility dive occurred when control began to return as Mach number slowly diminished at lower altitudes. When this happened the pilot would still have been pulling back hard on the control column and thus applying a considerable force in a nose-up sense. It was at this stage that the nose-down pitch at high Mach numbers started to diminish, a process that was accelerated during recovery as the aircraft's speed reduced rapidly during the pull out. It was thus important for the pilot to begin to relax his pull on the controls as soon as the recovery was initiated so that the aircraft was not over-stressed in the pull-out manoeuvre. Although the practice was discouraged in the strongest terms, some pilots may also have been tempted to seek the assistance of the elevator trimmer to help get the nose up during a dive. This would have the effect of increasing the nose-up pitch on recovery, a situation that would be made worse by any degree of longitudinal instability, such as might be expected when flying with an aft CG, which would be likely to produce light stick forces and result in over-controlling, severe accelerations and a possible structural break-up.

During the trial at Farnborough the Spitfire easily out-performed the Mustang reaching a maximum Mach number of 0.89 at 29,000 feet after commencing a dive from 40,000 feet. The Mustang was limited by its poor altitude performance and could only reach 0.80M following a dive from 28,000 feet. With both aircraft the maximum Mach number was reached after a dive of 11,000 feet and there was little point in extending the dive any further as Mach number slowly decreased as altitude was lost. In contrast as height was reduced, indicated airspeed started to increase significantly which had no benefit as the prime requirement was to study compressibility effects. All it did was to increase the loads that were likely to be experienced when pulling out of the dive. On one occasion with the Mustang the dive was continued at its peak Mach number down to a height of only 10,000 feet, with a final pull-out at 7,000 feet. This late recovery produced evidence of a small range of elevator movement over which control was lacking, one that was probably due to cable stretch or distortion under the higher loads that the aircraft had been subjected to. One factor that the trial did show, however, was that although the Spitfire and Mustang were both subject to the effects of compressibility to an extent, pilots generally had little to fear from these aircraft, unlike the Thunderbolt which hit trouble much earlier and was liable to be out of control rather longer.

In May 1943 reports were received in the UK from the British Air Commission in Washington relating to compressibility phenomena experienced by US personnel with the P-47 Thunderbolt. One sortie flown by an anonymous pilot on 8 January 1943 was reported on as follows:

Having completed a climb to 37,800 feet, I carried out a speed run at 37,500 feet. My oxygen was running low, so I decided to lose no time in getting down below oxygen height. I closed the cowl flaps, set the oil cooler and intercooler shutters to neutral, reduced the turbo revolutions to 10,000, the rpm to 2,400 and the manifold pressure to 26 in Hg. Starting from 155 mph IAS I did a gentle wingover to the left towards base. I had straightened out and was in a 50 degree dive at 310 mph IAS by 30,000 feet. At approximately 29,000 feet, the aircraft suddenly started to shudder, the control column tried to jump out of my hand-vibrating in a fore-and-aft direction and the nose of the aircraft dropped to about 70 degrees. It felt as if the tail was coming off, but looking in the mirror, I could see the radio mast, vertical fin and tail planes vibrating badly. Certain in my own mind that it was not just the mirror vibrating, I turned in my seat and could see the tail planes vibrating through about six inches. At the same time I wound the elevator trim tab fully back, but with no result.

I then closed the throttle and rpm lever, but the nose dropped further until it was vertically down. I still could not pull back the stick and hold it back enough to get the nose up because of the violent vibration, however, the ailerons were not vibrating and there was no lateral vibration of the stick. I then remembered that previous experience had shown that it was easier to pull out of a dive with engine on, than with no engine, so I opened the throttle and rpm levers fully and the nose immediately began to rise, and the trimming started to take effect. I corrected for over-trim, and the vibration had ceased altogether by the time that I was at 18,000 feet in a gentle dive of about 15 degrees. At no time did the IAS exceed 390 mph, and I feel certain that I never exceeded an acceleration force of 3g during the pull out. The aircraft carried a normal load of ammunition (275 rounds per gun), and at the time the shudder was experienced, the auxiliary fuel tank had been used completely and about 50 gallons out of the 205 gallons contents of the main fuel tanks. The aircraft was on a 'red diagonal', having had its wing roots wrinkled by a heavy landing. The crew chief later said he considered the wrinkle, especially in the left main spar, to be appreciably worse after this flight in which the shudder was experienced than it was before.

Two months later on 6 March 1943 another pilot had a similar experience when diving a P-47 from high altitude:

This afternoon I took P-47 airplane, No. 41-6127, to 25,000 feet to test its rate of climb. I stayed at the altitude for about ten minutes waiting for the cylinder head temperatures to decrease, so it would be possible to close the cowl shutters for a level maximum speed test. After finishing the test, I dived under a cloud and pulled back up to 25,000 feet. At this point the following existed – airspeed 170 mph, 25 inches of Hg, no turbo and 2,400 rpm. I made a half roll with the intention of levelling off at 20,000 feet for another speed test. Just as the nose of the ship was straight down, I noticed a vibration that seemed to come from the tail. The airspeed was 400 mph IAS. Just as I relaxed pressure for a second, the stick jerked from side to side about four times before I was able to stop it. At the same time I jerked the throttle and propeller pitch back. I tried pulling back with both hands but with no luck, then adjusted the elevator trim tab completely back and tried again with eventual success.

Somewhere during this time I opened the canopy with the idea of getting out but gave it up when I felt the wind. A mist inside the cockpit disappeared with the canopy open, so I was able to see white condensation over the wings. I could see that the ailerons were damaged and that the wings were rippled before the plane started out of the dive. As near as I can remember, the right wing had a two foot ripple about the centre toward the rear of the wing. Both wings had a small ripple near the leading inside corner of the gun cover. The glance was brief and no other ripples were noticed. The pull out was not over 5g as there was no tendency toward a black out. Also the plane seemed to have slowed down considerably as there was no pull up after levelling off and the airspeed did not take long to decrease to 230 mph, the first time that I was able to look at the ASI.

When the plane had slowed down and I found that I could still control it, the airspeed was 230 mph, altitude 3,000 feet. Needless to say, the plane was very unstable, taking two hands and a knee to hold the thing level. The landing gear came down OK but the flaps did not work. Because of the tendency to roll when the throttle was cut, I brought it in under power and landed or flew it into the ground at about 170 mph. The right tyre went flat after the plane was taxied back to the line and parked. Damage in general consisted of two bent and broken ailerons, rippled tail surfaces, torn engine cowl on the left side and slightly rippled wings. The gas load was about 150 and 175 gallons and 2,200 rounds of ammunition.

In response to a number of incidents similar to those recorded above the USAAF put out a technical order with various speed limitations for the P-47 as follows:

Height	Speed
0–10,000 ft	500 mph IAS
10–15,000 ft	450 mph IAS
15–20,000 ft	400 mph IAS
20–25,000 ft	350 mph IAS
25–30,000 ft	300 mph IAS
30–35,000 ft	250 mph IAS

Further high-speed diving trials were carried out at RAE in 1944 by Squadron Leader Tony Martindale, the long-suffering Spitfire XI EN409 again being the test aircraft. The trials were not without incident and the following is a report compiled by Martindale following a flight on 27 April 1944:

I took off and climbed to 40,000 feet with the altimeter at 1,013 mb. At ceiling I began to feel slightly anoxic due to the low oxygen flow and flew level for a time at 2,850 rpm full throttle and worked the ASI round to 170 mph. I then most carefully set the rudder and elevator trims, selecting an intermediate position on the latter between the extremes I have tried. I switched on the camera and dived the aeroplane. I bunted steadily keeping the 'g' low so as to reduce drag and closed the throttle slightly. When I was down to 32,000 feet the altimeter was spinning merrily and the dive was very steep and I was pulling back on the stick in the usual way due to the change of trim at the shock stall.

I glanced at the altimeter and saw it drop from 28,000 to 27,000 feet and I knew I was past the high speed. I began to think of pulling out of the dive when there was a fearful explosion and the aircraft became enveloped in white smoke. I incorrectly assumed that a structural failure had occurred as I knew this to be the danger. The aircraft shook from end to end and I knew I could not bale out at such speed so sat still. The aircraft was doing nothing startling but the screen and hood were now quite black and I could see nothing.

Automatically I eased the stick back and discovered by looking backwards through the oil film that I was climbing. The airspeed was falling as the noises were dying down. I realised I could now bale out and opened the hood, but the aircraft was under partial control at least and so I switched off the camera and began to think I might be able to get the aircraft down and save the film and other apparatus. I still did not know what had happened as I could not see through the windscreen.

I pointed the aircraft towards base and called up on the radio. As I tried to look round the screen my goggles were whipped away, but the engine clearly was not going and I could see no propeller. Bits of engine were sticking out and it seemed to have moved sideways. I reported this to base. I consulted the Chief Test Pilot as to the advisability of lowering the wheels, supposing they would go down. The hydraulics were u/s and I had pressure for flaps. The CTP advised a wheels down landing and I glided 20 miles or so and saw I could reach base. This I reached at 6,000 feet, the aircraft gliding very nicely without its propeller. On landing I saw that the propeller and engine reduction gear had gone and a main engine bearer had buckled.

The method of entry, which involved a bunt into a dive of around 45 degrees, was carried out so as to 'unload' the aircraft so that it accelerated quickly and reached its highest Mach number at a safe altitude. The alternative would have been a half roll and pull through which would have led to high 'g' levels and a much wilder ride for the pilot which, in turn, would have lowered the safety factor considerably. The maximum Mach number attained during this dive was 0.92, the highest ever recorded by a piston-engined fighter. Although there is no doubt that he possessed great bravery, Tony Martindale had another advantage in that at 6 ft 2 in and 17 stones he also had great strength which allowed him to apply the very heavy stick forces that were needed to retain control at these exceptional speeds.

Following his accident in EN409 Martindale continued the programme of high speed dives. On 15 August he was preparing to dive Spitfire XI PL827 when the engine began to over-speed (probably due to a failure of the constant speed unit) and the supercharger exploded, resulting in an engine fire. The fire soon went out but once again his windscreen was covered in oil that prevented him from seeing high-tension cables on his approach to land in a field near Woking. As a result he crash-landed and suffered back injuries but he still had the presence of mind to collect the valuable recording camera from his burning machine, an act for which he was later awarded the Air Force Cross (AFC).

To an extent the trials at Farnborough with the Mustang I had been unrepresentative as it could only be dived from 28,000 feet due to its low-altitude rated Allison engine. By 1944 the Merlin-powered Mustang was in widespread use and high-speed dive tests were carried out from heights of up to 40,000 feet on a P-51D (44-14134) by the Flight Research Branch at Wright Field, Dayton, Ohio. Although the P-51D was dived up to 0.85M it was recommended that the aircraft be limited in service to a Mach number of 0.80 as compressibility difficulties became increasingly dangerous above this point.

At Mach numbers as low as 0.70 the Mustang was subject to longitudinal instability or 'porpoising', a condition that was often pilot induced and was likely to be the result of any sudden elevator movement. Any effort on the part of the pilot to counteract this effect was liable to lead to a fore-and-aft motion of increasing amplitude and it was best to hold the stick firmly in one position, or to trim forward gradually to near zero stick force as the dive was entered, thus reducing the amount of forward stick necessary to maintain the required dive angle. As 0.76M was approached a true consequence of compressibility became evident in the form of airframe vibration which was a combination of compressibility effects on the wing and horizontal stabiliser. This condition increased in severity as Mach number was increased to the point where it could eventually cause a primary structural failure.

In an attempt to discover the maximum combat limit the Mustang was dived on several occasions to 0.84M and on one occasion to 0.85M. In each case the pilots involved in the trial reported that vibration levels had become extremely heavy by 0.80M and in every dive to 0.84M or above, the buffet levels were so severe as to cause damage to the aircraft. This included buckling of the leading edge skin of the wing flap, a cracked coolant radiator and a broken hydraulic line. As a result of the above it was considered that in an 'extreme war emergency' the Mustang could be flown to 0.83M (400 mph IAS at 25,000 feet), but only if a very gradual pull-out was made. Even a relatively low acceleration could result in a primary structural failure if the 'g' loading was applied when the aircraft was subject to the vibration experienced at high Mach numbers.

Care had also to be taken when entering the dive and it was best to gently lower the nose or to execute a diving turn. Entry to a dive from a half roll and pull through was not recommended since high Mach numbers could be reached in a matter of a few seconds and when this was attempted at rated power at heights above 36,000 feet structural failure was again a very real possibility. After completing the dive, the recovery had to be very gradual and made with extreme caution since relatively light stick forces or the rapid application of trim could easily result in excessive load factors.

Although aerodynamically the P-51 Mustang was the most advanced of all the Second World War piston-engined fighters, its behaviour in the transonic region of flight was disappointing and was inferior to the Spitfire which had been designed in 1935. From the flight testing carried out in 1943/44 it gradually became clear that the thickness/chord ratio of the wing was the most important factor in delaying the steep drag rise as an aircraft approached its limiting Mach number. Even a wing of conventional section, where the peak suction was generated over the first 25 per cent of wing chord, could be superior to a laminar flow wing if its t/c ratio was of a lower value. In addition to the testing of service fighters, the emergence of jet and rocket powered aircraft in the early war period opened up new avenues for high speed research. As these aircraft were exceptionally 'clean', low-drag machines and were unencumbered with a large-diameter propeller for propulsion, much was expected of them, and the following chapter looks at jet aircraft developed in Britain and the USA during the war years.

CHAPTER FIVE

Early Allied Jets

Much has been written about the trials and tribulations experienced by Frank Whittle in his single-minded quest to produce a gas turbine engine capable of powering an aircraft in flight. As this form of propulsion was to be one of the major factors that brought about the greatest advance in performance ever seen, it is discussed in detail in the following chapter, however, by 1939 Whittle's first jet unit was producing sufficient power for the Air Ministry to order a flight engine and an experimental aircraft to accommodate it.

Through a former acquaintance at RAF Cranwell, Wing Commander J.H. McC. Reynolds, who by 1939 was the Air Ministry representative at Gloster Aircraft, Whittle was introduced to Gloster's Chief Designer, George Carter, and the timing could not have been better. Carter immediately saw the potential of the Whittle engine and, by coincidence, had already penned an aircraft that would be capable of accepting the new powerplant. This was a twin-boom design which had been created to comply with Specification F.18/37 and had the advantage of offering minimal thrust losses due to its short jet pipe. In the event concern that the jet efflux might adversely affect the tail unit led to this scheme being abandoned and it was replaced by a more conventional looking design to Specification E.28/39.

As Whittle continued to develop his jet engine at his works at Lutterworth, the E.28/39 began to take form at Gloster's factory at Brockworth and eventually emerged in March 1941 with the serial number W4041. Although it had a relatively portly fuselage to provide sufficient space for the centrifugal jet engine, its lines were sleek enough and it featured a low wing which tapered to rounded tips. The horizontal stabiliser was mounted on top of the rear fuselage, with the fin set slightly forwards, and the jet pipe exhausted behind the trailing edge. Unusually for the period, a Dowty-designed tricycle undercarriage was incorporated, the lack of a propeller allowing the use of very short undercarriage legs with minimal ground clearance. The first engine installed in the E.28/39 was a W.1X which was not cleared for flight but produced sufficient thrust for taxi trials to be performed. Following the successful conclusion of this part of the test programme the aircraft was taken to Cranwell for its first flight, a convenient location as it possessed a long runway and was well away from populated areas which helped to preserve the air of secrecy surrounding the project. It was at Cranwell that the W.1 engine of 860 lb thrust was fitted and the E.28/39 was flown for the first time in the evening of 15 May 1941 by Gloster Chief Test Pilot, P.E.G. 'Gerry' Sayer.

During its early testing W4041 was fitted with a high-lift wing of NACA 23012 section, but this was later changed for a 'high-speed' aerofoil of EC.1240-0940 section which tapered from 12.5 per cent thickness/chord ratio at the root to 10 per cent at the tip. Although delays were experienced due to engine snags, including a cracked turbine blade and problems with the oil supply, the trials programme made excellent progress and in May 1943 the aircraft was fitted with a Power Jets W.2/500 engine of 1,700 lb thrust. In the meantime a second E.28/39 (W4046) had been built and this was first flown by Gloster development test pilot John Grierson on 1 March 1943 under the power of a Rover W.2B of 1,200 lb thrust, however, it was soon to be fitted with a developed version which produced 1,526 lb thrust.

On 3 May 1943 W4046 was flown to RAE Farnborough where it was due to undergo performance testing. On one occasion during level speed tests at low level it ran out of fuel, the pilot taking advantage of its low drag to glide back to Farnborough for a dead-stick landing. In the course of further trials several aspects of jet handling were experienced for the first time, including compressor stall which produced a noise rather like a machine-gun being fired. This could be cured by throttling back, but on another occasion the engine flamed out due to fuel starvation as a result of modifications to the fuel system to allow inverted flight. Luckily a relight system had, by now, been fitted and the first airborne relight was successfully performed. During its time at Farnborough concern was expressed as regards aileron control which at times was excessively stiff. On 30 July W4046 was being flown by Squadron Leader Douglas Davie to determine its climbing performance but at an altitude of 37,000 feet an application of aileron led to the controls seizing solid and the aircraft rolled onto its back and entered an inverted spin. As the E.28/39 went through a series of gyrations, Davie was hurled from the cockpit at a height of around 33,000 feet and thus became the first pilot to 'bale out' of a jet aircraft. His experiences during the descent were recorded in his report of the incident:

After being ejected from the aeroplane I found myself spinning, head downwards. I watched my boots fly off. I then wondered if I had left my parachute behind as I had come out so fast, but I was reassured by feeling it still there when I put my hands up. I thought

I had better wait a bit before pulling the rip cord as I was still going pretty fast but then remembered that I might pass out due to anoxia [now referred to as hypoxia] and pulled it. There was a faint jerk as the parachute opened and found myself swaying around in comparative comfort and silence. I then heard the oxygen escaping from my emergency supply tube and discovered that my helmet and mask had disappeared and also my left glove. Fortunately the supply line had become detached at the mask fitting and I therefore put this end in my mouth and sucked it on the way down.

The time of descent was 20 to 25 minutes. It was exceedingly uncomfortable as I was intensely cold and kept trying to vomit which in turn hurt a bruise I had sustained in my groin. I was conscious throughout the descent although pretty dopey at times. The landing was gentle and I was quickly despatched to hospital by the Civil Defence Services, the police and sundry spectators. I requested the first policeman who arrived to get in touch with Farnborough and to send out a guard to the aircraft impressing on him the importance of keeping people away from it.

Considering the altitude at which he had been thrown out of his aircraft, Davie escaped relatively lightly and only suffered minor frostbite during his descent. Various theories were put forward as to the cause of the aileron seizure including control rod friction due to moisture causing expansion of the fibre fairleads and differential thermal contraction as a result of the extremely cold temperatures experienced at altitude.

The demise of W4046 left W4041 as the sole remaining E.28/39 and having completed its trials programme with the manufacturers, this aircraft was also delivered to RAE at Farnborough where it was to be used to determine its characteristics at the upper end of the speed range. The arrival of W4041 coincided with the Establishment's investigations into flight at speeds approaching the speed of sound and it was particularly welcomed as it offered the chance to test an aircraft that was free from nacelles and the problems that were experienced with propeller-driven types. As the E.28/39 had a single jet propulsion unit in the fuselage with a nose-mounted air intake, the wings were free from any form of interference. The aircraft was still fitted with the 'high-speed' wing which had been designed to keep excess velocities over the upper surface to a minimum. During the trials particular attention was given to the measurement of incidence, aileron angles, elevator angle, stick force, aircraft drag and the drag and pressure distribution of a special test section of the starboard wing. For the tests the ailerons and elevator, which were normally fabric covered, were replaced with metal covered surfaces as it was anticipated that buffeting and elevator trim changes would be experienced. With the co-operation of Power Jets Ltd, a more powerful W.2/700 engine was installed in W4041, however, structural limitations at the rear of the fuselage, in particular the size of jet pipe that could be used, tended to restrict maximum thrust.

Initial testing was hampered by longitudinal pitching which set in at only 0.72M but this was quickly cured by fixing lengths of 3/16 inch cord to the top and bottom surfaces of each elevator which allowed further flights to be made up to a maximum Mach number of 0.816. At this speed the pilot reported that buffeting had set in, together with a general yawing, pitching and rolling of the aircraft and no attempt was made to increase Mach number any further. The normal technique was for the aircraft to be climbed to an altitude of 37–40,000 feet before it was put into a dive at a steady angle until the maximum Mach number desired for the particular test was achieved. For the recovery the aircraft was pulled out of the dive with a normal acceleration of around 2–3g.

The usual nose-down trim change at high Mach numbers was also apparent with the E.28/39 and was one of the largest yet measured by RAE, however, due to the small size of the aircraft it was possible for the pilot to hold relatively large changes of elevator angle. Although it was radically different from other aircraft in terms of its method of propulsion, the airframe was conventional to the point where it did not possess an elevator trimmer. The only method of elevator trimming was by small metal tabs which could be adjusted on the ground. To relieve the pilot of strain during the long climb to altitude these tabs were set to trim the aircraft to fly 'hands off' at about 250 mph EAS. Consequently a considerable push force in the order of 30 lb was required to maintain the correct dive angle, this changing to a pull force of nearly 60 lb during the pull out at 0.81M.

The results of the tests with the E.28/39 highlighted several important aspects of the 'high speed' wing design. The elevator trim change and the stick forces accompanying the trim change were much larger than for similar aircraft with wings of conventional section (i.e. Spitfire XI). Similarly there was a much greater rise in profile drag than that of the Spitfire XI at the same Mach number. The pressure distribution data obtained from the test section on the starboard wing indicated the development of powerful shock waves on both surfaces, the pressure coefficients at 0.81M being much greater than those recorded on the Spitfire XI. The trials appeared to confirm wind tunnel test information that had recently been obtained from Germany which showed that 'high speed' design profiles, although having a higher critical Mach number, were subject to a much more rapid increase in drag above this Mach number than a section of conventional design. Although RAE were keen to carry on with the high speed trials with the E.28/39, in particular to fit the aircraft with its original

NACA 23012 wing for comparative testing, this was not possible as the aircraft was required for 'exhibition' purposes. Shortly after the war W4041 was placed on display at Britain's Aircraft Exhibition which was held on the site of John Lewis' bombed department store in Oxford Street, London in June 1945. The fact that the E.28/39 was put on show instead of being used to further research into high speed flight goes some way to show where Britain's priorities lay at the cessation of hostilities.

The first jet aircraft designed in the USA was the rather ponderous looking Bell XP-59 Airacomet. The fact that America was able to enter the field of jet-powered flight was largely down to General Henry H. 'Hap' Arnold, Chief of Staff of the US Army Air Corps, who had come across the work of Frank Whittle during a fact finding tour of Britain in March 1941, before the United States had entered the war. In quick time arrangements were made for a Whittle W.1X to be sent across the Atlantic and General Electric were selected to build the engine as the Type I-A. Bell Aircraft of Buffalo received a contract for three examples of its XP-59A, the first of which was taken on its maiden flight on 2 October 1942. This was roughly five months before the Gloster F.9/40 (later named Meteor) was flown for the first time, the prototype airframes in the meantime having been gathering dust at Bentham awaiting flight-cleared engines.

The XP-59A was a rather ungainly looking straight-winged design with its twin jet-engines mounted in fairings each side of the fuselage, although this location did at least make the pilot's task much easier in the single-engined case. One of the first to fly the Airacomet was Frank H. Kelley Jnr who was effusive in his praise following a familiarisation sortie on 16 November 1942:

> The simplicity of starting and the smoothness of operation made it hard to believe that any form of motivating power was actually in operation. While taxiing to the take-off position, it is apparent that the throttle calibration between the left and right powerplants was just about as far out of phase as possible. Taxiing at identical rpm the left throttle seemed completely closed while the right throttle appeared fully open. Visibility from the ship is excellent although not quite as favourable as the P-39 series [this assessment was later refuted by other test pilots]
>
> Upon opening the throttles for take-off the airplane handled and acted like any conventional airplane. In fact throughout the flight and even after landing, I did not consciously think of anything other than flying a normal twin-engine airplane. After shutting down the powerplants, I desired to throw on the battery switch to check fuel quantity and without thinking called out to the men standing around to stand clear of the propellers! It was quite obvious to this

pilot that the transition to this type of airplane will be extremely simple, even to the inexperienced service pilot.

The overall flying characteristics of the airplane are amazing for a prototype. I have never before seen such a completely finished experimental ship. The general handling qualities are good although the controls are heavy and will require future modifications before being suitable for combat. The landing characteristics appeared excellent although the impression was gained that insufficient elevator area existed to permit a fully stalled landing. It was somewhat disconcerting to find that due to the high powerplant idling speed that considerable thrust necessitated a long, shallow, floating approach to landing. It seems that if the idling speed cannot be lowered, spoilers of some sort will be necessary to increase the gliding angle and shorten the landing run. Although neither helmet nor headphones were worn, the ship was very quiet throughout the flight with the exception of the landing gear warning horn which blew practically continuously. All in all the flight was very exciting and a unique experience and future flights in this airplane are looked forward to with enthusiasm.

The XP-59A was quickly taken up to a speed of 320 mph IAS in its test schedule and was also flown to +4.6g without any evidence of flutter, although considerable elevator movement was needed to produce this level of acceleration. It was also assessed by Wing Commander H.J. 'Willie' Wilson of the RAE. The elevator forces were found to be acceptable but the ailerons were extremely heavy at any speeds above 200 mph IAS and the rudder was practically immovable. Lateral control was subsequently improved so that the aircraft could be manoeuvred up to speeds of 375 mph IAS, however, the response was not immediate and the stick did not return to the neutral setting on release.

Flight at high altitude brought evidence of a new phenomenon with the revolutionary jet engines as at 37,000 feet a series of intermittent 'explosions' were heard occurring about once every thirty seconds. When height was increased to 40,000 feet the explosions were being heard every one and a half seconds and the left-hand engine had to be shut down. This was the first sign of engine surge, but subsequent modifications allowed flight to over 42,000 feet before it reoccurred. The trials programme progressed reasonably smoothly although one flight to obtain climb data had to be abandoned when the pilot reported 'interference by a P-38 whose vain antics in attempting to catch the XP-59A proved sufficiently amusing to distract my attention from the more serious work at hand.'

During performance testing with the first XP-59A in its normal finish a maximum speed of 385 mph was obtained at 20,000 feet with the engines set to 16,500 rpm. After all cracks had been filled with putty and the surface cleaned up, a speed of 399 mph was obtained. During a prolonged high speed dive from 35,000 feet in which a speed of 390 mph IAS was reached at 7,000 feet, a sharp crack was heard and the elevator trimmer ceased to function. After landing it was found that other damage had been inflicted including several popped rivets and torn fabric to the flaps. Although speeds of this magnitude had been flown on many previous occasions, this was the first occasion when high speed had been maintained for a long period.

In July 1944 the RAE at Farnborough received an example of the Airacomet for test purposes. This was the first pre-production YP-59A (42-108773) which carried RAF markings and the serial number RJ362/G. Performance testing showed a maximum speed of only 356 mph and an initial rate of climb of 2,400 ft/min at sea level. This was way below the performance of the latest piston-engined fighters and the YP-59A proved to be slower even than the Meteor I which entered squadron service at the same time as the trial was being carried out. The Airacomet was clearly unsuitable for service use and with a limiting Mach number of only 0.65 was also of little use for high speed flight research, however, it did provide pilots with useful experience of jet-powered flight and acted as a test bed for the first Whittle-based jet engines to be produced in the USA.

The first Allied jet fighter to enter service was the Gloster Meteor which can be traced back to a preliminary brochure which was submitted to the Ministry of Aircraft Production in 1940 by George Carter, the chief designer of the Gloster Aircraft Company. This led to Specification F.9/40 being issued to cover the design and eight prototypes were ordered on 7 February 1941. Due to the low power levels of the early jet engines the F.9/40 had of necessity to be of twin-engined design to provide adequate performance and these were carried in mid-wing nacelles. The structure was purely conventional with straight-set wings, the only concession to modernity being the use of a tricycle undercarriage and high-set tailplane to remove it from the jet efflux. The first prototype (DG202) was ready for taxi trials in the summer of 1942 but delays with the Rover-produced Whittle W.2B engines meant that the first aircraft to take to the air on 5 March 1943 was DG206 which was powered by the Frank Halford-designed H.1 that was developed into the de Havilland Goblin.

The Meteor was first flown by No.616 Squadron in July 1944 and saw limited service during the last few months of the Second World War. It was initially powered by two Rolls-Royce Welland Is of 1,700 lb thrust which endowed a performance little better than contemporary piston-engined fighters and so it was not until the arrival of more powerful engines that the high speed characteristics of the Meteor could be fully explored. The first major variant of the Meteor to be built in substantial numbers was the F.4 which featured Rolls-Royce Derwent V engines offering double the amount of power at 3,500 lb thrust. Whatever else might be said of the Meteor, the later variants did not lack power and this meant that it was relatively easy for pilots to get into trouble with compressibility. An early production F.4 (RA397) was tested at Boscombe Down to assess its handling characteristics at maximum attainable Mach numbers at high altitudes. The aircraft was trimmed in level flight at heights between 41,000 feet and 43,000 feet and then pushed into a dive to attain the maximum possible Mach number as quickly as possible. Continuous records of airspeed and height were taken by an automatic observer and the characteristics encountered were noted. The pilot also broadcast a running commentary during the dive. The Meteor F.4's behaviour at various speeds was recorded as follows:

TMN	IMN	Behaviour of Aircraft
0.79 to 0.80	0.78 to 0.79	Slight and rapid fore-and-aft control column movement promoting moderate porpoising. Aircraft nosing up with increase of IMN. Slight buffeting.
0.81	0.80	Change of longitudinal trim to nose down, but forces of small magnitude.
0.82+	0.81+	Porpoising and buffeting. Tendency to drop port wing. Wing could be raised with aileron, stick forces very heavy.
0.83	0.82	Alternate wing dropping. Ailerons not effective in controlling motion. Wing could be raised with rudder, but on assuming level attitude the opposite wing dropped. Use of rudder produced snaking, which, with lateral motion, resulted in Dutch rolling. Longitudinal trim became nose-up, and a heavy push force was required to hold the dive. Marked buffeting.
0.84 and above	0.83 and above	Complete loss of control and violent drop of either wing through 60 to 90 degrees. Ailerons quite ineffective and very heavy. With roll, the nose dropped and the angle of dive became very steep. Buffeting and Dutch rolling in the dive. Elevators only just effective, but application of small 'g'

TMN	IMN	Behaviour of Aircraft
		available increased buffeting and the aircraft continued in the dive. On occasions when 0.83 IMN was exceeded by making the initial dive steep, the aircraft became inverted when final wing drop occurred, and then nosed into a very steep dive.

The maximum true Mach number attained during the trial was about 0.85 but acceleration above 0.82 was slow and it was difficult to increase the angle of dive once the Mach number had risen appreciably above 0.81. The main factor affecting recovery was the small reserve of lift coefficient that was available at high Mach numbers and so any pilot who hauled back on the stick a little too much was liable to set up a high speed stall. The best recovery technique was to extend the air brakes but when these were not used around 20,000 feet was needed to regain level flight. It was noted that the Meteor's wing dropping was typical of high speed aircraft of the day, as was the ineffective nature of the ailerons. The opinion was expressed that this phenomenon was likely to constitute a serious problem for aircraft of the future that were intended to operate at higher Mach numbers in level flight. Although the Meteor was rapidly becoming obsolescent by the late 1940s, it was to remain in first line service with the RAF and other air forces well into the 1950s by which time it was something of an anachronism. It was severely limited by its low critical Mach number at high altitude and the fact that it had to remain in service far longer than it should have was due in no small part to the British government opting out of high speed flight research at the end of the Second World War.

Although it did not see active service in the Second World War, the de Havilland Vampire was a close contemporary of the Gloster Meteor and was flown for the first time on 20 September 1943. It had a straight, tapered wing of relatively thick section but the tailplane was carried on twin booms. This allowed a short fuselage pod which in turn resulted in jet pipe length being kept to a minimum. The prototype Vampire (LZ548) was powered by a single Goblin 1 engine of 2,700 lb thrust designed by Major Frank Halford of de Havilland's engine division; production aircraft having the Goblin 2 of 3,100 lb thrust.

During an evaluation of the Vampire as an interceptor, the Central Fighter Establishment (CFE) assessed the type's characteristics at high Mach numbers as follows:

The Machmeter on the Vampire is subject to fairly large variation and normally under reads. At the top end of the scale true Mach will be about 0.02 greater than indicated. During the dive the aircraft becomes increasingly tail heavy as speed is increased and should be trimmed into the dive. At about 0.73 IMN there is slight elevator buffet and vibration accompanied by a change of trim to nose down. At about 0.75 IMN the stick moves backwards about 3 inches although no large change of trim or direction is evident. At 0.76 IMN a lateral oscillation commences accompanied by aileron buffeting and snatching on the stick. At this point, and as speed is increased, the aircraft starts a quick irregular pitching in the fore-and-aft plane. At 0.77 – 0.78 Mach there is a tendency for one wing to drop. The fore-and-aft porpoising is difficult to check by use of the elevators and may in fact be aggravated by an attempt to correct it by movement of the stick. The porpoising was found to be fairly gentle and the aircraft automatically tends to pull out, and will only continue porpoising if held in the dive.

Stick forces at high Mach numbers are light and care must be taken in handling all controls, particularly the elevators. Good aileron control is retained throughout. As the aircraft is pulled out of the dive, however, considerable forward stick is required as it becomes increasingly tail heavy until it decelerates to 0.75 IMN when the tendency dies out. Above 15,000 feet or so the compressibility effects are similar to those encountered at low level but they can, of course, be more easily induced. The longitudinal trim tendency is, however, to tail heavy, this becoming well marked at 0.79–0.80 IMN. The aircraft shows no unpleasant handling characteristics up to a true Mach number of 0.80 but for operational handling it is considered that the present restriction of 0.78 is correct. The behaviour of individual aircraft varied a good deal and the effect also seems to depend on the speed at which the aircraft is initially trimmed.

The Vampire was also tested at A&AEE Boscombe Down and in addition to the porpoising that set in without warning at 0.78 IMN, a marked buffeting and juddering was also noted, plus a slight tendency for the aircraft to wallow laterally, although this could be corrected by use of the ailerons. The fore-and-aft pitching was difficult to control but, once again, the Vampire showed that it was willing to recover from the dive unaided if the push force on the control column was relaxed. At altitudes around 15,000 feet the Vampire showed similar characteristics to the Meteor but there was a general feeling of unsteadiness, with pronounced buffeting and fluctuating stick forces which meant that control was anything but pleasant. Unlike the Meteor there was no hint of directional snaking at high speeds.

Although the Vampire was a very pleasant aircraft to fly it would bite if mishandled. This was particularly apparent when pulling out of a high speed dive, and if the control column was pulled back too sharply the aircraft was liable to flick one way or the other. As the Vampire was to spend much of its operational life as a ground attack machine pilots had to be wary of this characteristic as considerable height could be lost in the recovery process.

The Vampire was also used by a number of Advanced Flying Schools to provide realistic training for the first-line squadrons and it was here that many RAF pilots had their first experience of compressibility. Bob Hillard was a trainee pilot in 1949 at No.203 AFS at Driffield and recalls his introduction to high speed flight:

> On one of my early Vampire sorties it seemed about time to find out about this compressibility I had been hearing about, so I set off 'luft-wards' to a reasonable height. Leaving the throttle wide open, I started a dive and watched the Mach number increase. The trim changed, becoming quite tail heavy. As Pilot's Notes suggested that different machines reacted in different ways it was a case of waiting to see what happened. Even so, I was startled by the sudden oscillations, quite violent I thought, sufficiently so as to make it hard to grab the throttle and airbrakes, which were eventually used and normal flying was resumed. I don't think I had been authorised for that particular exercise and, having done it once, I could not see any value in repeating it!

Due to the fact that it tended to recover automatically if pushed too far in a high speed dive, pilots had to try very hard indeed to get into trouble with the Vampire, a quality which potentially made it an ideal trainer. Its operational life was relatively short and it was replaced in front-line units in 2nd Tactical Air Force by the Venom in 1952/53. It was developed as a side-by-side trainer as the T.11 and was to remain in this role until 1967 when the last Vampires were retired at Leeming in North Yorkshire. During its career as a trainer the Vampire was the means by which over 3,000 pilots attained their wings and it proved itself an ideal aircraft in which the basic techniques for high speed flight could be taught.

CHAPTER SIX

Jet and Rocket Engine Development

Although advances in aerodynamics, in particular the development of the swept wing, were one of the major factors in the quest to conquer the sound barrier, any amount of aerodynamic redesign would have been doomed to failure without the development of jet engines and rocket motors in the late 1930s. By the end of the Second World War the most powerful piston-engined fighters, as epitomised by the later versions of the P-47 Thunderbolt and Hawker Tempest, were fitted with engines of around 2,500–2,800 hp and were capable of speeds of 450–500 mph. Even larger engines were being proposed but in terms of outright speed the limit had already been reached. The dives carried out by Spitfires at Farnborough in 1943/44 were exceptional and could only be achieved at high altitude where Mach number was high and indicated airspeed was low. These flights represented the ultimate for a propeller-driven fighter and unsubstantiated claims by pilots that they had flown faster in other types of aircraft owed everything to the large position error that afflicted the airspeed indicator during high speed dives. For flight above 500 mph some form of jet propulsion was necessary and this only came about as a result of a few visionaries who had to battle against the reactionary views of technical gurus within the military hierarchy.

The idea of a gas turbine was nothing new, the basic principle having been demonstrated by Hero, a citizen of Alexandria in the first century AD. The process of experimentation with gas turbines accelerated throughout the 19th century until by the early 1900s they were a commercial proposition with Brown-Boveri of Zurich manufacturing turbines for blast furnaces. It was not long before the idea of a turbine was being considered as a means of powering aircraft but most of the early designs were hopelessly impractical. It was not until 1929 when Frank (later Sir Frank) Whittle, at that time a Flight Lieutenant in the

56

RAF, first proposed a design for a gas turbine to produce jet propulsion (instead of being used to turn a conventional propeller) that real progress was made. Whittle's difficulties with getting his revolutionary idea accepted have been well documented but with the setting up of Power Jets Ltd in March 1936, Britain at least had a chance to be at the forefront of what would be one of the major new technologies of the 20th century.

Unfortunately the enthusiasm that Whittle possessed for his new concept was still not shared by the vast majority of others within the industry and he continued to struggle on with a shoestring budget. His first jet engine was the WU (Whittle Unit) which featured a double-sided centrifugal compressor, a single-stage turbine and an elongated combustion chamber which curled around the engine. It was designed and built by the British Thomson Houston Co of Rugby and was run for the first time in March 1937 but was soon damaged when the impeller came into contact with the casing. After repairs, further trials were commenced but the engine showed a marked inclination to runaway out of control, a situation that produced an increasingly loud shrieking noise together with overheating of the combustion chamber casing which glowed red hot. This was enough for the assembled technicians to run for cover but even with the fuel shut off the engine continued to accelerate for a time before it eventually stopped. It transpired that this was due to excess fuel that had pooled at the bottom of the combustion chamber and when this was drained the engine ran under control.

Following two rebuilds, the second being enforced as a result of the turbine disintegrating when it contacted the nozzle, the WU re-emerged in rather different form with ten separate reverse-flow combustion chambers. By mid 1939 the engine was being run to 16,500 rpm and was showing considerable promise, so much so that it was arranged for Dr D.R. Pye, the Air Ministry's Director of Scientific Research, to witness the WU in operation. Pye had previously been sceptical of the jet engine but after the demonstration he had something of a change of heart and immediately sanctioned the building of a new engine, the W.1, which would develop sufficient thrust to power a research aircraft (the Gloster E.28/39). The W.1 was developed over the next eighteen months and was run for the first time in April 1941 by which time it was capable of producing a thrust of 850 lb at 16,500 rpm. It was with this engine that the E.28/39 first took to the air at Cranwell on 15 May 1941 to become the first British jet-powered aircraft to fly.

By now the apathy that Whittle had had to put up with in the early years was a thing of the past, but unfortunately it was replaced by something equally restrictive as the project became embroiled in politics. At the instigation of the Ministry of Aircraft Production (MAP), Whittle's engines were to be built by Rover who were given the power to make modifications to the original design, however, many of these were made without discussion with Power Jets. Over a period of time the working relationship between Power Jets and Rover plummeted to the point where the whole jet engine programme stalled, this at a time when Gloster were churning out brand new examples of the F.9/40 (later to be called the Meteor) which could not be flown because there was no flight-cleared engine available. The whole mess was eventually solved by the intervention of Rolls-Royce who did a deal with Rover to take over jet engine production in return for a tank engine factory. Thanks to the technical expertise and drive of Rolls-Royce, Whittle was at last able to make significant progress and his W.2B engine of 1,600 lb thrust was fitted to an F.9/40 in June 1943. As the Rolls-Royce Welland I, this engine powered the first production Meteors to enter RAF service. The basic Whittle centrifugal jet engine was further developed towards the end of the Second World War as the RB.26 Derwent of 2,000 lb thrust, however, the ultimate derivative was the RB.41 Nene which had double the mass flow and produced 5,000 lb thrust.

Due to the development difficulties that had arisen out of the situation between Power Jets and Rover, the first Gloster F.9/40 had flown with jet engines designed by Frank Halford of de Havilland. In July 1941, with the encouragement of Sir Henry Tizard (then Technical Advisor to the MAP) de Havilland began work on an engine to power a new jet fighter. As it was decided that the aircraft (later the DH.100 Vampire) would be single-engined it was clear that the new engine would have to develop considerably more thrust than the Whittle jets and so a design aim of 3,000 lb was chosen. Rather than use a double-sided compressor as on the WU, Halford went for a single-sided compressor which had the advantage of increasing pressure at the inlet as a result of the ram effect, but it necessarily meant that overall diameter was increased. At first an annular combustion chamber was proposed, but eventually a more conservative approach was taken with sixteen straight-through combustion chambers, unlike the reverse flow type as adopted by Whittle.

The engine was initially known as the Halford H.1 and, from the issue of the first technical drawings, was completed in the remarkably short period of 248 days. The H.1 was run for the first time on 13 April 1942 and progress was relatively trouble free so that by 26 September nearly 200 hours of bench running had been carried out. Although the H.1 had quickly attained its design power output of 3,000 lb thrust at 10,500 rpm it was to take some time before reliability was achieved and it did not pass its Type Test until July 1945. In the meantime the first flight of the Vampire had taken place on 20 September 1943 with the H.1 (now known as the Goblin) restricted to 9,500 rpm and 2,300 lb thrust. The production version of the engine was the Goblin 2 of 3,100 lb thrust and an up-rated

Goblin 4 of 3,750 lb thrust powered VW120, the high-speed DH.108, which was the first British aircraft to fly faster than sound in 1948. The Goblin was developed into the 4,850 lb thrust Ghost which powered the successor to the Vampire, the DH.112 Venom.

Although Whittle and Halford had both favoured centrifugal jets, another design stream preferred the more compact axial-flow engine. This was a more ambitious approach to jet propulsion but was technically much more difficult than the simple, more rugged centrifugal. The first work on axial compressors in Britain was carried out by Dr A.A. Griffiths at RAE Farnborough. By the late 1930s others were working in the field, such as Hayne Constant of the RAE who was thinking more in terms of a turboprop and designed a compressor known as the B.10 that was built by Metropolitan-Vickers of Manchester. Of all the engineering firms in existence in Britain at that time, Metrovick was in a better position than most to embrace the new form of propulsion as they had already produced steam turbines of axial design.

Having discarded the turboprop as designed by Constant and knowing that Whittle was working towards a pure jet, Metrovick moved in the same direction and began work on the F.2 which employed a nine-stage compressor and an annular combustion chamber. The engine was run for the first time in late 1941 and by November the following year was producing around 1,800 lb thrust. Although its frontal area was smaller and it operated at a higher pressure ratio, the axial engine was heavier and more complex. The F.2 was first tested in the back of a Lancaster in 1943 and was also used to power one of the F.9/40 proto-types (DG204). This aircraft was first flown on 13 November 1943 but was lost on 1 April 1944 when one of the engines disintegrated during high speed testing, killing RAE test pilot Squadron Leader Douglas Davie. The basic Metrovick F.2 was developed into the F.2/4 (later named Beryl) which had one extra stage added to the compressor and eventually gave a thrust of 3,850 lb. Bench testing of this engine began in January 1945 and two were to power the Saro SR.A/1 jet-powered flying-boat fighter which was flown for the first time on 16 July 1947. The final design to emerge from Metrovick was the F.9 Sapphire, the development of which was taken over by Armstrong Siddeley Motors in 1948. The Sapphire was produced in large numbers and powered two variants (F.2 and F.5) of the Hawker Hunter and the Handley Page Victor B.1.

The USA were slow starters in the field of jet propulsion and other than a design study, very little progress had been made before USAAC chief General H.H. 'Hap' Arnold made a fact finding mission to Britain in April 1941 during which he became aware of Frank Whittle's work. As already stated, a Whittle engine was quickly despatched to the USA. In contrast to the slow progress being made by Power Jets/Rover, General Electric forged ahead and produced its Type I in April 1942. The improved Type I-A of 1,250 lb thrust was ready by the following October and two of these engines powered the first Bell XP-59A Airacomet. Production P-59As were fitted with the 1,600 lb thrust General Electric I-16 but even more was to come with the I-40 of 4,000 lb thrust. Unlike the I-16 which was virtually a copy of the W.1, the I-40 featured straight-through combustion chambers and was the equal of anything produced back in Britain. As the J-33, this engine was to be taken over by Allison and was to power the Lockheed P-80 Shooting Star which became one of the major types in the post-war USAF.

By the end of the war General Electric also had an axial turbojet under test. This had come about following a study into a turboprop and was known as the TG-180. It was bench run for the first time in April 1944 and although it produced virtually the same thrust levels as the centrifugal I-40, the similarity ended there. Like any other axial turbojet the TG-180 offered reduced frontal area but was much more complex and was 500 lb heavier than the I-40. It was also to be developed by Allison and as the J-35 powered some of the first generation of USAF jet fighters including the Republic F-84 Thunderjet.

Not to be outdone, the US Navy had requested its first turbojet from Westinghouse in December 1941 and this had led to the Type 19 (the number referring to the engine's diameter) which was first tested in March 1943. Unlike the development of the jet engine under the USAAF, US Navy sponsored designs owed nothing to the work of Frank Whittle and were wholly original in concept. The Type 19 was later to be referred to as the J30 and produced a modest 1,600 lb thrust. Two J30s were used to power the straight-winged McDonnell XFD-1 (later FH-1) Phantom which was the world's first purpose-built naval jet fighter. Only sixty examples of the FH-1 were produced and it was followed by the F2H Banshee which was powered by two Westinghouse J34s rated at 3,000 lb thrust. This engine was of slightly larger dimensions (24 inches diameter) and had first been run in its early form in 1944. The Banshee was capable of a maximum speed of 587 mph at sea level and was to remain in service in small numbers until the early 1960s.

Although Frank Whittle is largely credited with having invented the jet engine, his later work was closely matched chronologically with that of Hans Pabst von Ohain in Germany, however, this owed something to the different attitudes that existed towards the new technology as von Ohain was able to progress from conception to first flight in a little over four years, or only one third of the time that it took Whittle. Von Ohain had studied at the University of Gottingen where he had become aware of the patents that Whittle had filed. His first attempt at producing a gas turbine in 1934 was not particularly successful but it encouraged him to carry on and in April 1936 he took his ideas to Ernst Heinkel who was sufficiently impressed to take him on, together with his engineer, Max Hahn. The two immediately began work on the HeS 1 which was first run on hydrogen in April 1937 and throughout 1938 the first flight engine, the HeS 3, was built. It was first tested in the air under a Heinkel He 118 and achieved the first jet powered flight on 27 August 1939 in the Heinkel He 178, despite the fact that the amount of thrust developed was only just over 800 lb. Heinkel continued to be active in jet engine development throughout the war, the most advanced being the 109-011 which was to have developed 3,500 lb thrust. This engine, however, was only ever flown on a Junkers Ju 88 test bed.

In the run up to the Second World War Germany possessed almost an embarrassment of riches when it came to experiments in jet propulsion. As well as von Ohain at Heinkel there were three other mainstream firms active in the area, BMW, Bramo (the latter being acquired by BMW in 1939) and Junkers. These companies were working towards axial turbo-jets, the end products being the BMW 109-003 and the Junkers 109-004. Of these, the Junkers design was the more conservative and this was reflected in the service careers of the two engines as it took nearly two years to develop the compressor of the BMW 109-003 to an acceptable level of reliability by which time it was too late to play a significant role in the war. The production model of the Junkers 109-004 (the 004B) was to power the Messerschmitt Me 262 fighter and was rated at 1,980 lb thrust.

Although Germany was ahead of the rest of the world from a technical viewpoint, as the war progressed it became increasingly desperate for high-quality metals to withstand the high temperatures in the hottest parts of the engine and much development work had to be undertaken to reduce temperature in certain areas. An example of this was the ducting of air from the compressor to slots in the turbine. Late production examples of the Junkers 109-004B had hollow turbine blades so that cooling air could be passed through to reduce temperature even further. Despite advanced measures such as these the overhaul life of the 109-004B was still only 25 hours at the war's end.

As well as being at the forefront of the advancement in jet propulsion, Germany was also developing rockets and ramjets which could be used for high speed flight. By 1939 advanced rocket motors were capable of generating high levels of thrust but this had to be set against a very short burn time and the hazards as a result of the extremely volatile fuels that were used. The rocket motors developed by Hellmuth Walter which were used in the Messerschmitt Me 163 are fully described in the following chapter, however, this was not the only rocket interceptor to appear in the skies over Germany.

Of even more radical appearance was the Bachem Ba 349A Natter, a small vertical take-off interceptor which used the same power source as the Me 163 and was almost ready for operational use when the war ended. It was designed as the ultimate point-defence fighter and took off vertically from a launch tower under the power of a single Walter HWK 109–509A-2 bi-fuel rocket motor of 3,750 lb thrust, plus four Schmidding 109–533 solid fuel rocket boosters of 1,200 lb thrust each. These boosters were fully expended after just ten seconds and were then automatically jettisoned. Thereafter the Natter (Viper) was intended to accelerate to the height of the bomber stream where its load of unguided rockets contained in the nose would be fired in a single pass at any suitable target that presented itself. After the attack had been completed and all the fuel used up, the aircraft would be dived to lower altitude where explosive bolts would separate the short fuselage, allowing the rear section containing the rocket motor to descend by parachute, while the expendable nose section fell to earth. The pilot in the meantime would be making his own separate parachute descent. Before the war ended only one manned flight was attempted. Although the launch appeared to have been completed successfully, shortly afterwards the canopy was seen to detach and the aircraft passed over the vertical, after which it dived vertically into the ground killing the pilot, Oberleutnant Lothar Siebert.

Although the Ba 349 was severely limited operationally, it had impressive performance with a top speed of 500 mph at low level and an initial rate of climb of 37,000 ft/min. At the end of the war an improved Natter (the Ba 349B) was under development. This would have been powered by a more powerful Walter 109–509C rocket motor of 4,400 lb thrust and wind tunnel testing had shown it to be capable of speeds just below that of sound. In the event the concept of the rocket fighter as epitomised by the Natter came to nothing but the idea was to remain in vogue in several countries for the next ten years or so, with interest being shown in fighter aircraft powered by both a turbojet and a rocket motor.

Use of the rocket motor as a means of aircraft propulsion was also experimented with in the Soviet Union, the most successful designs being those of Leonid Dushkin. This led to the development of the Berezniak-Isayev BI-1 fighter which was of wooden construction and was powered by a D-1A motor of 2,400 lb thrust that used RFNA (red fuming nitric acid) and kerosene as fuels. The BI-1 was a clean looking design with a straight, low-mounted wing and after initial handling trials as a glider, the first powered flight was made on 15 May 1942 but the test programme had to be postponed pending modifications to the rocket motor. When trials were recommenced in March 1943 serious compressibility problems were encountered and the third prototype was lost when it dived straight into the ground. This was due to a strong nose-down pitching moment that occurred at high speed (around 550 mph) and plans to build further aircraft were shelved. This setback led to something of a hiatus in pure rocket-powered flight in the USSR and of two other designs, the Kositkov 302 was cancelled in 1944 and work on the Polikarpov Malyutka ended when its designer Nikolay Polikarpov died in July 1944. It was not until after the war with the acquisition of German research information and actual hardware that there was a revival of interest in rocket-powered aircraft.

For a brief period the turbojet and the rocket motor were joined by the ramjet which was the simplest of engines as it comprised a duct which acted as a combustion chamber. Air entering at the front was then mixed with a fuel spray which was then ignited aft of the intake. This worked on the principle that as an aircraft flies faster, the need for a compressor (and hence a turbine) as on a turbojet becomes less necessary as the ram effect of the air creates ram compression. As ramjets become more efficient as speed is increased they are ideally suited to high speed flight, but their major drawback is the fact that they cease to function when forward speed is reduced to zero and so any ramjet-powered aircraft need, either to be air-launched, or have some other secondary means of power. The greatest champion of the ramjet was Rene Leduc who was working towards this method of propulsion in the years immediately preceding the Second World War. His post-war development of ramjet-powered aircraft is described in Chapter Twelve. Perhaps the most famous use of the ramjet was in the Fieseler Fi 103 flying bomb (V-1), the first of Hitler's terror weapons.

CHAPTER SEVEN

Germany Shows the Way

In terms of piston-engined fighter development during the Second World War, Germany matched very closely the products of the British and American aircraft industries, but in the realms of jet-powered flight it managed to forge ahead and by the end of the war it was developing some extremely advanced projects. The basics were all in place by 1942 as Germany's most talented designers were able to embrace the new technology offered by a burgeoning gas turbine industry which had grown up following the pioneering work carried out by Pabst von Ohain. They were also able to take advantage of vast amounts of data that was beginning to come from wind tunnel research into high speed flight so that some of the designs that were produced in the last two years of the war were way ahead of anything contemplated on the Allied side. This whole process was given further impetus by Germany's increasingly desperate situation as there was a need to produce fighter aircraft that could out-perform Allied aircraft by a considerable margin in an attempt to regain the initiative from a numerically superior foe. As a result the rate of technical innovation accelerated when it was most needed. By comparison with what was to follow, however, the first jet aircraft to fly in Germany appeared almost toy-like

By 1939 von Ohain had developed the HeS 3b jet turbine which was capable of delivering a thrust of around 1,100 lb. To accommodate this engine Ernst Heinkel designed a small, shoulder-wing aircraft designated the He 178. The fuselage was a simple metal monocoque with a nose-mounted intake and an efflux at the rear. The tapered wings were of wooden construction and featured modest dihedral, the trailing edge incorporating large flaps inboard of the ailerons. Following taxiing trials, the He 178 was flown for the first time on 27 August 1939 by Erich Warsitz, thereby becoming the first jet-powered aircraft to fly and beating the Gloster E.28/39 by the best part of two years. The flight was not a resounding success, however, as the undercarriage refused to retract and a bird was ingested into the engine after take-off, necessitating a rapid return to Heinkel's airfield at Marienehe. Problems with the undercarriage were set to continue and despite the fitment of a more powerful HeS 6 engine of 1,300 lb thrust, an increase in weight meant that the power-to-weight ratio of the aircraft was actually worse. The length of the jet pipe from the fuselage-mounted engine also led to thrust losses so that the maximum speed ever achieved was a modest 373 mph. As directional stability was also a problem with the design the He 178 was quickly dropped in favour of the twin-engined He 280.

This process of evolution was the mirror of that at Gloster with the E.28/39 and the F.9/40 (Meteor) and was due to the low power-levels offered by the early jet engines and the high thrust losses incurred by single jet units mounted in the fuselage. The He 280 solved this problem neatly by mounting two HeS 8 engines under the wings. It was of all-metal construction with a mid-set wing displaying a straight leading edge and rounded tips. The inboard trailing edge of the wing was also straight, but with a pronounced curve on the outer section. The tail unit comprised a horizontal stabiliser mounted high on the rear fuselage with twin fins and rudders. A tricycle undercarriage was adopted. Following initial testing of the He 280 as a glider, it flew under its own power for the first time on 2 April 1941.

Development of the He 280 was disrupted by the HeS 8 engines which were down on power compared to what was expected from them and even by early 1943 thrust levels were only around 1,300 lb. The aircraft was also flown under the power of Junkers Jumo 109-004 engines, the same as fitted to the Messerschmitt Me 262, but even though the He 280 possessed a better top speed, rate of climb and service ceiling, the Augsberg machine was the one that was chosen to equip the *Luftwaffe*. Political considerations may have come into play in making this decision but the He 280 was inferior to the Me 262 as regards endurance and armament and there was also concern about its tail assembly which was prone to flutter. Having been rejected for service use, the He 280 prototypes were used in various research programmes including one in which He 280 V7 was used as a glider to investigate high speed flight. During one dive, a speed of 578 mph was attained without any problems being encountered.

The aircraft that the He 280 lost out to, the Me 262, was to become the first operational jet fighter and it was to develop a fearsome reputation following its service debut as it was approximately 100 mph faster than the best Allied piston-engined fighters of the late war period. Its history can be traced back to early 1938 when the RLM asked Messerschmitt to carry out a study to ascertain the performance levels of a fighter powered by a gas turbine engine. At the time there was very little research data on aerodynamics at compressibility speeds and so the design of what would become the Me 262 progressed on the 'best guess' principle. At first a twin-engined design was proposed but as Messerschmitt had been informed that engines under development at BMW and Junkers would have a static thrust of around 1,500 lb, the design team began to prefer a single engine layout in a conventional fuselage. This was soon discarded, however, due to the likely thrust losses that would be incurred with the nose-mounted intake and lengthy jet pipe, together with excessive weight and drag. For a time a twin boom installation was considered but this was also rejected because wetted area was actually greater and there would be increased interference at the nacelle and twin boom attachment points. The next attempt was a pod-and-boom configuration which, although better, did not meet performance expectations. Rather reluctantly Messerschmitt returned to their original ideas for a twin-engined machine even if this went somewhat against the grain as the company's philosophy was to keep size and weight to a minimum.

Both mid and low-wing designs were looked at, before finally settling on the latter, and having considered mounting the engines centrally on the wing, it was eventually decided that they should be housed in under-slung nacelles which were structurally simpler. A fuselage of triangular cross-section was chosen as this, together with the low wing layout, allowed ample space for the main wheels to be accommodated when retracted. At this time the Me 262 still had a tailwheel undercarriage. Until a very late stage in the 262's development the aircraft possessed straight wings but the latest projections by BMW showed that their 003 engines were larger and heavier than had been envisaged. This caused Messerschmitt serious problems in keeping the centre of gravity (CG) within acceptable limits and ultimately the only recourse was to employ sweepback on the outer wing panels. The fact that sweeping the wings would delay the sudden drag rise at transonic speeds was not fully appreciated at the time.

Due to the late delivery of flight-cleared engines from BMW, the Me 262 V1 was first flown on 18 April 1941 under the power of a Junkers Jumo 210G 12-cylinder liquid cooled engine. This was retained for the first flight of the 262 fitted with BMW 003s on 25 March 1942 which was just as well as both engines suffered compressor blade failures so that the aircraft had to land on the power of its piston-engine alone. Severe problems with the BMW 003 engines led to the adoption of the Jumo 004 which, although larger and heavier, was rather more reliable. The final revisions to the original design of the 262 were the adoption of a nose-wheel undercarriage and an increase in chord at the wing root so that wing sweep was constant along the whole of the leading edge. Despite a lack of relevant information, from an aerodynamic point of view Messerschmitt got it exactly right without even realising what they had done. Having reluctantly chosen a twin-engined design, the design team had come to accept that they would end up with an overpowered aircraft that was unlikely to be able to utilise all the power that it possessed in terms of pure performance. By a fluke, the sweeping of the wings for CG purposes was to transform the aircraft in a direction that no-one at the time could have envisaged and was to be a significant factor in turning the 262 into a design classic.

Compared with its closest rival, the Gloster Meteor, the Me 262 was much more refined aerodynamically. Both aircraft were of similar configuration and entered service within a few weeks of each other in the summer of 1944, however, the RAF chose to keep the Meteor well away from the front line until the last few weeks of the war so that there was no jet versus jet combat in the Second World War. Officially the reluctance on the part of the RAF to use the Meteor offensively in northern Europe was to prevent the secrets of its Rolls-Royce Welland engines from falling into German hands should one be shot down, but privately there were fears that the early Meteors were not up to the job. The superiority of the 262 over the Meteor became apparent after the war. In May 1945 Flight Lieutenant Clive Gosling was flying Meteor IIIs with 616 Squadron but as a former production test pilot with Supermarine he got the chance to fly an Me 262 which the squadron managed to 'liberate' from a former *Luftwaffe* airfield. He reports:

Compared with the Meteor III, the 262 was a much better fighter, it had better, lighter controls, more fire power and a very good view. However, it was not an aircraft for the inexperienced – it had to be flown. The engines had a very short life and unless a failure in flight was caught immediately, it would go into a spiral dive from which there was no recovery. In both aircraft it was inadvisable to dogfight with conventional fighters. In the Meteor as speed decreased, so did power and acceleration and you were easily outfought. If you played with piston-engined fighters you kept your speed up and dived and zoomed. With a wing loading of about 60 lb/sq ft, the 262 touched down at about 125 mph and took some stopping. It also had a longer take-off run. With reliable engines, I would sooner have gone to war in a 262 than a Meteor.

As well as flying captured examples of the 262, German personnel who had been involved with the aircraft were interrogated by the RAF after the war. Gerd Lindner, a former test pilot with Messerschmitt, gave a full account of his experiences with the Me 262 to officers of the

Aerodynamics Flight at RAE, Farnborough which included an assessment of the 262 during dives at high Mach numbers. This programme had not been without incident as a colleague, Wilhelm Ostertag, had been killed when his aircraft had dived into the ground at high speed on 18 April 1943. Several other Me 262s were lost in similar circumstances and the problem was eventually traced to the variable incidence tailplane which was liable to bring about an unwanted trim change.

According to Lindner the maximum speed attained by the 262 in a dive of 20–25 degrees was 600 mph at an altitude of 13,000 feet. Dives from 26,000 feet resulted in a corrected Mach number of 0.86 but at 0.83 the 262 began to show typical compressibility effects. At that speed the nose started to drop and Lindner said that he had to pull back on the stick with both hands, exerting a force estimated at 33 lb. As the Mach number increased, a violent buffeting commenced with a very alarming high-frequency banging noise which appeared to emanate from just behind the canopy. The nose-heaviness increased so that at 0.86M a force of up to 110 lb was needed to prevent the nose falling any further. As was to be expected the aircraft could be pulled out of the dive at lower levels when Mach number decreased on entry into the denser air at low level. One of the results of the dive tests with the Me 262 was that service pilots were warned not to exceed a speed of 590 mph, although several did with fatal results.

In addition to developing advanced jet-powered aircraft, Germany also pioneered the use of liquid-fuelled rockets as a means of providing the necessary thrust for high speed flight. There had been great interest in this method of propulsion during the inter-war years and in June 1928 Fritz Stamer had successfully flown a glider powered by solid-fuel rockets that had been designed by Alexander M. Lippisch. Further experiments with solid-fuelled rockets eventually gave way to the more promising liquid-fuelled rocket and the first flight with this type of motor took place in 1936 when a Heinkel He 72 biplane trainer was used to test an early rocket designed by Hellmuth Walter that offered a thrust of around 300 lb and a burn time of forty-five seconds. Three examples of the Heinkel He 112 fighter were also converted to rocket power and were fitted with a liquid oxygen/alcohol motor that had been designed by Werner von Braun. With a thrust of 2,200 lb, this unit appeared promising but it proved to be unreliable under test and although it was flown by Erich Warsitz, two of the He 112s were destroyed when the rocket motors exploded.

In the meantime Walter had been making excellent progress with his rocket motors and had developed a system whereby thrust could be varied in flight. With the promise of increased thrust levels, Ernst Heinkel was encouraged to design an aircraft to be powered solely by a rocket motor and this resulted in the He 176 which featured a streamlined, cigar-shaped fuselage with flush fitting canopy and a small, low-set wing of elliptical planform. The hydrogen peroxide and methanol propellants were stored in two tanks in the fuselage for the Walter RI motor which provided a maximum thrust of 1,100 lb. The He 176 was flown for the first time by Warsitz on 30 June 1939 and was later demonstrated before Hitler and Goering. Although Heinkel initially had high hopes for the He 176 its overall performance was not particularly impressive and it only achieved a top speed of just over 430 mph. Although a second machine was due to be built, the project was abandoned soon after the start of the war in favour of the Me 163 Komet interceptor designed by Alexander Lippisch.

The 163 could trace its ancestry back to the Storch I glider that was designed by Lippisch and first flown in September 1929. His next creation was the Delta which lived up to its name by employing leading edge sweepback with a straight trailing edge. Initially built as a glider, the Delta was later powered by a pusher 30 hp Cherub engine on which it could achieve a top speed of 90 mph. Various developments were flown over the next few years culminating in the DFS 39 Delta IVb which featured a 75 hp Pobjoy engine driving a tractor propeller. This aircraft proved to be of great interest to the German Air Ministry who proposed modifying it to incorporate a liquid-fuelled rocket. This led to Project X in which DFS were to build the wings with Heinkel being responsible for the rest of the airframe.

Lippisch continued to develop his ideas and came to the conclusion that the wingtip-mounted rudders, as used on the Delta IVb, were likely to be subject to flutter at the higher speeds that were going to be experienced under rocket power and so he came up with a more conventional fin and rudder for his DFS 40 and DFS 194. It was also at this stage that he realised that a swept wing with no dihedral would improve the aircraft's stability. By this time Lippisch had become disenchanted with the rate of progress of Project X and succeeded in having it transferred so that it came under the control of Messerschmitt AG at Augsberg. Under new management the prototype rocket fighter finally started to make headway and in early 1940 the DFS 194 was taken to Peenemunde-West to commence its flight trials. The engine fitted was a Walter HWK RI-203 of 1,650 lb thrust which ran on T-Stoff, consisting of 80 per cent hydrogen peroxide and 20 per cent water, and Z-Stoff, an aqueous solution of calcium permanganate. With turbojet engines in their infancy, rocket motors looked to be an ideal solution to the problem of achieving high speed flight as they offered high power levels for relatively little weight. After initial flights as a glider, the DFS 194 was cleared for tests using rocket power and it was flown by Heini Dittmar, eventually reaching a speed of 342 mph. The success of the DFS 194 led to the go-ahead being given for the development of the Me 163, the design of which featured an enlarged fin and rudder, increased trailing-edge sweepback and a revised, more capacious fuselage.

In its developed form, the Me 163B was powered by a Walter 109–509A-2 rocket motor with a thrust of 3,750 lb. It used concentrated hydrogen peroxide (T-Stoff) and a solution of hydrazine-hydrate in methanol (C-Stoff) as fuel. The wing, which was swept back 23 degrees on the quarter chord line, was of wooden construction with an 8 mm plywood skin covered with doped fabric. The root section of the wing had a maximum thickness of 14.4 per cent which reduced to 8.7 per cent thickness at the tip. There was a fixed leading edge slot of around 7 feet span which terminated just short of the wing-tip. Like the Me 262 the use of wing sweep was not an attempt to delay the sudden drag rise at compressibility speeds, but in this case it was incorporated merely to provide adequate stability due to the 163 having no tail. Lateral and longitudinal control was provided by differentially operated elevons with large longitudinal trimmer flaps fitted inboard of the elevons and behind the landing flaps. The latter were of the simple split type and could be lowered at any angle up to a maximum of 45 degrees. The fuselage was of metal construction with a single fin and rudder, the latter having an inset horn which carried a mass balance. The undercarriage consisted of a landing skid mounted on a small two-wheel trolley. On take-off the wheels were jettisoned automatically when the skid was retracted.

Early testing with the Me 163A V1 in the summer of 1941 was confined to flying the aircraft as a glider. One flight was witnessed by Ernst Udet, the Chief of the Air Ministry's Technical Department, who saw the Me 163 dive steeply and then flash across the airfield in excess of 400 mph. Udet, who was amazed at the speed of the small bat-shaped aircraft, turned to Lippisch and asked what type of engine it had, to which the latter, with only a hint of a smile, replied 'None!' Once powered flights were commenced the phenomenal performance of the aircraft was confirmed and very soon Heini Dittmar had unofficially broken the world absolute speed record which at the time was held by Fritz Wendel in a Messerschmitt Bf 109R at a speed of 469 mph. As fuel burn was limited to 4½ minutes, a powered take off or 'sharp start' meant that the maximum speed that could be attained before the fuel ran out was around 570 mph. It was obvious that the Me 163A was capable of much more, so to extend the performance envelope even further, level speed runs were made following a towed take-off behind a Bf 110C.

On 2 October Dittmar was towed to a height of 13,120 feet before breaking free and igniting the rocket motor. Taking full advantage of the increased acceleration time he achieved the unheard of speed of 624 mph, or just over 1,000 kph, which at the height that the run was made equated to 0.84M. This brought the aircraft into the realm of compressibility, however, which manifested itself in severe buffeting with a sharp nose-down pitch resulting in what later became known as the 'graveyard dive'. Dittmar's reaction was immediately to cut the motor and he managed to regain control as speed diminished. The results of this test flight were passed to the Air Ministry in Berlin where they were received with a certain amount of incredulity. To establish the claims, Peenemunde was visited by Dr Gothert who was the Director of the DVL, the German Aviation Experimental Establishment, but he eventually had to concede that the figures obtained by the ground tracking station were correct. To mark this particular flight Dittmar was later given the Lilienthal Award for Aeronautical Research.

To have flown nearer to the speed of sound than anyone else was a considerable achievement but the handling characteristics experienced at high speed were clearly unacceptable. The wing of the Me 163A was similar to that of the DFS 194 in that the 32 degree sweep angle of the outer wing was more pronounced than that at the root which only measured 20 degrees. The amount of sweep on the trailing edge was 6 degrees less. As the wing also featured washout, a reduction of incidence on the outer portion of the wing, the shock stall that had developed led to a sudden loss of lift which in turn produced a sharp nose-down pitch. In an attempt to cure this, a revised wing with a constant 23 degree sweep was devised for the operational version (Me 163B) with low-drag fixed slots on the outer sections of the wings, immediately forward of the elevons.

Although the Me 163 was clearly way ahead of anything that the Allies had under development, its advanced performance came at a price. The vicious handling characteristics at its limiting Mach number were bad enough, but they tended to be eclipsed by the hazards posed by the fuels used for its rocket motor. These were highly volatile substances which, when mixed in even small quantities, produced a violent explosion. There were many accidents during the development period of the Me 163 which led to a number of fatalities, one of the problems being inadequate flow of the calcium permanganate catalyst which induced large varia-tions in thrust with the consequent risk of explosion. On at least two occasions complete buildings where the rocket motors were being tested were raised to the ground. The later Me 163B had a more advanced RII-211 motor (later referred to as the 109-509A-2) which differed from the previous Walter rocket by using C-Stoff, a solution of hydrazine-hydrate, methyl alcohol and water as the catalyst. It was vital that the fuels be handled correctly. T-Stoff could only be stored in aluminium casks as it corroded any other type of container, and C-Stoff had to be kept in flasks made of glass or enamel for the same reason. Both liquids were colourless so it was vital for ground personnel to know which fuel they were handling as there was no room for error. One operative became confused and poured a quantity of C-Stoff into a container that had previously contained T-Stoff. The severity of the explosion meant that his end was at least quick, however, there was nothing left of the poor individual to bury.

Pilots, of course, were equally at risk should anything go wrong. The Me 163B was landed on a skid which was lowered hydraulically. The shock absorbing qualities of this system left a lot to be desired and if the touchdown was not judged to perfection the jolt on landing and those experienced during the subsequent ground run could cause serious back injuries. This happened to Heini Dittmar when his aircraft suddenly lost airspeed shortly before landing and he stalled on from a height of around 10 feet. The skid undercarriage took very little of the impact and Dittmar was to spend the next two years in hospital recovering from serious spinal injuries. A similar accident was experienced by Rudolf Opitz who joined the Me 163 test programme at Peenemunde in 1942. On one occasion prior to touchdown his landing skid failed to extend and the pummelling that his back was subjected to resulted in him being out of action for three months.

The greatest dangers for pilots, however, were caused by the volatile fuels that were stored just a few feet behind the cockpit. Any malfunction of the rocket motor after take-off usually resulted in a fatality as the chances of carrying out a successful forced landing were virtually non-existent. Even if a flight appeared to have been carried out successfully there was still sufficient fuel left in the tanks to cause an explosion and many pilots died when their aircraft flipped over at low speed having overrun the designated landing area. Although this fate was bad enough, pilots could be faced with an even more grisly prospect. Among its other qualities, T-Stoff would ignite if it came into to contact with anything organic. On 30 December 1943 *Oberleutnant* Josef Pohs of *Erprobungskommando* (Test Detachment) 16 made a 'sharp start' from Bad Zwischenahn but the wheeled dolly that was used for take-off, and was normally jettisoned at a height of around 50 ft, hit the ground and rebounded so that it struck the aircraft. The Me 163B climbed to a height of around 300 feet before sinking back onto the runway and eventually coming to a halt. Amazingly there was no explosion but by the time that emergency crews reached the 163 there was very little left of Pohs as it appeared that the dolly had punctured a fuel line and he had been dissolved alive by the T-Stoff that had leaked into the cockpit.

When it worked as it should the Me 163B offered a quantum leap in performance. On take-off the aircraft became airborne at a speed of around 200 mph after a ground roll of 1,100–1,300 yards and was then held down until the ASI was reading just over 400 mph. The acceleration was such that the force experienced by the pilot during take-off reached a maximum of 4.5g. The best climb speed was usually reached just beyond the airfield boundary and the aircraft was then put into a 45–50 degree climb which resulted in a climb rate of about 12,500 ft/min, or roughly three times the figure achieved by piston-engined fighters of the period. After a mere 2½ minutes the Me 163B was already passing 30,000 feet, and its service ceiling was 39,500 feet. For some the performance of the 163 took some getting used to. One pilot forgot to throttle back on reaching his operational level and climbed to an altitude estimated by ground radars as 52,000 feet. Without the benefit of a pressure suit, there appeared to be very little chance of survival, especially as the aircraft was later seen to be descending out of control. On passing 20,000 feet, however, those on the ground saw that a recovery had been initiated and this was followed by a successful landing. Having flown at such an extreme altitude, one that was way above the limit for the oxygen system, the pilot had suffered hypoxia but his exposure was sufficiently short for him to be able to recover in time to pull the aircraft out of its dive.

Top speed of the Me 163B at altitude was a little under 600 mph but this in itself posed a problem as this was around 350 mph higher than the cruising speed of the bomber formations they were meant to be attacking. This was just too much for the average pilot who was completely overwhelmed by the vast overtaking speeds which allowed very little time for the aircraft's guns (two 30 mm MK 108 cannon) to be brought to bear. Another big drawback with the Me 163 was the fact that its fuel was expended after only 6 minutes at full throttle which severely limited its operational flexibility. Fuel consumption was considerably higher than had been hoped and in a full power climb T-Stoff was consumed at a rate of 11 lb per second. Once the fuel had been used up the 163 reverted to being a glider which then placed it at the mercy of escort fighters during its descent.

In an attempt to obtain more endurance from the Me 163 Hellmuth Walter began to look at the possibility of incorporating an auxiliary cruising chamber which could be used once the aircraft had reached its operational altitude. This installation was tested on Me 163B V6 and V18, the latter inadvertently setting a new speed record for the 163 despite losing its rudder on the way. The pilot on this occasion was Rudolf Opitz who took off from Peenemunde on 6 July 1944 to test both the main and auxiliary rocket chambers in the climb. The flight was normal until an altitude of 13,000 feet had been passed when it accelerated beyond the pilot's control and exceeded its limiting Mach number. Opitz managed to cut the rocket motor but by this time the aircraft was in a steep dive from which he was able to pull out at very low level. On landing it was discovered that the rudder had been torn away as a result of flutter and it was later ascertained that the maximum speed achieved during the dive was a staggering 702 mph. This version of the *Komet* became known as the Me 163C but it was dropped in favour of a further development, the Me 163D. This aircraft was taken over by Junkers as the Ju 248 but changed its designation again to become the Me 263. Although the wing was similar to the Me 163, the fuselage of the new aircraft was completely redesigned to allow increased fuel tankage and it also featured a wheeled undercarriage. Flight tests showed that the aircraft's characteristics at high speed were inferior to the 163, however, as Mach-induced trim changes occurred at only 0.80M. Plans were made to put the aircraft into mass production but these had not been implemented before the end of the war.

Due to testing and production delays the Me 163B only saw service in relatively small numbers and had a minimal effect on the Allied bomber offensive. Despite its futuristic appearance, the 23 degree wing sweep angle employed on the Me 163 was not sufficient to bring about a significant delay in the drag rise experienced at compressibility speeds. It was beginning to run into trouble at 0.82M and was usually out of control at 0.84M. The severity of the trim changes at these speeds also suggested that the swept-wing tailless configuration might not be the best way to explore the transonic region, not that this stopped other aircraft manufacturers from trying.

After the war a captured Me 163B was tested by the Royal Aircraft Establishment in Britain. The aircraft was first flown in 1945 but owing to considerable maintenance difficulties, especially with the hydraulic system, the tests were not completed until November 1947. Even then the test programme had to be scaled back due to the problems that were encountered. During this period a Spitfire IX was used to tow the aircraft and all flights were made from Wisley or Wittering airfields since it was necessary to use a grass runway to land on the skid-type undercarriage. For the trials carried out by RAE the rocket unit was removed and an auto-observer was installed in its place so that the aircraft was flown solely as a glider. This was understandable enough as the post-war debrief of German personnel who had been involved in the operational use of the Me 163 had shown that 80 per cent of the total losses were sustained on landing or take-off due to the unstable fuels exploding. A further 15 per cent of accidents occurred due to fire in the air, leaving just 5 per cent as a result of combat.

The decision to use the Me 163 as a glider resulted in a considerable reduction in all-up weight, the normal loaded weight of around 9,000 lbs, which resulted in a wing loading of 43 lb/sq.ft, being reduced to only 3,800 lb (wing loading 18 lb/sq.ft). It also meant that it was not flown anywhere near to its limiting Mach number and as a result the trial did not shed any light on the adverse handling characteristics that were apparent with this type of aircraft when they were taken to their absolute limit. This lesson was only learnt in tragic circumstances with the death of Geoffrey de Havilland Jr in the crash of the second DH.108 (see Chapter Eleven).

Pilots' impressions of the general handling characteristics of the Me 163 were extremely favourable and it was considered that the behaviour of the aircraft differed little from that of a conventional aircraft with tail. It was flown at speeds up to 440 mph and all controls were found to be effective throughout the speed range. The most hazardous part of the trial involved a series of fast landings which were designed to simulate the likely high approach speeds of future designs such as those with a delta wing configuration. Three landings were made with touchdown speeds of up to 158 mph EAS but there were no difficulties either with the approach, or with lowering the aircraft smoothly onto the ground. However, as had been the case on many occasions in Germany, high vertical velocities were transmitted to the pilot's back due to the poor shock absorbing qualities of the skid, combined with the rough nature of the airfield. On the final landing the skid collapsed and jammed the rudder control fully over to port. The aircraft did not swing violently but followed a gentle curve on its landing run. The vertical shocks experienced during several bounces were very severe and caused instruments and fittings in the cockpit to become loose. The damage to the skid was so severe that the aircraft could not be repaired and as a result the trial had to be terminated.

At the end of the Second World War teams from Britain, USA and the Soviet Union were locked in a desperate race to discover the secrets of Germany's most advanced weapons programmes. The actual hardware that they came across was impressive enough and also included the Heinkel He 162 'People's Fighter' which had been designed in late 1944 for mass production. It was a relatively sleek straight-winged, twin-finned design, the clean lines of which were only marred by the addition of a single BMW 109-003 jet engine mounted pick-a-back style on top of the fuselage. Maximum speed was a little over 500 mph, interference from the unusual engine installation restricting limiting Mach number to only 0.75. Jet technology had also been applied to bomber and reconnaissance aircraft including the Arado 234 powered by two Jumo 004B turbojets which saw limited service towards the end of the war. Although it was slower than the Me 262, it was still capable of a top speed of just over 460 mph and could outrun most Allied piston-engined fighters.

One of the most extraordinary finds was the Junkers Ju 287 four-jet bomber which featured wings that were swept 25 degree forwards. This aircraft was schemed from mid-1943 by a team led by Hans Wocke, the aim being to develop a jet bomber capable of Mach 0.80 in level flight. The decision to use forward swept wings was sound as this type of wing worked just as well as a swept-back wing in delaying the drag rise at transonic speeds. It also had the advantage that the spanwise flow of air on a swept-back wing at low speeds (which led to tip stall, loss of aileron control and possible pitch-up) was actually reversed, so that with a forward-swept wing air tended to flow towards the root. This meant that near the stalling angle of attack the root would stall first so that the pilot still had aileron control. The big drawback with a forward-swept wing was that it had to be made stiffer, and thus heavier, because when the wing was loaded, its angle of attack, unlike a swept-back wing, tended to increase which would progressively raise the amount of twist that it was suffering. The first Ju 287 was taken into the air for the first time on 16 August 1944 but the decision to abandon the development of bombers in favour of fighters taken in the summer of 1944 led to its development coming to an end, although it did have a short reprieve just before the end of the war. Following the occupation of large areas of eastern Germany the two prototypes (Ju 287 V1 and V2) were acquired, and later evaluated, by the Russians with the assistance of German personnel who had been involved with the project. The second prototype was later modified with swept-back wings and was apparently flown to a speed of around 600 mph.

Of particular interest to those scouring the remains of the German aviation industry were the projected designs for future fighter aircraft. In 1944 the OKL (the *Luftwaffe* High Command) had put out a requirement to several manufacturers for advanced jet-powered fighter aircraft with a maximum speed of around 1,000 kph (621 mph) and the ability to climb to an altitude of 14,000 m (45,920 feet). A single Heinkel-Hirth 109-011A jet engine of around 1,300 kg (2,866 lb) thrust was specified. It was felt that such an aircraft was needed as intelligence assessments of Allied jet aircraft unfortunately tended to overstate their capability. In reality, although the development of turbojet engines was progressing well, Britain and the USA were still light years behind Germany when it came to aerodynamics with the result that the performance potential of the new form of propulsion was not being fully realised. In response to the specification issued by the OKL, designs were submitted by Blohm und Voss, Heinkel, Junkers, Focke-Wulf and Messerschmitt, those of the last two manufacturers being of particular note as they were to have a significant influence on post-war fighter design.

Work on an advanced swept-wing fighter at Focke-Wulf had, in fact, been started as early as 1942 when a team headed by Hans Multhopp began to study the problem. Their work polarised into two similar swept wing designs, later designated Ta 183. The more radical of the two designs had wings of 40 degree sweep angle mounted well forward on the fuselage in the mid-position. The elegant and slender fin was raked back at an angle of 60 degrees and had a T-type tail with dihedral. The relatively short fuselage was oval in section and was made up of two halves divided longitudinally, the upper section being the main structural member as it incorporated the fixing positions for the wings and tail and housed the pressurised cockpit. The lower fuselage section contained the engine, together with the ducting from the nose-mounted air intake, and provided sufficient space for up to four MK 108 cannons and the retractable undercarriage. The other scheme to be proposed by Focke-Wulf was not quite as extreme as it exhibited wing sweep of 'only' 32 degrees. The wing was still mid-mounted but it was moved back along the fuselage to a central position and the fin and rudder were of broader chord, the sweep angle also being considerably reduced. The horizontal tail was also moved to the base of the fin.

In the meantime Messerschmitt had been developing the P.1101, a design that had begun life as a private venture in early 1944. It employed a form once considered for the Me 262 as it featured a pod-and-boom type fuselage with the engine efflux located underneath the slender rear fuselage which also accommodated swept vertical and horizontal tail surfaces at its extremity. On the prototype aircraft the angle of sweep of the wings could be ground adjusted between 35 and 45 degrees to determine the most efficient setting and for the OKL competition, this was set at 40 degrees. The wings were mounted in the mid-position and were fitted with leading edge slats. In addition to the P.1101, Messerschmitt also submitted two further designs, the swept wing P.1110 and the tailless P.1111. The P.1110 had a completely new fuselage of smaller, circular section made possible by the adoption of side mounted air intakes to the rear of the cockpit. The P.1111 featured a 45-degree swept wing which was of broad chord at the roots which also housed air intakes for the engine. A large swept vertical tail was also of broad chord at the base, tapering to the tip.

The OKL met in February 1945 and selected the more radical of the Focke-Wulf designs as the competition winner to be put into production as the Ta 183 but although plans were made for prototype aircraft to be built, there was insufficient time for construction to begin before the factories were captured by the Allied ground forces. Of the advanced fighter projects proposed towards the end of the war, only the Messerschmitt P.1101 was actually built, this aircraft being around 80 per cent complete when it was found by the US Army. Its potential was recognised immediately and it was shipped to the USA where it was given over to Bell Aircraft for an evaluation to be carried out. This company went on to produce the X-5, which, although being completely different structurally and the first to employ variable wing-sweep, was nonetheless virtually indistinguishable from the P.1101 externally. A plan view of the P.1101 also bears a striking similarity to that of the North American F-86 Sabre which was rapidly transformed from a straight winged design to one with 35-degree wing sweep immediately after the war.

The secrets of the Focke-Wulf Ta 183 were to head in the opposite direction and were to have a significant impact on the thinking of designers in the Soviet Union whose work was made even easier by the generosity of the new Labour government in Britain which donated several examples of the Rolls-Royce Nene, the UK's most powerful jet engine of the time, to the Soviets. Thanks to this extraordinarily naïve gesture and the plundering of Germany's high speed research data, the first prototype of the MiG-15 was flown for the first time on 30 December 1947. The overall configuration of the MiG-15 closely resembled the less radical of the Focke-Wulf designs, its 35-degree swept wing also being mounted in the mid-position. Only at the rear of the aircraft were there any significant changes, with the fuselage being extended so that the jet efflux exhausted under the rudder and the horizontal stabiliser being mounted just over half way up the fin. Had the war continued, it is likely that the Ta 183 would have entered *Luftwaffe* service in early 1946 as the first production examples were scheduled to be finished by October 1945. If this had occurred the type could have been in widespread use fairly quickly as it was far simpler to produce than the Me 262 and it was estimated that each aircraft would only have taken 2,500 man hours to complete. As it was Germany's research into high speed flight only served to benefit its wartime enemies and the two different design philosophies would eventually be pitted against each other in the Korean War.

CHAPTER EIGHT

Meteoric Records

A lthough by early 1945 the German aircraft industry was the most advanced in the world, the collapse of the country at the end of the Second World War meant that only the USA and Great Britain were in a position to extend the boundaries of high speed flight. Of the two the British were to be the quickest off the mark launching an attempt on the World Absolute Speed Record in 1945 with the Gloster Meteor F.4 powered by two Rolls-Royce Derwent V jet engines specially cleared to produce 4,000 lb thrust. At the time the record was still held by Germany at 469 mph, the figure set by Fritz Wendel in the Messerschmitt Me 109R on 26 April 1939. To any serious student of British aviation history it will come as no surprise to discover that this initiative did not come from any official organisation, rather from Glosters themselves who were conscious that their product was in competition with the rival de Havilland Vampire in the UK and the Lockheed XP-80 Shooting Star in the USA. Any publicity to be derived from a successful record attempt would clearly be of great value to the company in securing export markets for the Meteor. With the backing of Rolls-Royce, an approach was made to the Ministry of Aircraft Production which gave its approval for the bid to bring the speed record back to Britain.

The attempt was to be made over a 3 km course at Herne Bay, Kent in late October 1945, a rather unfortunate time of year to be attempting a speed record as air temperature was a factor in ultimate performance, although in this case it was unavoidable if the bid was to be made that year. Two Meteor IVs were prepared – the camouflaged EE454 'Britannia' flown by Group Captain H.J. 'Willie' Wilson AFC, a former O.C. of the Aerodynamics Flight at Farnborough and then commandant of the Empire Test Pilots School, and the all-yellow EE455 (nicknamed 'Yellow Peril') flown by Gloster Chief Test Pilot Eric Greenwood. Some inform-ation had already been gathered on the Meteor's handling characteristics at high Mach number following testing of EE211, a Meteor I which had been brought up to Mark III standards with Derwent I engines of 2,000 lb thrust. This aircraft had also been used to prove the fitment of elongated engine nacelles, the previous shorter design having resulted in severe buffeting at a relatively low Mach number of 0.75. Although Wilson and Greenwood had some idea of what to expect, they were still entering a region of the flight envelope in which very little was known, a situation that was compounded by the speed record regulations which still stipulated a maximum height limit of 200 feet. It was obvious to everyone taking part that if anything went wrong at that height there would be very little time, if any, to sort it out.

Early runs over the course clearly indicated that the aircraft were encountering compressibility effects which were becoming more severe with every small increment in speed. At the top end of the speed range the controls were becoming extremely heavy and there was a marked increase in the amount of buffeting. After an initial nose-up pitch change on reaching its critical Mach number (approximately 0.78M), a further increase in speed resulted in the Meteor pitching nose-down. At the same time there was a significant increase in cockpit temperature due to skin friction. To explore these factors thoroughly, Wilson and Greenwood increased performance levels in small stages, much to the disgust of the members of the press covering the event who were desperate for headline news. Eventually the pilots were satisfied and with suitable weather conditions the record was attempted on 7 November. After a seemingly endless wait the official timings were eventually released, Wilson having recorded a speed of 606.262 mph with Greenwood just behind on 603.425 mph.

Having secured the record for Britain for the first time since 10 April 1934, when the Italian MC.72 surpassed Flight Lieutenant George Stainforth's speed of 406.94 mph set in the Supermarine S.6B following the Schneider Trophy event of 1931, thought was given to making a further attempt with the Meteor in 1946. Further testing of EE454 had shown that, even with more powerful engines, the Meteor would not be able to raise the record by any substantial margin, but with better weather it was hoped to achieve a speed of just over 620 mph (equivalent to 1,000 kph) which, was likely to put the record beyond the capabilities of the XP-80. At the time the Republic XP-84A Thunderjet was being developed in the USA, but reports received from the British Air Commission in Washington were of the opinion that its TG-180 axial turbojet was still a long way from delivering the thrust levels necessary for it to achieve speeds in excess of 600 mph. This assessment proved to be somewhat inaccurate as the XP-84A was flown to 608 mph at Muroc Dry Lake in September 1946.

During the record attempt at Herne Bay both pilots had complained of excessive buffeting at speeds above 600 mph, however it was felt that this could be improved by clipping the wing-tips of the Meteor to increase wing loading. This would also have the effect of reducing the area of the ailerons, but it was hoped that this would be offset by the decrease in inertia about the roll axis. Although the aileron geared tabs had been locked on EE454 and EE455, structurally there was no reason why a moderate amount of gearing should not be used and Gloster adjusted the tabs on later high-speed Meteors so that a pilot could not exceed 4½ degrees aileron movement above 600 mph. One major area of concern was the structural integrity of the hood which was cleared for flight at 600 mph TAS at an ambient air temperature of +15 degrees C. It was considered that raising speed to 630 mph at +30 degrees C would lead to a reduction in hood strength by as much as 40 per cent and so some form of strengthening would be necessary. In the event an aluminium canopy with small side vision panels on each side was used on the 1946 record-breaking aircraft. With the knowledge that the Meteor was capable of raising the speed record even further, the RAF wasted no time in resurrecting the High Speed Flight which was re-formed at Tangmere on 14 June 1946.

The Flight was commanded by Group Captain E.M. 'Teddy' Donaldson DSO AFC, a former Battle of Britain 'ace' and one of three brothers who served as fighter pilots in the RAF. The other members of the team were Squadron Leader W.A. Waterton AFC who had flown with the Air Fighting Development Unit (AFDU) at Wittering, and Flight Lieutenant Neville Duke DSO DFC, one of the RAF's top scoring fighter pilots during the Second World War with twenty-six victories. Three standard Meteor IVs were allocated for practice purposes (EE528, EE529 and EE530) and these were followed on 8 August by EE549 and EE550 which were the two aircraft to be used for the record attempt and were powered by up-rated Derwent engines of 4,300 lb thrust. They were also cleaned up as far as possible with the removal of the radio mast, faired-over cannon ports (armament and ammunition boxes were replaced by extra fuel tanks) and an overall high gloss finish. A completely new course was laid out over the English Channel just off Littlehampton in Sussex. The previous course at Herne Bay had involved flight over land as well as sea which had led to some unpleasant turbulence being experienced, but at Littlehampton the approaches to the measured 3 km section, together with the positioning turns at either end were all flown over water.

Prior to the record attempt further test flying was carried out by Gloster to check the Meteor's handling at high Mach number and at low level. As the aircraft used were standard Meteor IVs a dive was necessary to build up speed before pulling out at low level over the Bristol Channel. The pilots involved were Eric Greenwood, Philip Stanbury and Roland Beamont who recorded his experiences in his book *Testing Years* (Ian Allen, 1981)

In a series of exhilarating low flights down the Severn estuary from Moreton Valence in June and July of 1946, at times rendered difficult by heavy turbulence, we established that 612–618 mph TAS (depending on air temperature at the time) was practical at 100 feet or so in level flight. Clearing a handling margin above this was less easy as it was apparent that at these speeds the Meteor was encountering the onset of compressibility trim effects, in addition to buffet vibration and very loud airflow noise round the cockpit. In shallow dives from about 1,500 to 100 feet over the mudflats, passing Avonmouth and Weston-super-Mare in seconds, the controls at upwards of 600 mph were already heavy and slow in response and levelling out required a two-handed pull on the stick.

I was determined, however, to establish the optimum condition which might be encountered by the High Speed Flight. In a final sortie on 9 July, after a run at about 600 mph down to 150 feet to check atmospheric conditions which proved to be smooth and ideal in very hot sunny weather, I pulled the Meteor up in a wide climbing turn to the west over the Severn off Avonmouth. After tightening down the harness adjusters and checking instruments, I set up a diving turn at full power approaching the handling Mach limit for that height of 0.79. Straightening out over the mudflats with heavying controls we continued the shallow dive until passing 500 feet at about 605 mph indicated and increasing. With buffeting, wind roar, heavy vibration and near solid controls it was time to level out but at that moment the Meteor suddenly changed trim, pitching nose-down with the Mach meter touching 0.80.

With the two-handed pull that had now become vitally necessary to avoid bouncing off the Severn, I could not reduce power. There was a brief moment in which with maximum possible pull force on the stick the Meteor continued its apparently unchallenged flight path down to what now looked like an inevitable impact point only seconds ahead. Then the nose began to rise and, at something under 100 feet which seemed altogether too low for comfort at that speed, we levelled out with the ASI showing about 608 mph. The Meteor was not going to go faster than that at low level and survive. We returned rather gently to Moreton Valence for a somewhat sweaty debriefing with a very happy flight test engineer.

Beamont later claimed that when corrected for position error, instrument error and ambient air temperature, which during the run was +27 degrees C, his true airspeed had been 632 mph which raised a few eyebrows when it was inadvertently reported in the press the following day.

Back at Tangmere, preparations for the record attempt were continuing but there was a setback when one of the 'hack' aircraft flown by Bill Waterton suddenly lost power on the port engine at high speed, resulting in a strong yaw to the left. Throttling back the starboard engine, Waterton was able to regain control and fly back to base where it was discovered that the port engine was badly damaged. Initially it was thought that the aircraft had suffered a bird strike, but a lack of debris suggested otherwise. Not long after another aircraft flown by Neville Duke suffered a similar loss of power and it was discovered that the engine was ingesting small pieces of metal that had become detached from pop-rivets in the air intake. These were tending to chip pieces off the compressor which in turn were breaking the turbine blades. The problem was quickly solved by applying sealing fabric to the offending areas of riveting.

To maximise performance on the Meteors of the High Speed Flight the so-called 'Daunt-guards' had also been removed from the engine air intakes. These were metal grilles which prevented anyone being sucked into the nacelle when the engine was being run up on the ground and were named after Michael Daunt, the Gloster test pilot who had discovered what could happen when walking too close to the front end of a working jet engine. 'Teddy' Donaldson had an almost identical experience and was prevented from being pulled into the starboard engine of one aircraft by Squadron Leader George Porter, the engineering officer, who grabbed hold of Donaldson's legs and managed to hold on long enough for the engine to be shut down.

As the practice aircraft were fitted with standard Derwent V engines it was necessary to carry out a dive to investigate the handling characteristics at high speed. From the figures obtained it soon became evident that previous estimates of the Meteor's speed and Mach number had been somewhat optimistic. It was also apparent that as the altitude decreased so did the aircraft's limiting Mach number. From this it was soon realised that it would not be possible to fully exploit the extra power available on the record-breakers as airframe capabilities would be the limiting factor and the likelihood of exceeding Mach 0.82 at sea level would be remote. In actual practice the limiting Mach number proved to be in the order of 0.81.

The course was generally easy to fly, though, like Herne Bay, it was subject to considerable bumpiness. This was most evident at the eastern end off Worthing, owing to the shallows that were just offshore and areas of sand at low tide. Turbulence was also apparent at the mouth of the river Arun as it flowed into the Channel near Littlehampton. From the pilots' point of view the most difficult part of the course was the turn to seawards after completion of the timed runs as this involved a height limitation of 300 metres (985 ft) while turning with 55–60 degrees of bank. The timed section was flown at a maximum height of 75 metres (246 feet) and was marked by two large back and white chequered balloons at each end. During testing of the 'record breakers' (they were also referred to as Star Meteors) a significant discrepancy was noted between the two aircraft. Whereas the longitudinal trim characteristics were virtually identical, there was a marked difference in lateral behaviour as EE550 showed a worrying tendency to drop its port wing at the very top end of the speed range. As the course had to be flown at such a low altitude this was inevitably of great concern for Bill Waterton and Neville Duke, 'Teddy' Donaldson having conveniently got round the problem by allocating himself as pilot of EE549.

By early September all the various timing arrangements were functioning properly and despite temperatures being far lower than had been hoped for, the first attempt on the speed record was made on the 7th. Actual weather conditions included a solid overcast at 2,000 feet, a surface temperature of +15 degrees C and a slight onshore breeze bringing the threat of rain. Having already checked the course, Donaldson took off at 1745 hrs in EE549 for a record attempt. To enter the course he passed over the eastern outskirts of Chichester in a turn to port and straightened up two miles to the west of Bognor pier at 1,000 feet at an indicated speed of 580 mph. He then opened up to full throttle and by the time that Bognor pier was passed the aircraft had reached its maximum speed and remained fully compressed over the whole twelve miles of the course. During four timed runs in opposing directions the accelerometer in the aircraft recorded bumps of +4½ to -2½ g, almost entirely due to compressibility buffet. At the completion of the last run a slight drizzle started and Donaldson flew back to Tangmere, landing at 1808 hrs having used 208 gallons of fuel. The average speed recorded was 616 mph (991 kph).

Shortly after Donaldson's return, Bill Waterton was airborne in EE550. Passing over Bognor pier at 800 ft at a speed of 570 mph IAS, the engines were opened up to full power in a shallow dive so that by the time Littlehampton appeared the aircraft was showing a speed of 600 mph with a Mach number of 0.77 at 150 feet. At this point the Meteor was in the latter stages of compressibility with heavy buffet and a strong nose-down pitch. Although the port aileron had been 'tweaked' the aircraft had already begun to drop its left wing and this tendency got worse as speed was increased. Shortly before entering the timed section a particularly nasty bump caused the wing to drop even more and Waterton found that he was unable to prevent the aircraft veering to the left in a descending turn towards the coast. Having snatched the throttles shut and used every ounce of his fourteen stones in weight on the controls, the aircraft eventually began to respond but only after it had nearly collided with the marker balloons and had passed at very low level over the western edge of Worthing.

After this experience it was obvious that even brute force was insufficient to retain lateral control of the aircraft and so on his next run Waterton was careful to align the aircraft early and to brace his left shoulder against the port side of the cockpit so that his forearm was a physical barrier to prevent the stick moving to the left. In addition he selected right rudder trim and applied as much pressure to the rudder pedal as he could. Although the pain in his left arm was excruciating, this unorthodox technique appeared to work and he was able to complete four more runs before returning to Tangmere. Despite having to fly slightly out of trim Waterton had still managed a speed of 614 mph (988 kph).

Although the record had been extended there was no sense of euphoria as the cool weather that had been experienced in the early part of September had ensured that the figure of 1,000 kph had still not been reached, even though it was tantalisingly close. In the hope that warmer conditions would eventually prevail, the High Speed Flight remained at Tangmere and prepared for another go. The aircraft were cleaned up, ill-fitting panels were improved by filler, the cockpit cowling vents were sealed up and the external finish given an even higher gloss. A conference was held to discuss the tendency of EE550 to drop its port wing. The aircraft had already been looked at by Glosters who had been unable to effect any improvement and Donaldson was of the opinion that it should be left due to the limited number of engine hours remaining. It was also felt that any change in trim to improve the left-wing down tendency might cause problems of a different nature elsewhere.

The prospects of extending the record still further gradually slipped away as weather conditions remained poor for the whole month. Despite this further attempts were made on 24 September with Donaldson taking off at 0757 hrs. As the temperature was only +10 degrees C there was little likelihood of an improvement but the mean speed of six runs was still 613 mph. Bill Waterton was next up in EE550 and in the course of six runs he was forced to endure considerable discomfort once again as the control column tried to crush his left hand. At full speed considerable wing-tip vibration was noticed and the entire rear third of the outer wings was covered in a dense vapour. This could be seen forming just aft of the white of the roundels, the ailerons being invisible. Observers on the ground noticed that the entire wing nacelles and the centre section aft of their centres appeared to be covered in a dense fog. These effects were caused by a high relative humidity and were some of the first observed instances of shock waves forming around the wings being visible because of condensation. Teddy Donaldson made one further attempt at 0900 hrs but had to abort during the third run when a severe vibration set in. On return it was discovered that the mass balance weight attached to the lower part of the rudder had broken loose. This weight was all of 27½ lb and was attached via a steel bar with a diameter of over 1 inch but it had still sheered due to buffeting caused by compressibility.

After Teddy Donaldson had cleared the course Neville Duke was finally given the chance to have a crack at the record but, like Bill Waterton, his attempt was badly affected by the lateral handling problems of EE550. His flight report records an eventful trip:

Never having flown this aircraft before (previous experience with EE549) I had planned to make one run over the course to get the feel of the aircraft at speeds of around 600+ mph IAS. After take-off all was well until turning onto the course at Bognor Pier when the engines were opened up from cruising (13,800 rpm) to 15,200 rpm. The acceleration on opening up was rapid and speed jumped from 500 to 580 mph IAS very quickly. As this speed was attained the nose tended to rise strongly – it was of sufficient strength to require trimming out.

As speed was increased to the 600 mph IAS mark, the nose tended to go down steadily and strongly, again re-trimming being necessary, and at the same time the port wing started to go down. Although rudder trim was quickly applied, it was necessary to use both hands on the stick to keep the nose and the wing up. The wing low became so heavy that it was necessary to prop my elbow against the side of the cockpit to brace the control column. At the same time a very heavy and maximum foot load on the starboard rudder pedal was used to help the wing.

By the time the aircraft was at its maximum speed indicating around 603–605 mph below 300 feet (Mach No. approx 0.81+) a terrific amount of vibration and buffeting was occurring over the whole of the airframe emanating from the tail – all controls were vibrating and pressure was increased on these controls. Heat in the cockpit rose rapidly due to skin friction and on occasions a fore-and-aft pitching took place. Although the air was calm the accelerometer registered from +7g to -3g due to the buffeting of compressibility.

On the first run I was unable to keep the aircraft in a straight line on the course as the left wing was slightly down. On a third run the aircraft veered uncontrollably off to the left and I had to pull up to avoid the balloons marking the course. At the end of each measured 3 km stretch the aircraft was pulled up slightly and the throttles pulled back a little by a quick snatch – it being necessary to regain a hold of the stick with both hands quickly. The aircraft soon became decompressed – the speed when compressibility comes on being about 595 mph IAS (0.78M) and with this the nose tends to rise rapidly.

After landing from this abandoned attempt, the aileron trim was altered to make the aircraft right wing low. Experience on the second attempt was as before but right wing low up to 550 mph IAS, in trim 550 to 570 mph. Above this speed the trim was ineffective and the port wing went down as hard as before. A little more time was available, however, to get properly lined up on the course and maintained by having the right wing down slightly. Six runs were made, the official speed averaged 613 mph (one run at 625 mph).

The decision to alter the aileron trim on this occasion was prompted by the fact that Waterton had made his final attempt on the record and it was not of such importance if the adjustment proved to be unsuccessful. One final run was flown by Donaldson in EE549 later in the day but the weather conditions were considerably bumpier than in the morning and no improvement was recorded. Both EE549 and EE550 were returned to the manufacturers on 25 September, a day which, ironically, was clear and hot, conditions that may have allowed a speed of 1,000 kph to be achieved. Having raised the absolute speed record to 616 mph, Britain thus held onto the prestigious position of having the world's fastest aircraft for a little longer. The record was eventually broken by the Lockheed P-80R Shooting Star when it recorded a speed of 623.61 mph on 19 June 1947 at Muroc in California.

One of the most valuable lessons to come out of the record attempts was the need to limit the amount of 'g' on an airframe when operating at high speed. This was due to the fact that stressed portions of the structure were under greater strain as speed increased. The application of a certain amount of 'g' at, say, 200 kts IAS would only have a small effect on the safety margin of a structure, but the same amount of 'g' at 600 kts IAS, when the structure was already stressed close to its design safety factor, was likely to push it over the limit with disastrous results. Air density also affects structural strength so that the lower the altitude, the greater the stress for any given true airspeed. Flight in bumpy air was also noted as being hazardous, with large variations in positive and negative 'g' being noted on accelerometers. As these were of extremely short duration they did not cause the pilot to black out, but the structural effects could still be catastrophic. Overall, the recommendations were that excessive 'g' and pilot 'ham-handedness' were to be avoided when flying at high speed and that flight at low level in turbulence should be made at reduced speed. Sadly, this advice was to be ignored by many pilots who would pay with their lives when their aircraft disintegrated around them.

Although many valuable lessons were learned with the Meteor, its conservative straight-winged design with drag-inducing nacelles and various external appendages meant that it was ill-equipped to explore the transonic region of flight. The fact that it was able to make a successful attempt on the world speed record to offer any help at all was due to the rapid progress made with the centrifugal jets, the later Derwent V engine offering twice the power of the original Welland of the Meteor I. Effectively the Meteor was an object lesson in how not to design an aircraft for high-speed flight, not that this had been one of George Carter's design considerations when he first put pen to paper. To delay the drag rise due to compressibility it was necessary to reduce the thickness/chord ratio of the wing to the lowest value that was practically possible and this was done with the Miles M.52, a futuristic straight-winged design that was commenced in 1943 and one which held the very real prospect of achieving a speed in excess of Mach 1.0.

CHAPTER NINE

The Miles M.52 Fiasco

Although it was destined never to fly, the Miles M.52 has gone down in British aviation history as being one of the most controversial aircraft programmes of all time. Most of the subsequent debate has concentrated on its ultimate demise and the reasons for it, however, the requirement for a machine capable of flying faster than any other aircraft, and by a considerable margin, meant that right from the word go the M.52 was a project that was liable to provoke strong opinions. The fact that it was to be built by a manufacturer that was best known for producing all-wood light aircraft only served to heighten the degree of introspection that was to surround the project.

The M.52 was first conceived in the autumn of 1943 when the tide of the Second World War had only just begun to turn in the Allies favour. The requirement for a high speed research aircraft was not put out to tender, instead a contract was placed with Miles Aircraft as all other aircraft companies were fully committed with the production of aircraft for the RAF. Although Miles had not been involved with anything remotely like the aircraft that was needed, it did have a reputation for innovative design solutions including the Merlin-powered M.20 fighter, which went from drawing board to first flight in sixty days, and the M.39B Libellula twin-engined tandem-wing aircraft. It has also been alleged that Miles were given the work as their proposal for a transatlantic passenger aircraft (the X.11) was not given the consideration that it should have received from the Brabazon committee which had been set up to assess various designs for post-war civil transports. It was not until ten months after the first discussions were held that a specification (E.24/43) was finally issued to cover the project.

Over the years some confusion has arisen over the proposed top speed of the M.52. Several accounts have stated that its top speed was to be 1,000 mph in level flight, however, others have qualified this by saying that this was merely an inadvertent use of mph instead of kph by an unwitting member of the administrative staff at the Air Ministry. Any idea of the M.52 being capable of 1,000 mph in level flight in its original form was somewhat fanciful, instead during a discussion at RAE in November 1943 Miles were estimating the M.52's maximum speed at 700 mph EAS at 40,000 feet, while a month later RAE assessed the top speed of the preliminary version of the M.52 in level flight at 36,000 feet as 'about 600 mph'. Farnborough did, however, state that any short period increase in thrust by rocket assistance (or by increasing speed in a dive) could raise speed from 600 mph to 1,100 mph. Even if rather more was expected of the M.52 than it was capable of producing, there can be no doubt that the task facing Miles was an immense challenge as the design of an aircraft capable of flying at such speeds was, in Britain at least, a complete step into the unknown.

This was in marked contrast to the situation in Germany where there was a well established research programme, aided by data obtained from the world's first supersonic wind tunnels, which were helping to evolve configurations to delay the drag rise of compressibility, so that the elusive prize of flight at the speed of sound was becoming tantalisingly close. The problem facing Germany was that due to the incessant bombing of the homeland and the severe pressure being placed on supply routes, the resources that were needed to facilitate an advanced aircraft programme were becoming hard to come by. In the UK the situation was largely reversed in that high quality alloys for aircraft structures and heat resistant materials for jet engines were available, but virtually nothing was known about the advanced planforms that were needed to make aircraft go significantly faster. Back at Woodley aerodrome near Reading, the Miles design team, headed by its director George Miles, turned to the only avenue that offered any guidance, the science of ballistics.

As bullets and shells had been happily travelling at supersonic speeds for a long time, Miles came to the conclusion that an aircraft designed along similar lines would stand the best chance of success. The fuselage of the design that eventually emerged was noticeably bullet shaped with a pointed nose cone that enclosed the cockpit, a cylindrical body which housed the jet engine and fuel tank and an aft section which tapered to the jet efflux. The basic form of construction was to be high-tensile steel with an external alloy skin. A straight wing was employed and initially the intention was to build two different wings, one of 7½ per cent thickness/chord ratio and 5 to 1 aspect ratio and the other of 5 per cent t/c ratio and about 4 to 1 aspect ratio. The wing was far removed from any other contemporary wing section as it was of bi-convex design, but by February 1944 Miles had decided to go for a t/c ratio of 7½ per cent at the root and 4 per cent at the tip [this compares with corresponding figures of 13 per cent and 7 per cent for the Spitfire which had the thinnest wing of the piston-engined fighters of the day].

The planform of the wing revealed a pleasant slender elliptical shape with splayed tips, the trailing edges incorporating split flaps. For the first flight it was proposed by Miles to build up the wing to 10 per cent t/c ratio by means of 'plasters', an idea that was welcomed as it would save much time compared with the original idea of producing two different sets of wings. A moderate sweep angle was adopted for the tailplane and the vertical tail possessed a profile very similar to the outer section of the wing. Normal aileron and rudder controls were provided but there were to be no elevators, instead the tailplane was to have variable incidence. It was also the intention to have irreversible (electric) controls for flight at high speed, switching to direct mechanical control for take-off, landing and manoeuvring.

As the wing was virtually solid, fuel was contained in a 200-gallon saddle tank that fitted around the profile of the Power Jets W.2/700 centrifugal engine which provided 2,000 lb thrust, air being admitted to the engine via an annular intake just to the rear of the cockpit. The fuselage also had to accommodate the tricycle undercarriage, the main wheels retracting into wells adjacent to the wings with the nose wheel ending up between the pilot's feet. The cockpit was extremely cramped and could only be accessed by a pilot of small stature, the seating position being semi-reclined. In case of emergency the nose cone was to be detached from the airframe by activating explosive charges in the mountings, a parachute then being deployed to slow the nose section down so that the pilot could make his own parachute descent when it had reached lower levels.

By December 1943 RAE had changed its view somewhat and was estimating top speed at 'only' 570 mph. It was felt that the slope of the drag curve was so steep that speed was not likely to be affected appreciably by changes in power. Despite this assertion it was suggested that a jettisonable bi-fuel rocket could be used, along the lines of the rocket assisted take-off gear (RATOG) that had recently been developed. It was considered that a unit producing a thrust of 5,000 lb for twenty-five seconds would be suitable, although this installation would weigh 1,500–2,000 lb. Despite this possibility it was still felt that the greatest possible thrust should be demanded from the main engine and that the drag of the aircraft should, if possible, be reduced still further by decreasing wing thickness. Without any means of assistance from increased thrust or reduced drag it was felt that the only means of getting to speeds in the region of Mach 1.0 was by diving. Preliminary calculations showed that the dive angle need not be steep but in order to get to a suitable altitude to commence the dive, the aircraft would need to have a good rate of climb and reasonable economy. Drop tanks containing a further 880 lb of fuel were considered at first but were later discarded when it was calculated that the M.52 would be able to reach its optimum height on internal fuel and still be able to return to base.

One particular area of concern was the low speed handling characteristics of the bi-convex wing. As a wing of this section had not been tested before, it was decided to build a full-size wing out of wood and fit it to one of Miles' single-engined light aircraft, an M.3B Falcon. The aircraft used was L9705 which, with the sharp-edged wing fitted, became known as the 'Gillette Falcon'. It was eventually flown in this condition by Mr H.V. Kennedy on 11 August 1944 and confounded the critics by displaying excellent aileron control at low speeds. There was, however, a large drag rise with increase of incidence and if the stick was eased back after take-off the aircraft sank back to the ground. The Falcon was also modified to have a narrow track undercarriage similar to the main gear of the M.52. Miles had also requested that a Spitfire IX be delivered so that it could be modified to test the variable incidence tail that was proposed for the M.52. In January 1944 F.G. Miles wrote to the Ministry of Aircraft Production (MAP) to say that the firm was being handicapped on the design side by the aircraft's non-appearance. He then went on to ask whether anything could be done to speed up the arrangements that had been made. Several weeks later Joe Smith, the chief designer at Supermarine, offered his assistance in connection with the work that Miles were doing on the moveable tail, but eventually the all-moving tail was tested on the Falcon.

One person who had been involved from the very start was Frank Whittle of Power Jets Ltd whose W.2/700 was to power the M.52. This was the last of Whittle's own designs and featured reverse-flow combustion chambers which did nothing to reduce frontal area, but the engine was at least reliable. Testing of the W.2/700 began in 1943 with the engine mounted in the back of a Wellington test bed. It was of innovative design in that it employed an 'aft fan' behind the normal turbine to draw air from around the engine and compress it before expelling it via an annular jetpipe that was situated around the hot core exhaust. From an early stage it was envisaged that thrust could be increased by burning fuel in the exhaust tube. This was known at the time as 'supplementary heating' and comprised a number of combustion chambers mounted in the jetpipe to which fuel could be introduced and burnt to increase thrust. This was the first example of what later became known as an afterburner. Whittle was quick to grasp that, unlike a piston engine, a gas turbine uses only a small proportion of the available oxygen that passes through it and so thrust could be substantially increased for little additional weight by burning extra fuel aft of the engine. Another advantage which was particularly useful in the early days of jet engine development was that the temperature of the gas flow in the jetpipe could be much higher than that passing through the turbine which had to be limited to avoid damage to the turbine blades.

By April 1944 concerns over the way the M.52 was progressing were already apparent at the MAP, in particular an increase in all-up weight which led J.E. Serby to comment as follows, 'the firm seem to be rather adrift on weights . . . if this goes badly astray the whole aeroplane will be useless.' It was true that weight had increased from the initial estimate of 5–6,000 lb to an all-up figure of 7,493 lb that was being quoted by RAE in July 1944, but this would not have stopped the aircraft from reaching supersonic speeds in a dive. Even at this early stage one almost gets the impression that a number of people were just waiting for the aircraft to fail.

In July 1944 the RAE published a technical note on the M.52 which gives a good idea of what was expected from the aircraft when it eventually flew. It was thought that the speeds likely to be reached by the M.52 were sufficiently high as to be interesting and that valuable results would be obtained from the design. Despite the concerns that had been raised as regards low speed handling, RAE thought that the aircraft would be satisfactory from an aerodynamic point of view at low speeds and that lateral and longitudinal stability would be adequate. It was also suggested that slightly higher speeds and greater safety could be obtained by using a conventional wing section instead of the bi-convex section as proposed. The estimates of drag that had been made also showed the benefit of keeping the fuselage diameter to a minimum and it was felt that an alternative power unit of reduced dimensions would provide the maximum thrust per square foot of frontal area.

The performance calculations showed that there was no hope of the M.52 reaching Mach 1.0 in level flight and it was thought that the best that could be achieved was 0.95M. It was also estimated that the greatest height that could be attained with the bi-convex wing was 50,000 feet, however, this could be increased to 56,000 feet if a conventional wing section was used. Because of this it was thought that higher speeds would be attainable in a dive with an aircraft fitted with a conventional wing section and that the safety factor would be increased as more height would be available for the recovery. It was calculated that the best technique would be to push over into a dive so that a condition of zero 'g' was maintained for as long as possible to keep drag to a minimum, and it was expected that maximum Mach number would be reached at a dive angle of 45 degrees. To avoid all airspeed limitations a 3g recovery was recommended so that the pull out manoeuvre was complete on reaching 30,000 feet.

The progress of the M.52 was discussed at the monthly meetings of the 'supersonic committee' which looked at various ways of obtaining relevant data, including attaching small aerofoil test sections to the rear end of existing rockets, the construction of a very high speed rail track and the dropping of heavy bodies from high altitudes. These meetings were normally chaired by Sir Ben Lockspeiser, the Director of Scientific Research, and had been set up in 1943 because interrogation of prisoners of war had indicated that the Germans had already flown an aircraft capable of supersonic speeds. This, of course, was something of an exaggeration, but at least it prompted the British into action. Of all the various schemes that were overseen by the committee, the M.52 was the most important as it offered the most effective way of discovering aircraft behaviour at transonic speeds.

The first doubts on the M.52 began to be expressed in June 1944 when Mr R. Smelt of the RAE voiced his concern over the increase in all-up weight. This meant that estimated ceiling had been reduced from 60,000 feet to 50,000 feet and he felt that it was now doubtful if the M.52 would reach supersonic speed in a dive owing to the height required to pull out. He also expressed concern over the predicted high drag rise of the bi-convex wing and questioned whether it would be successful. Professor Sir Melville Jones asked whether, in view of the fact that British and American jet-propelled aircraft were already reaching high speeds, the M.52 should be proceeded with (by 'high speed' he was presumably referring to the Meteor I and the P-59A Airacomet!), and A.R. Howell of RAE suggested that the M.52 was not large enough for a supersonic aeroplane, preferring instead a specially designed aeroplane and engine. Mr Smelt raised the idea of using rockets of bi-fuel type for boosting thrust, but again the question of weight increase was thought to be the decisive factor.

By October 1944 Dr. H.M. Garner, the Deputy Director of Scientific Research, was raising the possibility of a successor to the M.52 which had been made a possibility as a result of the rapid rate of development in jet engines. This prompted a further discussion on rocket power, but Sir Ben Lockspeiser ruled that under no circumstances should this supersede turbine work. Over the next few months there was little to report on the progress of the M.52 but by March 1945 the prospect of acquiring supersonic data by the use of rocket-propelled aircraft of some sort had improved considerably. Garner was of the opinion that this would be the quickest method of obtaining information on supersonic flight, but Lockspeiser stated that he still preferred to see a piloted aircraft as he felt that actual flying experience was needed at the kind of speeds under consideration. This subject was debated again on 10 April with Lockspeiser reaffirming his position which was opposed by Mr R.

McKinnon Wood (MAP) who felt that the aircraft should be radio controlled for reasons of safety. Mr R. Smelt pointed out that scale models could be used initially with a full scale piloted aircraft to appear later when more information had been obtained. It was suggested that Barnes Wallis of Vickers Aircraft would be able to assist with the design of the models and he was to be approached by the Chairman. Wallis, of course, was famous as the designer of the 'bouncing bomb' that was used to devastating effect by No.617 Squadron in May 1943 to breach the Moehne and Eder Dams in the Ruhr and he had also devised the geodetic form of construction used on the Wellesley general purpose bomber and the twin-engined Wellington which formed the backbone of Bomber Command in the early years of the Second World War.

The next meeting was held on 12 June (with Barnes Wallis in attendance) and produced some of the strongest criticism yet of the M.52. Mr H.F. Vessey reported that wind tunnel testing had shown that there was a serious decrease in longitudinal stability with increase in Mach number. This effect commenced at about 0.5M and got worse up to 0.8M which was the limit of the wind tunnel. RAE had recommended that the cure was to move the centre of gravity further forward but this would lead to higher tail loads and it was anticipated that severe structural difficulties would be encountered. As a result of this the whole question of whether or not to proceed with the M.52 was raised. The Chairman expressed the opinion that as time went on the aircraft had become less and less likely to succeed, although he did state that he was not sure of the results of the wind tunnel tests as various difficulties had been encountered in interpolation of results in the past.

The following month Vessey had to backtrack from his previous position as he reported that the M.52's stability problems were not as serious as had been thought and that it was proposed to fit a larger tailplane for the later trials to involve high speed flight. Mr McKinnon Wood then threw a spanner in the works by calling to attention the advantages of wing sweep on an aircraft of this type, stating that the M.52 should be discontinued as it was 'out of date'. His comments reflected the recent acquisition of German technical information, however, Sir Ben Lockspeiser declared that the M.52 should proceed at the same level of priority, but that the work on small expendable rocket-propelled aircraft should proceed with the highest priority. As regards the latter it was agreed that the first stage would be the use of small pilot-less expendable aircraft (which Barnes Wallis was to investigate), followed by similar, but controllable aircraft, and finally the production of a larger piloted machine.

The question of stability was discussed further in September 1945, however, Mr Smelt of RAE pointed out that all aircraft showed the same longitudinal characteristics as those of the M.52 which it was now thought would only experience instability at some point above 0.82M. As it was expected that the aircraft would be stable again on reaching Mach 1.0, it followed that the period of instability would be fairly short and it was now considered that this was not a serious difficulty after all. Just when it seemed that the M.52 was about to be painted in a slightly more favourable light, it received another body blow when the problem of pilot escape was discussed. It was estimated that it would take another year to develop a satisfactory method of using explosive charges to detach the nose section from the rest of the airframe. The following month Mr Vessey stated that latest wind tunnel tests had shown that the pilot of the M.52 would only be able to vacate his craft if he could invert it. Sir Melville Jones said that no one would willingly send a man up in an aircraft from which there was no means of escape in an emergency. The Chairman agreed that the whole question must be reconsidered in the light of the latest information.

The future of the M.52 finally came to a head in early 1946 when a flurry of memos between the various departments that were overseeing the project had just one thing in common, that the project was in serious trouble and was unlikely to produce anything worthwhile. It was noted that although the contract had been placed with Miles on 13 December 1943 'as a matter of urgency', progress thus far did not seem to have been very rapid. It was also stated that the firm had spent £73,000 in the previous three years and had estimated that it would cost at least £250,000 to complete. Phrases such as 'in these circumstances you may wish to reconsider the project', were commonplace, but remarks like 'if it is decided that it should continue, will you please obtain additional financial approval on the basis of the estimate of final cost' were guaranteed to cause the Treasury to have a fit.

Mr H.F. Vessey (ADARD) summed up the M.52 project as far as he was concerned in a memo on 18 February 1946:

> The matter was raised at DGSR's supersonic committee on 12 February 1946 but no firm decision was reached. The opinion of the committee was unanimous that there was no case for continuing on the grounds of obtaining information at transonic or supersonic speeds (the reason for placing the contract). A case was put forward for the completion of the aircraft for use as an engine test bed. It was developed especially for the E.24/43 and although it is not one in which we are seriously interested, it is an engine on which useful information on ducted fans and afterburning could be obtained.
>
> The aircraft was designed purely for supersonic investigations

but the amount of space available for instrumentation is extremely limited. In addition, engine accessibility is very poor. Considerable development is required to make the aircraft fly even at low speeds and the outstanding points are:

Pilot escape – the main problems of its design have yet to be solved

Power operation – bench tests of the power operating system to be fitted to all flying controls have been promising but considerable development is required

Landing speed is very high and is outside present experience

The firm's estimate is at least £250,000 representing a future expenditure of at least £150,000. Past experience with the firm, particularly on E.24/43, leads us to regard this as an underestimate.

Dr H.M. Garner concurred with the above and added the following:

Although we had the best scientific advice in the country, we made two bad mistakes (at least) in the design. These were the square [sic] wings and the annular intake. We found from German information in 1945 of the great advantage in swept back wings and recent experiments have shown that the annular intake has low efficiency at high speeds. This information came to light nearly two years after the project was launched.

All that was needed now was for final approval to be given for the M.52 programme to be terminated. Although he had resisted calls for the M.52 to be cancelled on several previous occasions, Sir Ben Lockspeiser went along with everyone else and said that the project had been a case of 'putting the cart before the horse'. He was also of the opinion that there would be no more supersonic aircraft until 'our rocket propelled models and wind tunnels have given us enough information to proceed on a reliable basis'. Now that the whole thing was over, the collective sigh of relief must have generated even more hot air than usual in the corridors of power at Whitehall.

The fact that the M.52 had been cancelled was communicated to Miles in the form of a letter from the Ministry of Supply (formerly the Ministry of Aircraft Production) which was received on 20 February 1946. Not surprisingly the news was greeted with stunned disbelief and for a time F.G. Miles was unable to tell the rest of his workforce that the aircraft they had been working on for the last three years was no more. Instead he queried the decision but when it was confirmed that work was to end forthwith, he was left with no choice. If this was not bad enough, Miles were apparently requested to despatch all of their data to Bell Aircraft in the USA so that it could be used on their own straight-winged research aircraft, the rocket-powered XS-1, although it is debatable as to how much benefit the Americans would have derived from this information, with the possible exception of the slab tail. As was the case with all aircraft cancellations, the material evidence of the M.52 was quickly disposed of with jigs and tools being broken up, together with the mock-up, although photographic evidence exists that the nose cone of the M.52 survived until at least 1948 on the dump at Woodley.

The true role of Barnes Wallis in the M.52 debacle will probably never be known. Several writers have alleged that he was instrumental in the eventual cancellation of the E.24/43 programme, however this author has found no direct evidence to support any interference on his part. Despite this it has to be said that Vickers would be the chief beneficiary of any move away from manned supersonic flight. Wallis had achieved great success there as the Chief Designer (Structures) and by 1945 was the head of a research department within the company. It is also well documented that Wallis had been appalled at the loss of life during the Dams raid, so his views would have fitted in well with others on the supersonic committee who were unwilling to risk the lives of test pilots in an extremely risky testing programme.

Having become increasingly disenchanted with the M.52, the possibility of using nice 'cheap' models to do the same job was a convenient way out of what was perceived at the time as being an impossible situation. Unfortunately for Britain the project was surrounded by so many unanswered questions that it was easy for experts in their field to rally against the aircraft if they so desired, as they could be certain that anything they came up with was unlikely to be contradicted. In the light of the importance of acquiring supersonic flight data, the committee's views on safety has to be called into question, especially as there were pilots willing to take the challenge. Although the chances of a successful bale out in an emergency were slim (it is assumed here that detaching the nose cone was not possible), it has to be said that the likelihood of a pilot getting out of the Bell XS-1 in one piece was equally as bleak and this did not stop the Americans. It is not intended to doubt the sincerity of some of those who made up the committee, but following the M.52's cancellation the fact that pilots would not be put at risk could be used to distract attention from the real reasons why the project was being terminated, i.e. lack of money, a total misreading of the supersonic potential of the aircraft and a complete lack of will to maintain Britain's pre-eminent position in world aviation.

The sequel to E.24/43 was the eventual testing of radio-controlled models. This was known as Operation Neptune which turned out to be one of the most aptly named projects of all time as the trials were carried out over the Atlantic and all the hardware ended up at the bottom of the sea without having produced any useful data whatsoever. It was also to account for an expenditure of £500,000 which was five times the sum spent on the M.52. So much for taking the 'cheap' option!

While the Americans were left to develop the Bell XS-1, which apart from its rocket motor and the positioning of its horizontal stabiliser was remarkably similar to the M.52, the British instead took the 'Airfix' option. In 1945 a contract was placed with Vickers for the design and construction of several test vehicles. At first it was envisaged that these would be simple models utilising solid-fuel rockets, but when the extent of German rocket testing became evident it was decided to modify the design to incorporate a bi-fuel rocket motor using an alcohol-hydrogen peroxide propulsion system. This extended the duration of flight so that an auto-pilot was required and a radio telemetering unit was needed as no other means of data recording was feasible. Due to the increased level of complexity, what had started out as a simple vehicle with a con-structional timescale of weeks, grew into a complicated aeroplane in miniature requiring months for manufacture. The models were to be 3/10 scale versions of the M.52 (except that the annular air intake of the full scale aircraft was omitted) and for drag and stressing reasons the operational altitude had to be in the stratosphere to which altitude the test vehicles were carried under a Mosquito XVI. Two pilots were allocated to the Flight, Squadron Leader D.A.C. Hunt and Mr Keith Butler.

The main fuselage of the model was of stressed skin construction on cylindrical Z and U-shaped formers, to the front of which was attached a machined ogival nose section forming the fuel tank and to the rear was a similar shaped shell structure housing the tail unit and the combustion chamber. The centre section was split on the centre line to permit the insertion of the full span mahogany wing above and below which were the various units contained within the shell. To maintain CG it was necessary to include a large balance weight of almost 10 per cent of all-up weight in the foremost section of the nose. The layout was further restricted by the need to maintain a constant CG position during the consumption of the fuels. To achieve this, the various fuel tanks were carefully placed along the length of the fuselage together with the rest of the equipment that was carried. The single piece bi-convex wing extended the whole span and was of mahogany with dural inserts at leading and trailing edges which formed a convenient dipole aerial system for the telemetering unit. The all-moving tailplane was of similar construction.

It was not until the summer of 1947 that the programme had progressed sufficiently for an actual test firing to be considered but on 30

May during a last check flight, the parent aircraft inadvertently descended into a storm cloud at 22,000 feet which immediately sent it out of control. By the time that the Mosquito had been recovered at 8,000 feet, test vehicle A1 had parted company and had disappeared into the murky waters of the Bristol Channel. This was a particularly serious setback as the model had been carrying the prototype examples of all the instruments and equipment.

By early October test vehicle A2 was ready at the operating base at St Eval in Cornwall and was fuelled in the early hours of the 8th prior to being slung under the Mosquito. Before the sortie could be flown a peroxide leak into the combustion chamber was discovered and a hazardous, but ultimately successful, operation was carried out in which the PVC rupture discs in the oxidant lines were replaced while the vehicle was fully fuelled. In the event the take-off was only slightly delayed and the Mosquito with its precious cargo flew to the drop zone which was to the west of the Scilly Isles. On release the test vehicle rolled onto its back without any sign of control and the telemetering was deranged by a small explosion which was followed by a large explosion that led to the model being completely destroyed. Later experience showed that failure of the two fuels to ignite spontaneously was characteristic of their behaviour at low temperatures and pressures. The next twelve months were taken up in tests of wingless models in an attempt to cure the ignition problems. It was eventually found that ignition at high altitudes could only be guaranteed by the use of an igniter torch which, by providing an intense flame in the combustion chamber on which the fuels impinged, enabled the all important initial chemical combination to take place.

The next attempt at exceeding the speed of sound occurred on 9 October 1948 by which time the original Bell XS-1 had been taken to Mach 1.45 and John Derry had achieved Mach 1.02 in the DH.108. Test vehicle A3 was positioned under the Mosquito in preparation for the flight. The model was carried externally except for the tail fin which was buried within the bomb bay through a large slot cut out in the bomb doors. A cradle structure slung from the existing strong points on the bomb bay arch steadied the vehicle in the correct position and provided the anchorage for various connections. The model had to be released in a nose-down attitude, as otherwise it tended to float under the parent aircraft after release, which was potentially serious with the fin protruding into the bomb bay.

The release height was 35,500 feet with the Mosquito flying at a Mach number of just less than 0.5. The vehicle fell away cleanly and after six seconds the rocket motor fired. It then accelerated smoothly in a straight and more or less level course, there being no indication of any appreciable rolling, yawing and pitching. The rocket motor burned for about a minute, the maximum speed attained corresponding to a Mach number of 1.4, after which there was a deceleration but it maintained its course. After all the fuel had been expended full positive elevator should have cut in automatically to pitch the vehicle into a dive but this did not happen and it continued out to sea. The radar echo was lost after around seven minutes by which time the vehicle was at a range of about sixty miles, but telemetered signals, interrupted by more and more noise, continued until about eight minutes after release when they ceased abruptly.

By the time that test vehicle A3 had performed satisfactorily the decision had already been taken to wind-up the model tests in favour of other work. As originally conceived the experiment had been intended as an investigation into the problems of flight at transonic speeds, however, due to the complex nature of the test vehicle that was eventually chosen, three years had been lost just trying to get the rocket motor, telemetering gear and autopilot to work. This led to a considerable amount of experience and knowledge in the flying of pilotless aircraft, together with the use of peroxide at high altitudes, but the programme contributed nothing to the knowledge of high speed flight. The results did no more than highlight the drag rise and the nose-down trim change that occurred at transonic speeds, but by 1948 this was not exactly news.

The whole sorry story of the Miles M.52 and the subsequent model trials took up around five years and accounted for approximately £600,000 in development funding. No worthwhile data was obtained during this time and the only benefits were entirely secondary in nature. Even the fact that the model tests had proved the M.52 configuration to be practical was completely worthless as the Bell XS-1 had already done this a year earlier. The lamentable decision making on the part of those who controlled the M.52 project ultimately led to adverse repercussions for the British aviation industry. This was admitted in a White Paper published in February 1955 which stated that the cancellation had 'seriously delayed the progress of aeronautical research in the UK'.

Perhaps if just one member of the supersonic committee had really believed in the M.52 then the outcome might have been different. Then again, if any of the assembled experts had been able to point out that a straight wing, if made thin enough, was just as good as a swept wing, then Britain might have been first in the race to Mach 1.0 after all. Another lifeline would have been the use of the aircraft as a test bed for the development of powered controls and the all-flying tail, the latter being a noticeable omission on British aircraft for the next ten years.

Unfortunately the development of the M.52 staggered from one perceived setback to the next, until the weight of negativity that surrounded it was finally too much. As far as Britain was concerned the M.52 was the first jet-powered aircraft to be cancelled but it was not to be the last.

CHAPTER TEN

The Barrier is Broken

W ith Britain having opted out of the supersonic race for the time being, the field was left entirely to the various research programmes that had been set up in the USA. Contrary to popular belief the result was to be extremely close and there is a vociferous growing minority in the United States which is of the opinion that the wrong man was given the credit for being the first to break the sound barrier.

In the early 1940s with piston-engined aircraft encountering compressibility on a regular basis, the need for research aircraft became paramount and steps were taken by the USAAF, US Navy and NACA in 1943 to implement programmes to produce aircraft capable of flying faster than the speed of sound. This built on work already carried out, notably by John Stack of NACA, who came up with a hypothetical high speed aircraft in 1934 during a study on compressibility effects, and Major Ezra Kotcher of the USAAF who was intrigued by the subject of high speed flight and whose ideas were encapsulated in a proposal for a 'Mach 0.999' research machine.

Discussions throughout the latter half of 1943 led to formal approval for the building of a research aircraft, but differing opinions as to the method of propulsion (rocket and turbojet) led to the USAAF sponsoring the rocket-powered Bell XS-1 (later X-1) with the US Navy backing the Douglas D-558-1 Skystreak, which was powered by a General Electric TG-180 jet engine. The choice of the Bell Aircraft Corporation to take on the XS-1 was made in similar fashion to the issue of Specification E.24/43 to Miles in Britain, as all other aircraft manufacturing companies were fully occupied with the production of aircraft for the war effort, however, it was not until the end of 1944 that Bell began work on the project. By this stage much was known about the design of the rival Miles M.52 and the aircraft that emerged at Bell bore a strong similarity.

Like the M.52, the Bell XS-1 had a 'bullet-shaped' fuselage which was of conventional stressed skin construction but was immensely strong as it was built to withstand loadings of +/-18g. The straight wing had

103

moderate taper and was mounted in the mid-position with the horizontal stabilizer located towards the base of the fin. The controls were manually operated, except that the tailplane could be trimmed via a switch in the cockpit to assist the elevator to provide longitudinal control. Two different wings were proposed, one of 8 per cent thickness/chord ratio and one of 10 per cent. In an attempt to maintain tailplane control at high Mach numbers the t/c ratio of the horizontal stabiliser was 6 per cent and 8 per cent respectively. As the XS-1 was intended to take off normally, a wheeled undercarriage was used and power came from a Reaction Motors XLR-11 rocket which burned liquid oxygen and diluted ethyl alcohol. There were four separate combustion chambers (each of 1,500 lb thrust) which could be fired in any number and total burn time amounted to 5 minutes. The Bell XS-1 was slightly larger than the M.52 (length was 30 ft 11 in compared with 28 ft 7 in), however, due to its heavy fuel load, its gross weight was significantly greater at 12,250 lb (the all-up weight of the M.52 was 7,710 lb). The only means of escape for the pilot was to detach the entrance panel on the right-hand side of the cockpit and bale out in time-honoured fashion.

The first Bell XS-1 (46-062) was completed in late 1945 and was flown under a B-29 Superfortress to Pinecastle Army Air Field in Florida on 19 January 1946. By this time the first major problem had already been experienced in that the turbopump for the rocket motor could not be made to work. This was required to transport the fuel and oxidiser from the tanks to the engine and instead an alternative arrangement had to be provided which consisted of a high-pressure nitrogen system to pressurise the fuel tanks and force the fuel through the engine. This unfortunately imposed a considerable weight penalty and halved the amount of fuel that could be carried which reduced the burn time of the XLR-11 rocket to a mere 2½ minutes. Any hope of ground launching the XS-1 was dashed as a result, leaving air-launch as the only option.

The first unpowered flight was made on 25 January 1946 by Bell test pilot Jack Woolams. The aircraft's handling characteristics were explored up to 275 mph IAS with the XS-1 exhibiting excellent control with light stick forces and good response. Ten more flights were made before a move was made to Muroc Army Air Field in California but, sadly, Woolams was to play no further role in testing the XS-1 as he was killed on 30 August 1946 in a P-39 during practice for the Thompson Air Race. His place was taken by Chalmers 'Slick' Goodlin who flew his first glide flight in the second XS-1 (46-063) at Muroc on 11 October 1946. This aircraft replaced 46-062 which had gone back to Bell to have the thinner 8 per cent wing attached, the original 10 per cent wing being fitted to 46-063. On 9 December this aircraft made the first powered flight and it was to continue to be the sole test aircraft until the return of 46-062 on 5 April 1947. No time was wasted and Goodlin made his first powered flight in this aircraft on 11 April. By the end of May a total of twenty powered flights had been made which proved the XS-1 up to 0.8M and thus fulfilled Bell's contractual obligations. The first aircraft (46-062) was then turned over to the USAAF to explore the upper end of the speed range while 46-063 was taken on by NACA to explore stability and control.

The trials with the XS-1 were complicated by a number of factors that would not have been encountered in the flight testing of normal jet-powered aircraft. This was due entirely to the use of a rocket powerplant, in which thrust could only be varied in increments of 1,500 lb, making it difficult to obtain steady flight conditions. In addition, the high rate of propellant consumption that was inherent with rocket engines tended to cause large changes in the weight and CG positions. During the course of a 3 minute engine burn, the wing loading changed from 94 lb/sq.ft at the time the aircraft was dropped from the B-29, to 54 lb/sq.ft. At the same time CG moved forwards from 22.5 per cent mean aerodynamic chord to 20.3 per cent at the completion of powered flight but the jettisoning of the remaining propellants meant that CG moved back again to 24.2 per cent mean aerodynamic chord. As the duration of powered flight was so short, it was difficult to obtain steady flight or any series of manoeuvres at high Mach numbers.

The head of USAAF flight testing, Colonel Al Boyd, raised a few eyebrows by choosing Captain Charles E. 'Chuck' Yeager to lead the XS-1 test programme with Lieutenant Robert A. 'Bob' Hoover as his back up and Captain Jack Ridley as project engineer. Yeager was a junior member of the flight test establishment but Boyd saw qualities in him that were ideally suited to the difficult task of getting to Mach 1.0. His ability as a pilot was backed up by the perfect temperament and extremely quick reactions. Yeager first flew the XS-1 on 6 August 1947 on an unpowered flight which once again highlighted the aircraft's excellent handling characteristics. His first powered flight took place on 29 August and during this sortie Yeager reached 0.85M (even though he had only been cleared to 0.82M). The test schedule stipulated that speed be increased in stages of 0.02M to avoid any nasty surprises, but at 0.86M there was the first sign of airframe buffet due to compressibility and the starboard wing began to drop, however, control could still be maintained without too much trouble.

Progress was relatively straightforward up to 0.94M at which point a worrying lack of longitudinal control was discovered. This was potentially serious as it meant that any compressibility trim changes could not be trimmed out, leading to loss of control. What was happening was that at this Mach number a shock wave was developing at the hinge point of the elevator, the end result being zero response when the control wheel was pulled back. At first the situation appeared bleak but then it was realised that control might still be possible via the variable-incidence tailplane. The aircraft was modified with a quicker responding actuator and the crunch came when Yeager replicated the previous flight. Having tested the system at lower speeds, he attempted to manoeuvre at 0.94M and found that he had just enough authority to control the aircraft in pitch. Any feeling of elation quickly disappeared, however, as the windscreen suddenly iced up which held the prospect of a blind landing. He was assisted by the aptly named Dick Frost who was flying as chase pilot in a Lockheed P-80 and Frost guided Yeager down to a safe landing on Rogers Dry Lake.

With the elevator problem solved, there was nothing to hinder the continued exploration of the flight envelope and the next test flight was scheduled for 14 October 1947. Two days before this Yeager broke two ribs in a riding accident at the infamous guest house and drinking establishment run by Florence 'Pancho' Barnes, a former holder of the women's world air speed record, which doubled as a stable. Not wanting to miss out on the opportunity to be the first pilot to break the so-called sound barrier, Yeager did not tell the USAAF of his injuries but instead was treated by a private doctor who patched him up as best he could. Although he considered that he would still be able to fly the aircraft, there remained the problem of getting into the XS-1 from the B-29 mother ship and then locking the cockpit door. Yeager was of the opinion that he could make it into the cockpit but it was Jack Ridley who came up with the solution for locking the door by adapting a broom handle to the required length so that Yeager could use it in his left hand.

With the authorities completely in the dark as to Yeager's condition, the B-29 with its precious cargo slung underneath took off to begin its slow climb to 25,000 feet. As the climbing speed of the B-29 was 180 mph and the stall speed of the fully fuelled XS-1 was around 240 mph, Yeager did not climb into the cockpit until a height of 12,000 feet had been reached as it was considered that a successful recovery could then be made if the XS-1 was dropped prematurely. The XS-1 was launched in a shallow dive from 25,000 feet to increase speed but this was still too slow for the heavily laden rocket plane and it began to stall. Only by applying positive elevator was Yeager able to maintain control and as speed started to increase in the dive he fired all four chambers of the rocket motor in sequence. Speed quickly increased to 0.88M and the aircraft was climbed to 36,000 feet. At this point he reduced power to 50 per cent but speed continued to increase to 0.92M. Having levelled off at 42,000 feet he selected one of the remaining two rocket chambers which very quickly propelled him to an indicated reading of 0.96M.

This was faster than any previous flight and the amount of buffet was notably reduced at the higher speed so that the elevators became effective once more. The Machmeter then went to 0.965 before moving right off the scale. Down on the ground a sonic boom was heard and it was confirmed that the XS-1 had gone supersonic, the subsequent data analysis showing that it had achieved 1.06M. For all the prognostications of doom and of aircraft breaking up on reaching Mach 1.0 the actual milestone was reached without drama, the difficult part had been just getting there. To the disappointment of everyone involved in the programme, it was decreed that the XS-1's feat was to remain a secret but enough people knew of the achievement that it was inevitable that word would get out eventually. On 22 December 1947 *Aviation Week* published an article on the XS-1 and informed the world that it had exceeded the speed of sound. This displeased the USAAF intensely but despite rumours that legal action was in the offing, no action was taken.

In the meantime the programme continued and a conference was held by the USAF and NACA in early 1948 to discuss the flight research that had been carried out with the XS-1, an important part being an assessment of the aircraft's stability and control characteristics at high Mach numbers with the 10 per cent thickness/chord ratio wing fitted. Longitudinally, the XS-1 was subject to a gradual nose-down change in trim between 0.78 – 0.99M with a change in the nose-up direction to 1.0M, however, once above the speed of sound there was a further nose-down trim change. Elevator effectiveness decreased markedly at higher Mach numbers and was so low at Mach numbers above 0.93 that it was difficult to obtain stabilised trim conditions in the short amount of powered-flight time that was available. Elevator effectiveness was at a minimum at 0.99M, increasing at Mach numbers above and below this value. This change in effectiveness caused a disturbance in decelerating from Mach numbers above 1.00. The actual elevator forces that were required to fly to a Mach number of 1.05 in level flight at 40,000 feet were relatively low and were of the order of 30 lb. Rudder effectiveness was approximately constant as Mach numbers increased from 0.35 to 0.90 but this had almost vanished at 0.99M. Some snaking was encountered at supersonic speeds and it was thought that this was affected by both lift coefficients and the actual Mach number. It was, however, noted that the XS-1 fitted with the thinner wing appeared not to be affected by snaking to quite the same extent.

Flight testing continued at Muroc and on 26 March 1948 Yeager attained a speed of 957 mph (1.45M) in 46-062, the fastest speed ever achieved by the XS-1. Other aspects of the aircraft's performance were then tested including its absolute ceiling and on 3 August 1949 Major Frank Everest reached an altitude of 71,902 feet. Shortly after 46-062 was taken to Wright-Patterson Air Force Base prior to being placed on display in the Smithsonian Institute. The second XS-1 continued to be used by NACA until October 1951 and the highest speed it achieved was 792 mph (1.20M) when flown by John Griffith on 26 May 1950. A third machine was produced (46-064) which had a turbopump instead of the nitrogen system of the first two aircraft, but problems with its development meant that it was only available in 1951. It was somewhat ill-fated and was lost on 9 November 1951 in a ground explosion which also destroyed the B-50 carrier aircraft. Pilot Joseph Cannon managed to escape but suffered severe liquid oxygen burns which put him in hospital for nearly a year.

At the same time that Bell were heading towards Mach 1.0 with the XS-1, a team from North American Aviation (NAA) were developing an aircraft that would become one of the all time classic designs, the F-86 Sabre. Towards the end of 1944 work had begun on the jet-powered NA-134 for the US Navy which was to emerge as the XFJ-1 Fury, a straight-winged aircraft whose portly fuselage offered little to suggest that it had been produced by the same manufacturer responsible for the clean lines of the Mustang. The USAAF also had a requirement for a fighter with a top speed of 600 mph and North American submitted a design study based on the NA-134 but with a slightly thinner wing (10 per cent t/c ratio instead of 11 per cent) and a longer fuselage. The Air Force machine was given the company designation NA-140 and was referred to by the military as the XP-86. Performance projections were not promising as they showed that the likely maximum speed was only 582 mph at 10,000 feet which was no better than the rival Republic XP-84. In the summer of 1945, however, a significant decision was taken at NAA, the new fighter was to be redesigned with a swept wing and it would be this that would transform it into a world-beater.

The catalyst for this radical change was the amount of data and hardware that had been captured in Germany in the period leading up to, and immediately after the end of the Second World War. Although the basic theory of using swept wings to delay the compressibility drag rise had been around for some time, the sheer weight of research material coming out of Germany was overwhelming. This was backed up by the capture of German scientists and technicians who had been involved in the various research programmes. Many were later persuaded to continue their work in the West. At North American the design team, led by John 'Lee' Atwood with Ed Horkey as chief aerodynamicist, were convinced of the benefits of using a swept wing and they were successful in arguing their case with the USAAF. Work began on the new wing in August 1945 with early wind tunnel tests confirming that the design speed of 600 mph would be easily attainable. The design eventually chosen showed a leading edge sweep of 35 degrees, an aspect ratio of 4.79 to 1 with thickness/chord ratio of 11 per cent at the root and 10 per cent at the tip. To avoid stability problems at low speed the wing was fitted with leading edge slats which opened automatically at high angles of attack.

The prototype XP-86 Sabre (45–59597) was completed in July 1947 and was ready for its first taxi trials early the next month. These were completed at NAA's facility at Mines Field, Los Angeles, before the aircraft was sectioned prior to being taken by road to Muroc Army Air Field for flight testing. The first flight of the XP-86 occurred on 1 October 1947 and was carried out by company test pilot George Welch. It is at this point that the controversy begins as several sources in the USA maintain that Welch went supersonic on the very first flight of the XP-86, a full two weeks before Chuck Yeager achieved the same feat in the XS-1. During the 40 minute flight it is alleged that Welch took the Sabre up to 35,000 feet before rolling into a 40 degree dive during which he attained a speed of 520 mph IAS. As he watched the instruments, Welch became aware during the dive that the airspeed indicator appeared to stick before suddenly jumping to a higher value and on the ground there were a number of reports of a double boom being heard. Unfortunately the recording cameras were not functioning and the flight was not tracked by NACA personnel on the ground.

It seems almost inconceivable that Welch would have attempted to dive the XP-86 to supersonic speeds on its very first flight, although it is acknowledged that this is exactly what he did when he took the prototype YF-100 Super Sabre up for the first time in May 1953! Furthermore, Welch had already experienced undercarriage problems in the early part of the flight and it had taken several attempts to get the gear to retract. It had also been noticed by the chase aircraft that the nose undercarriage leg would not extend fully when flying at speeds greater than 150 mph. In view of the fact that a known problem existed, it seems unlikely in the extreme that Welch would have attempted anything other than general handling on that flight with a view to making sure that the undercarriage worked and that a successful landing could be made. In the event the nosewheel did lock down, but only after Welch had touched down on the main wheels and kept the nose up for as long as possible as the speed diminished.

It is also claimed that Welch went supersonic during a test flight in the morning of 14 October, a mere 30 minutes before Yeager broke the sound barrier in the XS-1. This is slightly more plausible as even the limited amount of testing that had been carried out in the previous two weeks had shown that the XP-86 was one of those rare aeroplanes that was right from the word go. Welch was airborne at 0900 hrs and as before carried out a full power dive, this time from 37,000 feet. Once again a sudden 'jump' was seen on the airspeed indicator and the dive was terminated at 25,000 feet. As he pulled out of his dive Welch saw the B-29 carrying the XS-1 slowly climbing to its release height and not long after landing he heard a muffled double boom that signified that Yeager had been successful in his quest. On speaking with those on the ground, however, it appeared that this was not the first boom to be heard that day as a louder noise had been heard about 20 minutes before, one that co-incided almost exactly with the time when Welch was making his dive.

Like all good conspiracy theories there are accusations of a political cover up. As the USAAF had invested heavily in the XS-1 programme it did not take too kindly to the possibility of being beaten to the barrier by the XP-86. W. Stuart Symington, the first secretary of the United States Air Force (as the USAAF had become on 18 September 1947) made it clear to North American that they were not to cause any embarrassment by achieving Mach 1.0 before Bell made their attempt. Unfortunately this message seems to have been lost somewhere between Washington and Muroc, although it would probably have been ignored by George Welch even if it had been received. What is known with certainty is that the XP-86 definitely went supersonic on 21 November 1947 as it was tracked at a speed of 1.03M by the same ground team that had been set up to record the flights made by the XS-1. This information was not released as the public were still unaware that the sound barrier had been broken by Yeager five weeks before.

News that the Bell XS-1 had gone supersonic was eventually leaked to *Aviation Week* magazine in December 1947, but the fact that the XP-86 had also achieved this distinction was not officially confirmed until May the following year when it was announced that it had been flown at a speed in excess of Mach 1.0 on 26 April 1948. This delay and the omission of any reference to the fact that the XP-86 had flown supersonically much earlier, allowed the team at Bell and Chuck Yeager to have their moment of glory and neatly avoided any awkward questions being asked as to whether the whole rocket-plane programme had been a waste of money [in fact this was just the beginning of the 'X-plane' programme which was to underpin the development of military aircraft in the US over the coming decades]. The withholding of this information also ensured that the XP-86 was kept under wraps until a time when the first production examples were about to enter USAF service. Unfortunately by that time the legend had already been created and the name of George Welch has largely been forgotten.

Regular service pilots got their chance to fly the F-86A (USAF desig-nations changed from 'P' for pursuit to 'F' for fighter in June 1948) in February 1949 when the first aircraft were delivered to the 94th Fighter Squadron of the 1st Fighter Group at March AFB in California. One of the first pilots to get the chance to fly the F-86 Sabre was Flight Lieutenant 'Paddy' Harbison, a Royal Air Force officer on an exchange posting:

Everyone who flew the Sabre in squadron service achieved Mach 1.0. It was one of the transition flights in the conversion to type. Set up was simple. Climb to altitude (the higher the better) roll over and dive as steeply as possible at full power whilst holding the aircraft in the dive. The F-86A would drop the port wing as it went supersonic, but the 'E' and subsequent marks did not. The supersonic bang could be aimed by using the gunsight. The citizens of Los Angeles, San Diego and the Naval and Marine airfields in southern California suffered greatly from supersonic bangs in 1949–50, some deliberate, some inadvertent! Likewise in 1953 the inhabitants of Cologne and Dusseldorf were alerted to the Sabres presence until standing instructions discouraged the practice. The Mach meter registered over 1.0 but the position error was significant. The bang produced on the ground was the best confirmation. Insofar as the pilot was concerned in the cockpit it was a non-event. Other aircraft in the path of the bang could experience a jolt.

Paddy Harbison's final comment has relevance in the Yeager/Welch controversy. If Welch did go supersonic on the morning of 14 October 1947, as Yeager was still aboard the B-29 mother ship as it climbed to altitude, there is a good chance that the latter experienced the tremor as the shock wave passed by and would therefore have known that he had been beaten to the barrier just before he did it himself!

Unlike their USAF counterparts, the vast majority of RAF pilots had to wait until 1953 for their first taste of supersonic flight when the first of 430 Sabres were delivered as a temporary stopgap to Fighter Command as the Hawker Hunter and Supermarine Swift were still nowhere near entering service. The testing establishments in the UK had already carried out an appraisal of the Sabre in 1950 when two USAF F-86A-5s were put through their paces at A&AEE Boscombe Down. At the time that these initial tests were carried out pilots were limited to a Mach number of 0.95 but this restriction was later lifted and in April 1951 a further trial was commenced to evaluate handling and performance in dives up to high limiting Mach numbers.

During the trial a total of six dives were made, each of which exceeded the speed of sound with a peak indicated Mach number of 1.20 (1.10 TMN) at 35,000 feet. Throughout the testing period the aircraft (FU-91279) behaved in a 'gratifyingly docile' manner and as far as the pilot was concerned there were no disconcerting characteristics at all which was in marked contrast to some British aircraft of the period (see

Chapter Fourteen). All the dives were commenced from an altitude of 42–45,000 feet with recovery around 20,000 feet and in the last two dives the aircraft was tracked by ground radar equipment so that true Mach numbers could be derived for comparison with the indicated figures recorded by the pilot. The method of entry was the same for each dive and with all trimmers set to neutral, the aircraft was rolled onto its back before being pulled through into a steep dive. In all cases the recovery was made by elevator alone without recourse either to tailplane adjustment or operation of the dive brakes.

The angle of dive was around 70–80 degrees from the horizontal and slight airframe buffet commenced between 0.89 and 0.97 TMN. At speeds greater than 0.97 TMN a nose-up change of trim began to assert itself and this gradually built up until the pilot had to apply a push force of at least 100 lb to prevent the nose from rising. The adjustable tailplane was not used to trim out this force because this may have affected the recovery and as the F-86 was something of an unknown quantity to the RAF at that time, it was thought best to allow a large safety margin. This had the effect, however, of reducing the peak value Mach numbers that were likely to be achieved.

With increasing Mach number there was a slight left wing down tendency but this was easily corrected with aileron. When the push force became too great to hold the pilot was forced to ease back slightly which brought about an immediate recovery and it was at this stage that heavy airframe vibration began to be felt together with the possibility of either wing dropping. The latter could generally be checked by use of aileron but during one dive the ailerons became temporarily ineffective, it being possible to move the stick laterally about 3 inches at the top, with no effect and very little stick force. As the indicated Mach number decreased so did the elevator push force necessary to maintain a reasonable recovery attitude. Engine rpm were maintained at the values on entry to the dive until the recovery was initiated, whereupon the engine was throttled back progressively for the remainder of the pull out.

The only problem encountered during the trial was a partial failure of the starboard elevator during the last dive in which a higher true airspeed was achieved and heavy vibration was felt during the pull out. The F-86A-5 was fitted with a revised three-hinge elevator to reduce the likelihood of this eventuality but it appeared that failures could still occur under certain circumstances involving high negative elevator angles. This type of recovery was not recommended for normal service flying and Pilot's Notes for certain Marks of the F-86 suggested that it was preferable to initiate the recovery from steep dives by extending the dive brakes, and that if this was ineffective, carefully to trim the aircraft out of the dive by means of the adjustable tailplane. Although the handling characteristics of the Sabre at high Mach numbers were probably better than any other contemporary aircraft, A&AEE did feel that it was unlikely to be satisfactory as a gun platform above 0.95M due to the wing dropping tendencies which occurred the moment any manoeuvre was attempted above this indicated Mach number that involved an increase in the normal acceleration.

The Sabre was also evaluated by Flight Lieutenant N.F. Harrison of the RAF Flying College's Handling Squadron whose findings showed that although the F-86 was just supersonic, it needed considerable effort on the part of the pilot:

The climb performance falls off noticeably after about 30,000 feet, but as there is no point in going very high the aircraft can be levelled off at, say, 38,000 feet to start the dive. After a general check, the Sabre can be pushed at full throttle into a dive of about 30 degrees. The speed and Mach number rise rapidly. Nothing happens until about 0.94 – 0.95M when either wing starts to get heavy, but this can easily be held with a small aileron movement. The wing heavying tendency may transfer to the opposite wing after a second or so, but at no time does it become worrying. By the time 0.97M is reached this period is passed and no further lateral unsteadiness is encountered. In a 30 degree dive the aircraft will not accelerate much past 0.97M and to reach supersonic speed the aircraft must be clean, the dive must be started from at least 35,000 feet and must be vertical, with the throttle fully open.

A dive of this sort is accomplished without approaching any of the aircraft's limits; during the whole performance the IAS remains well within the limiting speed of 600 knots. The only strain is that imposed upon the pilot's nervous system because, for the average cautious man it takes considerable determination and mental effort to half roll, pull through to a vertical dive at full power, and then deliberately to hold the aircraft in this unnatural attitude while the speed builds up. The wing-heavy period shows up as a few sharp wing drops that occur and disappear almost before they can be corrected, after which nothing more happens except for a nose-up change of trim which is easily held and which can be trimmed out by blipping the trimmer, taking care not to over-control as all controls are very sensitive at these speeds. There is no indication that Mach 1 has been exceeded, the Mach meter itself may not read more than 0.98–0.99M, but once its needle has slowed down and eventually stopped, there is no point in pressing on as this movement represents the Mach number terminal velocity. The Sabre, in other words, can only just reach supersonic speed with its present engine.

Recovery can be made either by throttling back and using the airbrakes or simply pulling out of the dive. The latter method uses up more sky but is quite straightforward; level flight being resumed somewhere around, or a little below, the 20,000 feet mark. There is one point that must be watched when opening the airbrakes, which incidentally are operated by a thumb switch on top of the throttle lever. The airbrakes are set so that on opening they cause a nose-up change of trim. This change is fairly strong at high indicated airspeeds and so must be anticipated and checked if necessary. Just for interest, the rate of descent at 30,000 feet is somewhere between 50,000 and 60,000 feet per minute, and even though you are at a fairly high altitude you are uncomfortably aware of the fact that objects below are getting bigger noticeably faster. And as the true airspeed is somewhere around 700 knots the racket set up by the airflow is appalling.

Not surprisingly, RAF pilots were delighted when they were given the chance to fly the Sabre having had to put up with the Meteor for so long. The fact that they had to wait so long for an aircraft of transonic capability, with equivalent British fighters still one to two years away from service, is a damning indictment of UK defence policy immediately after the end of the Second World War which had initially given up on high speed research. When it became obvious that tensions between east and west could precipitate further conflict at any time, a rapid u-turn was made, but such was the rate of progress in aeronautics at the time that British aircraft manufacturers spent the next ten years playing catch up. Part of that process involved the testing of the de Havilland DH.108, a tailless swept wing aircraft which had the potential for flight at very high speed, albeit in near vertical dives. Unfortunately at the top end of the speed range it possessed adverse longitudinal handling characteristics very similar to those experienced with the Messerschmitt Me 163 which was also of tailless configuration. Only three examples of the DH.108 were to be built and all were to be involved in accidents in which the pilot was killed.

CHAPTER ELEVEN

Flying the DH.108

I n marked contrast to the rapid progress being made in the USA, the unfortunate demise of the Miles M.52 meant that the research programme into high speed flight in Britain was thrown into complete disarray. The only aircraft that was capable of taking over investigations into transonic flight was the de Havilland DH.108, but at the time of the M.52's cancellation this machine was still three months away from its first flight.

The origins of the DH.108 can be traced back to the setting up of the Brabazon committee in December 1942 which had a remit to consider the types of civil transport aircraft that would be needed after the war. Various requirements were put forward including the Type 4 for a high-speed mail carrier with transatlantic capability. At the time de Havilland were developing the Vampire fighter powered by a Goblin jet engine and it seemed obvious to Geoffrey de Havilland that a jet-powered transport aircraft would steal a march over the Americans, one of the prime requirements of the Brabazon committee being to ensure that Britain would not be reliant on American aircraft post war. After further discussion the proposal for a mail carrier soon evolved into a swept-wing passenger plane, but the initial design did not have a horizontal tail, a layout that found favour at the time as it resulted in an appreciable reduction in drag. With such a radical layout the decision was taken to build a small, single-seat aircraft to test the configuration and Specification E.18/45 was issued to cover the construction of two prototypes. Even before the first of these was completed, however, the decision had been taken to employ conventional tail surfaces on the airliner project which was to emerge in 1949 as the DH.106 Comet I. As the principal area of research was not required any more, the two DH.108s were to be used purely for swept wing handling trials and the first prototype (TG283) was flown for the first time by Geoffrey de Havilland Jnr on 15 May 1946 from Woodbridge in Suffolk. Although it was often to be referred to as the Swallow, a name that came about as a result of its wing configuration, at de Havilland the aircraft was known only by its company designation.

The DH.108 was based on the fuselage of a Vampire F.1 with an extended aft section to accommodate an elegant fin and rudder which was swept 51 degrees and an elongated centre section for the wing which had leading edge sweep of 43 degrees. Due to the tailless layout both lateral and longitudinal control came via elevons mounted on the wing trailing edges outboard of the split flaps. As RAE had predicted that 'Dutch roll' was likely to be encountered at slow speeds, along with wing drop due to tip stall, the first DH.108 was fitted with Handley Page leading edge slats locked in the open position and anti-spin parachutes in wing tip fairings. In the event no adverse handling characteristics were experienced. The aircraft was powered by a Goblin 2 engine of 3,100 lb thrust but did not feature an ejection seat. TG283 was used for low speed trials and continued to provide useful data on swept-wing handling characteristics until it was lost in a crash on 1 May 1950 which claimed the life of Squadron Leader G.E.C. 'Jumbo' Genders AFC DFM, the O.C. of Aero Flight at RAE Farnborough. It was followed by TG306 which was to explore the upper reaches of the speed envelope. This aircraft was first flown on 23 August 1946 from Hatfield and took part in the Society of British Aircraft Constructors (SBAC) show at Radlett on 12/13 September. Compared with the earlier machine it featured leading edge sweep of 45 degrees, retractable leading edge slats, an uprated Goblin 3 of 3,300 lb thrust and a strengthened canopy.

As soon as trials got underway with TG306 it became clear that despite its relatively modest power, the DH.108 was capable of flight at speeds of well over 600 mph and de Havilland began to look at the possibility of making an attempt on the World Absolute Speed Record which, at the time, was in the process of being raised to 616 mph by the Meteor F.4's of the RAF High Speed Flight at Tangmere (see Chapter Eight). In preparation for an assault on the record TG306 had further modification work carried out to the canopy with metal sheeting reducing glazing to the absolute minimum and the airframe was generally cleaned up to give a high gloss finish. The fairings on the wing tips which accommodated the anti-spin parachutes were also removed. As the timing systems were still in place at the high-speed course recently vacated by the RAF's Meteors, the intention was to operate the DH.108 from Tangmere, but unfortunately it never made it.

As part of his preparations for the record attempt Geoffrey de Havilland Jnr took off in TG306 from Hatfield at 1726 hrs in the evening of 27 September 1946 to carry out a high speed handling assessment over the Thames estuary, involving a shallow dive from 10,000 feet up to a Mach number of 0.87, and also a straight and level speed test up to 650 mph IAS. At 1739 hrs the aircraft was observed a few miles from Gravesend flying on a north-north-easterly course at a height that was variously estimated as between 5,000 feet and 10,000 feet. When over Cliffe Marshes it appeared suddenly to accelerate but when over the River Thames near Egypt Bay it disintegrated and the fragments fell into the water along a line extending a quarter of a mile, west to east, a few hundred yard from high water.

The accident was witnessed by a number of people in varying locations, from Canvey Island to the north of the Thames estuary, to Rochester in Kent. The most qualified witness was a pilot, Flight Lieutenant H.W.A. Godfrey who saw the DH.108 come down from a vantage point at Canvey Island, although some aspects of his evidence are at odds with a number of other witnesses. Godfrey was first aware that something was amiss when he heard a very loud explosion with a decided crump. When he first sighted the aircraft it was at about 10,000 feet and one wing had detached and was falling near the island. The main body of the 108 with the other wing still attached was seen spinning down to a height of around 2,000 feet at which point it was lost to view. At the place in the sky where the 'explosion' had occurred there was a ball of pale orange smoke with several wisps in different directions.

Another witness was Mr R. Hall, also of Canvey Island who heard an aircraft apparently approaching from the south side of the River Thames as the noise of the engine seemed to be increasing. On looking up he saw the DH.108 which seemed to be in a shallow dive and travelling at high speed, although as it was heading towards him this was difficult to judge. He noticed that from each side of the aircraft there was a trail of white vapour extending behind it which was fairly thick and blurred. As he watched there was a tremendous explosion, Hall mentioning that he had heard German acoustic mines and ordinary sea mines blow up and the noise was just as severe as these. Almost simultaneously with the explosion he saw the aircraft burst into fragments although it all happened so quickly that he was unable to say which piece was the first to come away.

Most witnesses were of the opinion that the DH.108 lost both its wings quite early in the break-up including T. Fitness who saw the accident from Cliffe on the south side of the estuary. He observed the aircraft pick up speed very quickly whilst travelling in a north-easterly direction but after a few seconds light grey smoke was seen to come from the nose and the wings came off in a very short space of time. The engine and fuselage fell into the water at very high speed, the wings dropping like 'falling leaves'. The fall of the wings was also seen by Police Constable A. Briggs who was another to witness the break up from Cliffe. He had a clear view of the wings falling separately through the air about 4–500 yards apart. Mr S.M. Squire of Walworth in London was visiting Canvey Island with his wife and family and he also had a clear view of the wings, commenting that they seemed to take ages to come down. As they turned in the slipstream the sunlight occasionally glinted on the silver colouring and when they finally hit the water he could see the spray that was sent up. He also reported that after the first explosion, there was a further double explosion.

The break up was also seen in Rochester by Mr F. Mudge who saw a large puff of white smoke to the west, out of which two descending arcs were described in the sky which appeared as two bright white star lights, quite wide apart. In the centre of these lights he saw what he knew afterwards to be the remains of the DH.108 twisting earthwards. After an interval of 10-15 seconds he heard a very loud whistling note getting louder and this ended with a terrific cracking explosion. According to Mr Mudge, the time of the accident was 1738 hrs.

The weather at the time of the accident was good with a light south-south-westerly breeze of 7 knots, 3/10 cloud or less with a base at 3,000 feet and tops at 5,000 feet and a visibility of at least 8 miles. The wreckage fell in three main groups comprising the two wings and the tail cone and engine. The starboard wing was found at the western end of the wreckage trail with its elevon detached but lying within ten yards of it. A short distance to the east was the port wing which was the more extensively damaged of the two. Its elevon was broken in half along its chord line at the position of the control rod and was found some distance from the wing. The engine, together with the tail cone and jet pipe, was found further to the east. The cockpit was located near to the port wing but the canopy was found further to the west not far from the starboard wing. At the time of the accident the tide was high although it was on the ebb. Due to its location the wreckage was only uncovered at low tide and owing to the depth and softness of the mud in which it lay the salvage operation was carried out with extreme difficulty, and with some risk to those taking part. The body of Geoffrey de Havilland Jnr was not discovered until 7 October 1946 when it was washed ashore at Whitstable. A post mortem showed that he had suffered major injuries to the head and a broken neck and it was surmised that his head had come into violent contact with the canopy when the aircraft pitched sharply downwards. It was generally agreed that the forces would have been sufficient to kill him instantly.

A thorough investigation was carried out by the RAE who published their findings in August 1947. A separate analysis undertaken by the manufacturers based on automatic observer results showed that the

Designed by Louis Bechereau, the Deperdussin racer of 1913 was one of the first aircraft to be streamlined to reduce drag and increase speed.
(Philip Jarrett)

The Deperdussin floatplane that was flown into first place by Maurice Prevost in the 1913 Schneider Trophy race at Monaco.
(Philip Jarrett)

Although it was initially derided by the opposition, the little Sopwith Tabloid was dominant in the Schneider contest in 1914.
(Philip Jarrett)

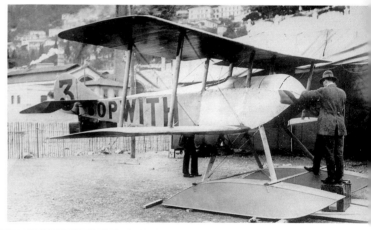

The S.E.4 of 1914 was initially powered by a 160 hp two-row Gnome rotary and was capable of a top speed of 135 mph.
(Philip Jarrett)

The Mars I racer (nicknamed 'Bamel') was designed by Henry Folland for the Gloucestershire Aircraft Company and established a British speed record of 196.4 mph in 1921. *(Philip Jarrett)*

A Curtiss R2C-1 which set a world speed record of 267 mph in November 1923. *(Philip Jarrett)*

The clean lines of the Curtiss R3C-2 Schneider racer are evident in this view taken on 30 September 1925. *(Philip Jarrett)*

Supermarine S.6B S1596 having its Rolls-Royce engine run-up on the slipway with mechanics draped over the rear ends of the floats to prevent the nose from dipping. *(Philip Jarrett)*

Flt Lt George Stainforth climbs out of the cockpit of S1596 having set a new world speed record of 379 mph on 13 September 1931.
(Philip Jarrett)

The XP-38 Lightning twin-engined fighter was one of the first aircraft to encounter serious compressibility problems.
(Philip Jarrett)

The Republic XP-47B Thunderbolt could exceed 400 mph in level flight but its relatively thick wing meant that it had a low critical Mach number which was soon reached in high altitude dives.
(Philip Jarrett)

An early production P-47B Thunderbolt with fabric covered rudder and elevators.
(Philip Jarrett)

The North American NA-73X which was the prototype of the outstanding P-51 Mustang. *(Philip Jarrett)*

One of the first British aircraft to experience severe buffeting and loss of control during high speed dives was the Hawker Typhoon. This is R7579, the fourth production aircraft. *(Philip Jarrett)*

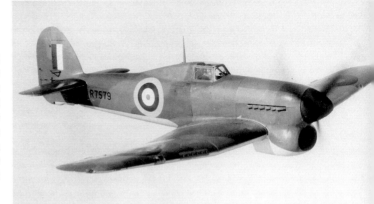

The Spitfire was able to record higher Mach numbers than any other fighter of the period thanks to its thin wing. This is a Spitfire XI flown by Jeffrey Quill. *(Philip Jarrett)*

Britain's first jet aircraft was the Gloster E.28/39 which was flown for the first time on 15 May 1941. *(Philip Jarrett)*

The E.28/39 after it had been painted in RAF markings and standard camouflage colours. *(Philip Jarrett)*

An air-to-air view of the Bell XP-59A Airacomet. Although its performance showed no improvement over piston-engined fighters of the day, it gave valuable jet experience. *(Philip Jarrett)*

Always renowned for their innovative design, de Havilland chose a twin boom layout for its Vampire jet fighter. *(Philip Jarrett)*

Although of poor quality, this photo shows the first flight of the Heinkel He 178 on 27 August 1939. *(Philip Jarrett)*

The Heinkel He 280 takes off on its first powered flight on 2 April 1941 with uncowled engines.
(Philip Jarrett)

An Me 163B begins its take-off run at Bad Zwischenahn.
(Philip Jarrett)

The most successful jet fighter of the Second World War was the Messerschmitt Me 262. This is an aircraft flown by Kommando Nowotny.
(Philip Jarrett)

By 1945 Germany had many advanced aircraft projects under way including the Messerschmitt P.1101 which was later evaluated in the USA. The basic layout was adopted for the Bell X-5.
(Philip Jarrett)

Top: The all-yellow Gloster Meteor F.4 EE455 which was flown by Eric Greenwood during the 1945 world air speed record attempt. *(Philip Jarrett)*

Centre: Meteor F.4 EE454 as flown by Gp Capt H.J. 'Willie' Wilson to break the world speed record on 7 November 1945 at 606 mph. *(Philip Jarrett)*

Bottom: 46-063 was the second of the Bell XS-1 aircraft and is now preserved at Edwards Air Force Base. *(Philip Jarrett)*

Top: Bell test pilot Chalmers 'Slick' Goodlin poses in front of 46-063.　　　*(Philip Jarrett)*

Centre: DH.108 VW120 shortly after taking off on a test flight.　　　*(Philip Jarrett)*

Bottom: Another view of DH.108 VW120. This aircraft became the first British
machine to exceed the speed of sound on 6 September 1948 when flown by
John Derry.

　　　(Philip Jarrett)

Top: The first Soviet rocket-powered aircraft was the all-wood Bereznyak-Isayev BI
which was capable of speeds in excess of 500 mph. *(Philip Jarrett)*

Centre: Another rocket-powered design to emerge from the Soviet Union was the
Mikoyan I-270 which was an adaptation of the Me 263. *(Philip Jarrett)*

Bottom: For the first generation of jet fighters the 'pod-and-boom' configuration was
popular with Soviet designers and was employed on the Yak-23. *(Philip Jarrett)*

Top: The first successful French jet fighter was the Dassault MD 450 Ouragan which
was powered by a Nene engine built by Hispano-Suiza.   *(Philip Jarrett)*
Centre: The tiny Gerfaut was the first French aircraft to exceed the speed of sound in
level flight on 3 August 1954.   *(Philip Jarrett)*
Bottom: The futuristic-looking Leduc 021 sits atop its Languedoc carrier aircraft at Le
Bourget in June 1955.   *(Philip Jarrett)*

The Nord Griffon comprised a huge duct for the ramjet with flying surfaces and a small nose compartment for the pilot. It had Mach 2.0+ performance but was abandoned in favour of the Mirage III.
(*Philip Jarrett*)

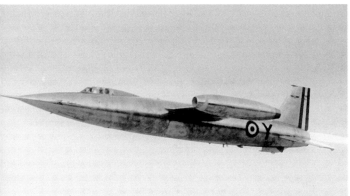

The SO.9000 Trident was designed as a point defence fighter and combined high speed with a prodigious rate of climb. Like all other mixed power (rocket/jet) aircraft, it lost out to pure jet fighters.
(*Philip Jarrett*)

A pleasant air-to-air view of the first MD 550 Mirage that preceded the larger Mirage III that was flown by the French Air Force.
(*Philip Jarrett*)

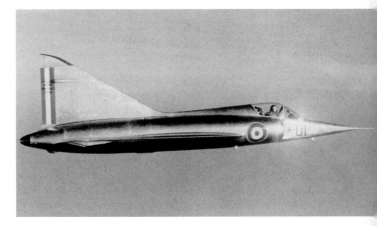

The Douglas D-558-1 Skystreak was funded by the US Navy for high speed research. It was just capable of Mach 1.0 in a dive.
(*Philip Jarrett*)

Douglas D-558-2 Skyrocket (BuAer No 37974) just after the point of release from the P2B-1S mother ship. *(Philip Jarrett)*

Another view of the Douglas Skyrocket taken from the P2B-1S shortly after it had been dropped over a typically barren desert landscape. *(Philip Jarrett)*

The Bell X-2 was designed to explore flight at speeds over Mach 3.0. This aircraft (46-674) was lost on 27 September 1956 as a result of inertia coupling. *(Philip Jarrett)*

The first X-2 to be completed was 46-675 which is seen here with booster tabs fitted to the ailerons. This aircraft crashed into Lake Ontario on 12 May 1953 after exploding under its mother ship. *(Philip Jarrett)*

A Republic F-84E Thunderjet, a stalwart of the USAF in the early post war years.
(Philip Jarrett)

The Convair XF-92A was the world's first delta-wing aircraft and paved the way for the F-102 Delta Dagger.
(Philip Jarrett)

Although it was designed to achieve Mach 1.25 in level flight, the YF-102 suffered from excessive drag rise at transonic speeds and would only go supersonic in a dive.
(Philip Jarrett)

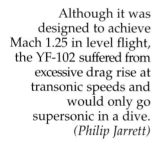

Following the failure of the original YF-102, the aircraft was redesigned to take advantage of the area rule theory as put forward by Richard T. Whitcomb of NACA. It re-emerged as the YF-102A as seen here.
(Philip Jarrett)

George Welch lands the prototype YF-100 Super Sabre after its first flight on 25 May 1953.
(Philip Jarrett)

An underside view of an F-100 showing the 45-degree swept wing and low-set, slab tail.
(Philip Jarrett)

One of the most elegant jet aircraft of all time, the Hawker P.1040 was developed into the Sea Hawk for the Fleet Air Arm.
(Philip Jarrett)

Hawkers next produced the P.1052 seen here piloted by Chief Test Pilot T.S. 'Wimpy' Wade.
(Philip Jarrett)

The second P.1052 (VX279) was re-engineered as the all-swept P.1081 but was lost on 3 April 1951 in a crash which claimed the life of 'Wimpy' Wade. *(Philip Jarrett)*

The prototype P.1067 Hunter WB188 was first flown on 20 July 1951 but did not enter RAF service for another three years. *(Philip Jarrett)*

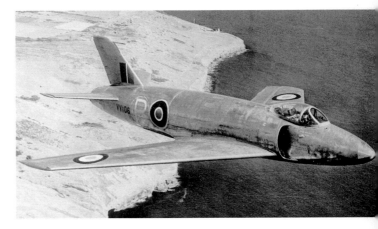

Having produced the straight-winged Attacker, Supermarine followed the trend towards swept surfaces with the Type 510 which handled rather better than Hawker's P.1081 in the transonic region. *(Philip Jarrett)*

The immediate precursor of the Supermarine Swift was the Type 535 (VV119). This aircraft was the star of the film Sound Barrier which was released in 1952. *(Philip Jarrett)*

A view of the first prototype Gloster GA.5 Javelin (WD804) before it was written off in a crash landing at Boscombe Down on 29 June 1952 following severe elevator flutter. *(Philip Jarrett)*

Following the fatal crash of the first DH.110, the type was eventually developed into the Sea Vixen for the Fleet Air Arm. This is the second prototype DH.110 WG240. *(Philip Jarrett)*

Having initially given up on supersonic flight, Britain eventually produced two outstanding designs to Specification ER.103. This is the Fairey FD.2 which claimed the world speed record on 10 March 1956 at 1,132 mph. *(Philip Jarrett)*

The other aircraft to emerge from ER.103 was the English Electric P.1 which went supersonic in level flight on only its third flight on 11 August 1954. It was developed into the Lightning interceptor for the RAF. *(Philip Jarrett)*

failure probably occurred in a shallow dive at about 7,000 feet and at 580 mph EAS (0.87M). A close examination of the wreckage led to the conclusion that the aircraft had broken up under down-loads on the wings and that the starboard wing had been the first major component to fail. No structural, mechanical or material defect was evident, neither was there any evidence of flutter, calculations showing that there was an adequate margin between the critical flutter speed and the speed that the aircraft had attained. Although it appeared as though the starboard wing had failed first, there was evidence of contact between the wing and the forward fuselage as the leading edge contained fragments of glass and synthetic resin glue which could only have come from this component. The break-up sequence was therefore of a general disintegration of the aircraft in down-load in which the starboard wing detached first, probably taking the front fuselage with it. The subsequent port wing detachment then disrupted the engine mounting so that the engine and tail cone finished up underneath the port wing with the lower engine cowlings sandwiched between them. The precise moment that the fin and rudder broke away could not be established, although it was stated with certainty that the failure was of a secondary nature and occurred after the main break-up.

Although it was a relatively straightforward task to establish the sequence in which the aircraft broke up, finding the cause was rather more difficult. The results of high speed wind tunnel tests eventually showed that at high Mach numbers there was a loss of elevon effect in the pitching plane which later changed to a reversal of control. This was accompanied by a nose down change of trim and reduced longitudinal stability. It was thought that these features were the probable cause of the accident since their continued effect would result in the aircraft nosing over into a negative incidence dive without possibility of recovery.

Despite the tragic loss of TG306, a third prototype DH.108 was quickly ordered and as the standard Vampire was now the FB.5, it was based on this particular variant. As had occurred with the first two machines, a fuselage was chosen from the Vampire production line at English Electric's Preston factory and transported to Hatfield for conversion. The new machine carried the serial number VW120 and compared with its predecessor it had a more elegant pointed nose for aerodynamic efficiency, a Goblin 4 engine of 3,700 lb thrust and a completely redesigned cockpit with a lowered canopy and an ejection seat. It was later to incorporate power boosted elevons which would allow an investigation into the top end of the speed range above 0.88M. VW120 was flown for the first time on 24 July 1947 by John Cunningham, who had taken over as Chief Test Pilot following the death of Geoffrey de Havilland Jnr, although much of the test flying at high Mach numbers was undertaken by his deputy, John Derry, who joined de Havilland from Supermarine in November 1947.

Having cut his teeth during high-speed dives on the twin-engined Hornet and the Vampire jet fighters, Derry became involved with testing the DH.108. The perilous nature of this type of work cannot be overstated as the aircraft's true potential in terms of top speed could only be reached in a near-vertical dive. In contrast, with the Bell XS-1 the Americans had the luxury of being able to carry out their own transonic research in level flight, a condition that the British could have shared if the Miles M.52 programme had not been cancelled. As the 108 was Britain's only potential 'supersonic' aircraft there was little choice but to continue, even though doubts still existed over its high Mach characteristics following the break up of TG306.

The test programme involving VW120 got underway in earnest in early 1948 with a series of shallow dives from 35–40,000 feet to obtain records of pressure levels at various locations over the wing. Speed was gradually built up in small increments towards the point where it was expected that the aircraft would encounter the pitching instability that had led to the demise of the first high-speed machine. One important difference, however, was that all dives would be carried out from very high altitude so that the aircraft was likely to be affected by compressibility factors alone, and not by any additional problems associated with high air loads at lower levels, as had been the case with Geoffrey de Havilland Jnr.

Britain finally became the second member of the supersonic club on 6 September 1948. The day dawned fine and bright and the task for John Derry was to take the 108 up to high level to undertake further pressure measurements over the wing and to confirm the readings taken previously. The intention was also to increase the dive angle slightly so that a speed of 0.96M could be attained. Derry climbed the 108 to 45,000 feet and after carrying out level speed checks he eased the aircraft into a 30 degree dive. As speed increased above 0.91M the aircraft became nose heavy and this was replaced by fore-and-aft pitching which set in at around 0.93-0.94M. Further acceleration saw a return of the nose-down pitch and at this point full power of 10,750 rpm was selected, although this did little to overcome the drag rise and it was necessary to move the stick forward slightly to maintain speed.

A further lessening of elevon angle produced a more violent nose-down pitch of around minus 2g and there was a general feeling of instability. Still more forward stick led to a sudden increase in the dive angle which caused the aircraft to go over the vertical within 1–2 seconds and producing a force of minus 3g. At this stage Derry still had some longitudinal control and he was able to reduce the dive angle to 60–80 degrees, but with speed increasing through 0.98M the stick force increased considerably so that it became impossible to hold the aircraft. As a result the dive angle steepened to the vertical once again and when it became clear that control had been lost Derry closed the throttle and used all of his strength to haul back on the stick. His actions had no effect, however, and by now the Mach meter was seen to be on the stops at 1.04M. With the aircraft not responding to normal control inputs, full trim flap was selected and almost immediately a gradual recovery was commenced with very low levels of 'g'. The aircraft was eventually levelled at 23,500 feet by which time speed had been reduced to 0.94M. At this speed the characteristic pitching oscillations set in again but these ceased as soon as the trim flap was fully returned to the neutral setting. During the dive it had become noticeable that at speeds above 0.98M the instability which had been apparent below this mark had virtually disappeared and the aircraft was much steadier with no buffet at all.

As John Derry flew back to Hatfield he could not be sure that he had broken the sound barrier, that would only be confirmed when the instrument readings had been corrected to give the True Mach Number. He did not have too long to wait, the correction showing a slight downwards revision of the indicated value to a true figure of 1.02M. At first the news was not made public but after a few days it was announced that Derry had become the first pilot to fly faster than the speed of sound in a British aircraft.

The series of high speed dives with the DH.108 did not end with the supersonic flight but continued well into 1949. Gradually more was learned of the DH.108's handling characteristics at high Mach numbers including the fact that the loss of elevon effectiveness that was experienced at 0.97M and above was due to the control surfaces coming up against the stops. Previously it had been thought that the power boosters or servodynes were incapable of overcoming the pressure of the air and the shock waves that were created at very high speeds. During one particular dive Derry had managed to exert a 280 lb pull force on the control column without realising that the elevons were already up against the stops so that all his exertions were of no avail. Eventually it was realised that the elevons were in the fully up position during the latter stages of the dive, but that this had no effect on longitudinal control.

On 1 March 1949 John Derry carried out four dives in the day, the last of which produced behaviour that had not been encountered before. The first three dives were carried out from 44–45,000 feet at a dive angle of 20–30 degrees and in each case a normal recovery was made having attained 0.97M. The fourth dive, however, was slightly steeper at around 35 degrees and after a slight pause at 0.97M, the Mach number increased to 0.98 at which point the now familiar nose down pitch occurred. Before the trim flap could be used to bring about a recovery, the aircraft pitched downwards even further and the application of full 'up' trim flap had no effect on its attitude. Throttling the engine also did nothing to halt the DH.108's plunge towards earth which was marked by a slight roll to port which had the effect of making the dive even steeper. By this time Derry was pulling back on the stick for all he was worth, whilst at the same time holding on full starboard aileron. The dive had now increased to around 60 degrees and after a brief hesitation, the slow roll to port recommenced. This could not be held on the controls and at the same time the aircraft was subjected to slight negative 'g' as the nose began to tuck-under leading to a true vertical dive.

By now the 108 was completely out of control but the nose-down pitch continued beyond the vertical so that the aircraft performed a bunt manoeuvre, the rolling motion continuing so that the 108 finally emerged upright in a dive at a shallower angle than before. In the latter stages of this extraordinary gyration a sharp 'bump' was felt as the aircraft left the area of negative 'g' and was once again subject to normal accelerations. During the dive the rate of descent had been higher than anything previously experienced and once again the speed of sound had been exceeded. As speed was gradually reduced, control slowly returned but the trim flaps and elevons did not become completely effective until the aircraft was in a shallow climb. On passing through the level flight attitude the Machmeter was still reading 0.98 with the airspeed indicator showing 490 mph. As the aircraft passed through 0.95M an undamped oscillation similar to those encountered on previous dives was experienced and the 108 was finally returned to straight and level flight at 29,000 feet.

John Derry was of the opinion that the dive recounted above was similar in many ways to his first supersonic dive of the previous year. The chief difference was that the nose-down pitch which was experienced at 0.98M had occurred at high altitude as the fore-and-aft oscillation that had set in during the first supersonic flight had tended to delay the progression of the dive so that this Mach number was only reached lower down. It was also evident on reflection that the bunt manoeuvre was effectively a resurgence of the nose-down pitching motion as the aircraft decelerated through 1.02M. So rather than continuing to fly faster, the maximum Mach number had been attained at some point when the dive was near the vertical, which suggested that at speeds above 1.02M the nose-down trim change was not as strong. This dive proved that as well as the elevons losing their effectiveness, the trim flaps also became ineffectual at 0.99M when diving from high altitudes, but that if the controls could be maintained in the correct recovery position, then the aircraft would begin to respond as it was approaching 26,000 feet. It was concluded that the highest Mach number the DH.108 could be taken to whilst maintaining a reasonable amount of control was 0.97M in dives of 20–25 degrees. Provided that these parameters were met the aircraft would not accelerate any further and could be recovered at any time.

On 19 August 1949 VW120 was transferred from de Havilland to the Ministry of Supply in whose ownership it was based at RAE Farnborough. It was here that it was flown by renowned test pilot Eric Brown who recounted his experiences with the DH.108 in his book *Wings on my Sleeve* (Airlife, 1978).

As I was already familiar with the low-speed characteristics of the 108 I started off immediately with the high speed tests. The first object was to get the plane going as fast as possible, as high up as possible and then gradually step down the height just as Geoffrey de Havilland Jnr had been doing when the aeroplane broke up at 10,000 feet. Our first series of tests were made at 35,000 feet and I reached Mach 0.985 after a dive from 45,000 feet. At this speed I had the stick right back against the stops, so it was obvious that this was the absolute limit that could be reached in controlled flight. It was exasperating to be so near the magic figure of Mach 1 and yet be so far – and all too easy to see how John Derry could have gone out of control in such a situation.

Then we repeated the tests at a medium altitude level of 25,000 feet, but this time I reached only 0.94. This time I was deliberately jerking the stick backwards and forwards to simulate the effect of the bumpy air which would have been met with at low altitudes such as that at which the world record run would have take place and Geoffrey de Havilland Jnr had been flying when he was killed. Even with the slightest sharp movement fore-and-aft, the aircraft began to oscillate to an extent that was becoming dangerous at this speed. I had had no trouble of this kind at 30,000 feet, but here was a warning signal that the Swallow lacked longitudinal damping at the higher indicated airspeeds met at lower heights. A long plank will always balance better than a short one, and in a conventional aircraft with a normal tail unit the inherent stability usually damps the oscillating motion before it becomes really dangerous. But it had long been suspected that a tailless aircraft would lack this steadying feature. It is rather like cutting off the tail of an ordinary machine and trying to re-balance it at a point much further forward.

With this very much in mind I descended to 10,000 feet, knowing all the time that it was at this stage that Geoffrey de Havilland Jnr had met disaster. At Mach 0.88 it happened. The ride was smooth, then suddenly went all to pieces. As the plane porpoised wildly my chin hit my chest, jerked hard back, slammed forward again, repeated it over and over, flogged by the awful whipping of the plane. My thoughts were grim. This was how it happened. This was how he had died. In the same second his head had cracked the canopy top and broken his neck, the wings had gone, the plane broken up. He was a big man, I was short, and I had had my seat lowered as far as it would go with this in mind. I wouldn't break my neck yet but this was the moment of truth.

I was going under fast and couldn't keep this up. The whole plane was oscillating as fast as a hand can wave goodbye. The 'g' was murderous and getting worse. Like another hand guiding me, the drill we had practised so hard took over. Both hands went out, both hauled hard back, one on the throttle, one on the stick. The motion ceased as quickly as it had started. I sat, head bowed, shaking. If this hadn't worked I would have been finished. But it was Q.E.D. We knew our enemy. Next time we would be better prepared. That is test piloting.

VW120 did not survive much longer as it was lost on 15 February 1950 in a crash that killed Squadron Leader J.S.R. Muller-Rowland DSO DFC, who was due to take over from Eric Brown as O.C. Aerodynamics Flight at RAE. Investigations were continuing into longitudinal stability and aeroelastic distortion at high Mach numbers and Muller-Rowland was briefed to carry out dives from 38,000 feet. Before the aircraft reached this height, however, control was lost and it dived into the ground at Birkhill near Bletchley in Buckinghamshire. During the subsequent enquiry that was set up to investigate the crash no fault could be found with the aircraft to explain its sudden descent and the theory was put forward that the pilot's oxygen supply may have been at fault.

Over the years the DH.108 has come in for a fair amount of criticism that stems from the fact that all three aircraft were lost in fatal accidents. Although in the end tailless swept-wing aircraft were to prove to be a design dead-end, the cancellation of the Miles M.52 in February 1946 meant that Britain had no alternative but to build a high-speed research programme around the DH.108 if it was to obtain the information that was necessary to develop transonic fighters to match those being produced in the USA and the Soviet Union. Despite being fitted with a relatively low powered engine, the 108 was capable of very high speed and although its handling characteristics at the very top end of the speed range could be capricious, once the flight envelope had been fully explored and its limitations were known there was little for the pilot to fear. Sadly, in getting to that stage Geoffrey de Havilland Jnr was to pay the ultimate price. His work was not in vain, however, as the experience that was gained with the little 108 was to be of great importance in the development of more advanced aircraft, in particular the DH.110 which was the forerunner of the Sea Vixen naval strike fighter.

CHAPTER TWELVE

Fighter Development in the USSR and France

During the Second World War the Soviet aircraft industry had a reputation for producing tough, workmanlike aircraft for its armed forces, however, the later products of the major fighter manufacturers, Lavochkin, Mikoyan and Gurevich (MiG) and Yakovlev were a match for anything built in the West. Although piston-engined fighter development closely mirrored that of other countries, very little progress was made towards producing a jet-powered equivalent. On the face of it, this was somewhat surprising as a design for a jet engine had first been proposed in 1937, but the German invasion of Russia on 22 June 1941 led to this work being shelved, the priority then being the building of large numbers of conventional fighters and bombers. It was not until the end of the war with the added impetus of large amounts of captured hardware being returned from Germany that Soviet experiments with jet and rocket-powered designs really began to take off.

Following on from the early testing of rocket motors as recorded in Chapter Six, several advanced German projects were continued in the Soviet Union after the war under the supervision of technicians who had been captured during the advance into Germany. One of these was the MiG I-270 which was based on the Messerschmitt Me 263 rocket-powered interceptor. The Me 263 had been developed as the operational effectiveness of the Me 163B Komet was severely affected by its limited endurance. The Me 263 thus had an enlarged fuselage for increased fuel tankage and there was also sufficient room for a tricycle undercarriage. The wing, fin and rudder were similar to those of the earlier machine. Unfortunately flight and wind tunnel testing showed that the aircraft's limiting Mach number was only 0.8 which was 0.02M lower than that of the Me 163B. At a late stage a fixed tailplane was being considered for the Me 263 and the completed I-270 was to appear with a slightly swept T-tail. Power was provided by a RD-2M-3V rocket motor which had a main chamber offering a thrust of 3,200 lb at sea level and a cruising chamber which provided 880 lb thrust. Two prototypes were built and powered flights were carried out in early 1947, but the rocket fighter concept was soon abandoned as it appeared that the turbojet offered much greater operational flexibility.

One of the most far sighted programmes in Germany at the end of the war was the DFS 346 which was similar in concept to the Miles M.52 and the Bell XS-1. Of the three aircraft, the DFS 346 looked the most futuristic as it possessed a slender fuselage and a mid-mounted wing which was swept back at an angle of 45 degrees. The horizontal tail surfaces were also swept and were mounted near the top of a broad-chord fin. Power was provided by two Walter 109-509B or C rocket motors, each offering a thrust of 4,410 lb. The DFS 346 was to have been carried by another aircraft to an altitude of over 30,000 feet and after initial flight testing as a glider, fully powered flights were to have been carried out up to the projected (and rather optimistic) top speed of Mach 2.6. After the war the project was continued in the Soviet Union and a glider version (the 346P) was flown in 1947 having been taken aloft under the wing of a captured B-29 bomber. Thereafter misfortune tended to dog further trials, with another airframe being badly damaged in a landing accident and a third being lost in a crash which killed the pilot. Despite its promise, the 346 was finally abandoned without having achieved its goal of exceeding Mach 1.0.

The first examples of German turbojet engines were seized during the advance westwards in late 1944 and these were transported back to the Soviet Union where copies were made, the BMW 109-003 becoming the RD-20 and the Jumo 109-004 becoming the RD-10. In a programme given the utmost priority, the fighter manufacturers were tasked with designing fighter aircraft to utilise these powerplants and the first to take to the air was the MiG I-300 (later designated MiG-9) on 24 April 1946 which beat the Yak-15 by a matter of a couple of hours. The I-300 was a straight-winged design which was powered by two BMW 109-003 engines in a pod-and-boom arrangement which found favour with several Soviet designers of the time. It was also the first Soviet aircraft to feature a tricycle undercarriage. Initial flight testing was disrupted by a severe vibration at high speed which was eventually traced to the jet efflux, but worse was to come when test pilot Alexei Grinchik was killed when his aircraft crashed during a high speed run at low level. He was replaced by Mark Gallai who was very nearly lost in similar circumstances when his aircraft hit compressibility and pitched violently nose down. Only by snatching back on the throttle was he able to reduce speed sufficiently to pull out of the subsequent dive. The MiG-9 entered Soviet Air Force service on 1 July 1948 and in all around 600 aircraft were produced.

The Yak-15 was a close contemporary of the MiG-9 and was based on the piston-engined Yak-3. It was powered by a single Jumo 109-004 which was mounted in the forward fuselage so that it exhausted under the centre section. Unfortunately in coming up with this arrangement no one had considered the tailwheel which promptly melted as it was directly in line with the jet efflux! A steel replacement cured the problem but led to a spectacular shower of sparks whenever it was in contact with the runway during take off and landing. The Yak-15 led to a family of aircraft, the next of which was the Yak-17 which initially employed the same layout as the earlier machine, but was subsequently modified to incorporate a tricycle undercarriage. The Yak-19 finally did away with the pod-and-boom design for a conventional fuselage with a long jet pipe exhausting at the rear. It was powered by an RD-10 turbojet which was modified to accept reheat, in which condition it produced 2,425 lb thrust. The Yak-19 was first flown on 8 January 1947 and was to become the fastest Soviet aircraft of its day with a top speed of 559 mph. It was developed into the Yak-25 (not to be confused with the later twin-engined Yak-25 Flashlight) which featured swept tail surfaces and was powered by the Soviet version of the Rolls-Royce Derwent, the RD-500 of 3,500 lb thrust.

Pavel Sukhoi was one of the most innovative of Soviet designers having dabbled with jet power as early as 1942. His first jet fighter was the Su-9 which outwardly resembled the Me 262 but was much more than a mere copy. Its fuselage was oval in section and the wings were not swept, although it did employ two RD-10 (Jumo 109-004) engines in underslung nacelles. The Su-9 was flown for the first time on 13 November 1946 and despite the fact that its performance was similar to the MiG-9, and in some respects was better, it was not ordered into production. The Su-9 was developed into the Su-11 which was generally similar except that it was powered by two Lyulka TR-1 jet engines of 2,866 lb thrust in nacelles that were now mid-mounted on the wing in similar fashion to the Gloster Meteor. Flight testing highlighted poor longitudinal stability, together with engines that were down on power, and the Su-11 was soon abandoned. A similar fate befell the Su-13 but in the case of this proposal, the axe fell before it had even flown. It was to have featured a wing of only 9 per cent thickness/chord ratio (compared to 11 per cent on the Su-11), sweptback horizontal tail surfaces and two RD-500 engines.

The other major Soviet fighter manufacturer was Lavochkin whose first jet design was the La-150 (later designated La-13). This was another straight-winged aircraft to have a pod-and-boom fuselage, with a nose mounted intake for a single RD-10 jet engine. Although at one stage the design was fitted with an RD-10 with reheat to become the La-150F, it was not proceeded with. The development sequence then moved onto the La-152, which was similar in configuration to the Yak-15, and the La-154 which was abandoned due to delays with its TR-1 engine. The La-156 had an RD-10 jet engine with reheat but although this aircraft made it into the air, its handling characteristics were criticised and development was terminated. The last straight-winged design in the development sequence was the La-174TK which was flown in 1948. This aircraft had a wing of only 6 per cent thickness/chord ratio but it was found that it was still inferior to the swept wing designs that were then being produced in prototype form.

The first Soviet swept wing design was the La-160 which was similar to the previous Lavochkin deigns but utilised wing sweep of 35 degrees. The engine used was a German Jumo 109-004 and the aircraft made its maiden flight on 24 June 1947. During trials it was flown to a speed of 650 mph but was used only for research purposes and was not ordered for production. The first Lavochkin design to have a conventional fuselage was the La-168 which was produced to the same requirement as the MiG-15. It was powered by a Rolls-Royce Nene engine and was flown for the first time on 22 April 1948 but ultimately lost out to the Mikoyan design. The last in this design stream was the La-176 which featured increased wing sweep of 45 degrees and was powered by an RD-45 (Nene). Although it was to lose out as a fighter, the La-176 had considerable success as a research aircraft and became the first Soviet design to exceed the speed of sound on 26 December 1948 when Colonel I.V. Fedorov attained 1.02M during a shallow dive from an altitude of 32,800 feet. It was later fitted with a VK-1 engine (an uprated Nene designed by Vladimir Klimov) but despite the aircraft's undoubted qualities it was not taken any further.

Having had his Su-9 and Su-11 designs rejected, Sukhoi began to look at a requirement for a fighter equipped with airborne interception radar which eventually emerged as the Su-15 in October 1948. It was a twin-engined design with the RD-45 engines being mounted in tandem in the fuselage and the wings were swept at 37 degrees. It was confidently predicted that the aircraft's top speed would be in the order of 640 mph but this could not be confirmed as the prototype crashed as a result of flutter which led to the whole project being cancelled. The reputation of Sukhoi had been on the wane in official circles for some time and the accident was a major factor in the design bureau being closed in 1949.

This led to the demise of the Su-17 which was to have undertaken transonic research, as well as being capable of development as a fighter. Its estimated top speed was 1.08M at 36,000 feet but concern over its susceptibility to flutter led to it being grounded before it had even managed to take to the air. Although it had been reluctant at first to move towards a swept wing, Yakovlev finally took the plunge with the Yak-30 which was powered by a single RD-500 engine. It was first flown on 4 September 1948 but despite the fact that it could achieve a speed of Mach 0.935, its performance was no better than the MiG-15 which was ahead in development terms.

The MiG-15 was the most successful design to come out of the Soviet Union in the immediate post-war years. It was first conceived in March 1946 when a requirement for a new fighter was formulated with a speed of not less than Mach 0.9 and a service ceiling of not less than 36,000 feet. For the time this was extremely ambitious and one of the major problems was to find a suitable engine. The most powerful engine in the world in 1946 was the Rolls-Royce Nene but the problem was how to obtain one so that it could be copied. The solution was staggeringly simple and involved a direct request to the British for the purchase of a small batch of the engines. When Stalin heard of the scheme he is reputed to have said – 'What fool will sell us his secrets?', but he had not reckoned with the naïvety of the new Labour government which as well as cancelling its own supersonic research programme (the Miles M.52) was apparently more than happy for others to reap the benefits of its advanced projects. A Soviet delegation arrived in Britain in 1946 and included amongst its number were Artem Mikoyan and Vladimir Klimov who successfully negotiated a deal. A contract was duly signed which led to the purchase of twenty-five Nene and thirty Derwent engines and these were soon being tested back in the Soviet Union or dissected prior to being produced on a massive scale.

With the engine problem solved, Mikoyan looked at the aerodynamic issues and having assessed both forward sweep and sweep back, opted for the latter at 35 degrees sweep angle, the wing being mounted in the mid-position. At first a conventional fuselage was proposed with a long jetpipe and a swept T-tail on top of a broad fin and rudder, but the tail was subsequently modified so that both the fin and rudder were swept and the horizontal tail was lowered to a position just above halfway up the fin. The rear fuselage was also cut back to allow a shorter jetpipe to reduce thrust losses. The prototype (known initially as the I-310) was flown for the first time on 30 December 1947 by Viktor N. Yuganov and underwent flight testing throughout 1948 which showed it to have extremely high performance. Following the loss of the second prototype during inverted spin tests, the third prototype (S-03) appeared with a beefed up structure and towards the end of 1948 it achieved a Mach number of 0.934.

Although in many respects the MiG-15 was equal, and in some cases was superior, to the F-86 Sabre, it lost out to the American fighter at the very top end of the speed range. Handling anomalies were discovered on a number of early production aircraft in that they possessed lateral instability at a Mach number of around 0.9. In these cases pilots were confronted with severe wing drop and even full aileron could not prevent the wing from going down. This problem had not been experienced on the prototypes and it was eventually found that it was due to manufacturing inaccuracies during production. Every effort was made to improve the situation by making sure that the correct tolerances were adhered to, but 'rogue' aircraft continued to appear. Some were subject to crude modifications comprising the riveting of a metal strip to the aileron of whichever wing was prone to drop. This was then bent to whichever angle was necessary for the aircraft to fly wings level over the full speed range. The MiG-15 also suffered from Dutch rolling which led to an initial limit of 0.88M being imposed, however, pilots found that it was almost impossible to avoid exceeding this speed and eventually the airbrakes were made to open automatically at 0.9M.

The basic MiG-15 design was subsequently developed into the MiG-15bis which was tidied up aerodynamically and had better systems, flying controls and armament. It also featured a more powerful engine as Vladimir Klimov had been quick to improve on the Rolls-Royce Nene which had been presented to the Soviets so fortuitously. By enlarging the compressor, the modified engine (known as the VK-1) was able to accept a 20 per cent increase in mass flow so that thrust was increased to 5,952 lb. This resulted in a weight increase of 140 lb and slight modifications had to be made to the internal fuselage structure as there was also a modest increase in diameter. The new aircraft replaced the original MiG-15 on production lines in 1949 and went on to be built in large numbers for the Soviet Air Force and the air forces of satellite countries. Much work went into improving the MiG-15's handling characteristics at high Mach numbers and this led to the development of the MiG-15LL research aircraft (also known as the SYe). This was fitted with an enlarged fin and had stiffened wings and revised ailerons. It was later fitted with more powerful BU-1 boosters for improved aileron control and in this condition the MiG-15LL achieved Mach 1.01 on 18 October 1949.

Although there was no immediate prospect of increased engine power, improvements could be made aerodynamically and this led to the MiG-17 which was flown for the first time as the SI on 13 January 1950. The most significant change was the adoption of a wing of 45 degrees sweep which was also extended in chord to reduce thick-ness/chord ratio. The rear fuselage was elongated to improve fineness ratio and the tail unit was redesigned with an extended fin and horizontal surfaces of greater span and increased sweep angle. Handling characteristics were much improved and on 1 February the aircraft was flown to Mach 1.03 in level flight. Development of the new aircraft was unfortunately delayed by nearly a year following the loss of the prototype when it dived into the ground as a result of a malfunction in the elevator control. It was not until the summer of 1951 that the testing programme was completed, during which period the aircraft achieved Mach 1.14 in a dive, although the MiG-17 was to be limited to a Mach number of 0.95 in service. The most important MiG-17 variant was the 17F which was powered by a VK-1F engine with reheat. This developed 7,450 lb thrust and restored the performance that had been lost with the introduction of airborne interception radar on the MiG-17P. The MiG-17 entered Soviet Air Force service in late 1953 and around 8,000 were to be built.

The success of the designs coming from the Mikoyan bureau tended to eclipse all others including those of Yakovlev. Having produced the straight-winged Yak-25, a 35 degree swept wing was adopted for the Yak-30 which also had swept tail surfaces and was powered by an RD-500 (Derwent) engine. The first prototype was flown for the first time on 4 September 1948 but despite the fact that it was found to possess excellent manoeuvrability and showed no undesirable handling qualities up to Mach 0.935, the dominant position that had been acquired by the MiG-15 meant that the Yakovlev design was not even subjected to air force trials. A refined version, the Yak-30D, was also flown but although its form was particularly neat, it was not proceeded with. Yakovlev also produced a design for an AI-equipped fighter which became the Yak-50 that was first flown on 15 July 1949. It was powered by a VK-1 engine and featured a mid-mounted wing which was swept at an angle of 45 degrees, but during testing it was discovered that the aircraft was prone to lateral instability at speeds above Mach 0.92 and the programme was cancelled in 1950. Yakovlev retained interest in this particular category of aircraft and went on to produce the successful twin-engined Yak-25 fighter.

Having produced a number of aircraft with transonic capability, the next step for Soviet fighter manufacturers was to come up with a design that could fly at supersonic speeds in level flight. They were helped in this task by the significant progress that was being made in engine design, particularly the products of Lyulka and Mikulin. In the quest for a supersonic fighter Yakovlev developed the Yak-140 with a 55-degree swept wing. As a fuselage-mounted, bicycle-type undercarriage was employed with wing-tip outriggers, the wing was thus unencumbered with a landing gear and could be made particularly thin, thickness/chord varying from 6–8 per cent. Power was to have come from a Mikulin AM-11 engine off 11,000 lb in reheat, but production delays meant that the lower powered AM-9D (7,165 lb thrust in reheat) had to be installed instead which reduced performance significantly. Even using this engine the Yak-140 was still expected to be capable of supersonic speeds at all levels, but the slippage in the programme was too much for the Ministry of Aircraft Industry which cancelled the project shortly before the aircraft was to have flown.

The trials and tribulations of the Sukhoi design bureau in the years immediately after the end of the Second World War have already been recounted, but with the death of Joseph Stalin in 1953 Pavel Sukhoi's reputation began to rise once more and he went on to produce swept and delta-winged fighters. Both configurations had their advocates which led to the swept-wing Su-7 (NATO codename Fitter) and the delta-winged Su-9 (Fishpot) entering service with the Soviet Air Force, the former as a ground attack aircraft and the latter as an interceptor. Apart from their differing wing planforms, the two aircraft were otherwise fairly similar but tended to go their own ways during the development process. The Su-7 was the production version of the original S-1 and had a long, circular section fuselage with a nose-mounted air intake and sharply swept-back wings with a sweep angle of 62 degrees. Power was provided by a Lyulka AL-7F jet engine offering 19,841 lb thrust in reheat. The S-1 prototype was flown for the first time on 7 September 1955 and was soon showing remarkable performance with a top speed approaching Mach 2.0. During performance testing of the Su-7, however, it displayed certain limitations as an interceptor and entered service as a tactical fighter in 1959. The delta-winged Su-9 stemmed from the earlier T-1 and T-3 designs and was powered by an AL-7F-1 of 21,165 lb thrust in reheat (this engine was also fitted to production Su-7s). Rocket assisted take-off was initially considered as a means of reducing reaction times and improving performance at altitude, but the aircraft proved to be more than capable on the power of its single jet engine and was flown to a speed of 1,367 mph at altitude which equated to Mach 2.06. The Su-9 entered service around the same time as the Su-7 and undertook first-line duties with the Soviet Air Force into the early 1970s.

Having become the premier design bureau in terms of fighter aircraft, Mikoyan followed up the MiG-17 with the MiG-19 which can be traced back to the I-350 which first took to the air on 16 June 1951. This aircraft was designed to a requirement for a supersonic fighter and was powered by a Lyulka TR-3A axial-flow turbojet rated at 10,141 lb thrust.

For its day the I-350 possessed an extremely radical wing with leading edge sweep of 60 degrees and it was built with sufficient torsional rigidity for conventional outboard ailerons, something that North American conspicuously failed to do with the F-100 Super Sabre. Concerns over possible aileron reversal at supersonic speeds meant that the latter had inboard ailerons. Although it had much potential, the I-350 was blighted by the lack of development of its TR-3A engine with the first five test flights all having to be curtailed because of engine-related problems. As the rival AM-5 axial engine designed by Mikulin was ahead in development terms it was decided to abandon the I-350 in favour of the I-360.

As the thrust rating of the AM-5 was only 4,740 lb, two engines were mounted side-by-side in the fuselage and were fed by a nose intake. This arrangement had first been tried on an experimental version of the MiG-17, the I-340, which was first flown in March 1952. The I-360 had leading edge sweep of 57 degrees and, at first, a high set tail, although this was soon lowered to a position at the top of the rear fuselage. This was carried out to eradicate a lack of effectiveness at high Mach numbers and to avoid buffeting due to wake turbulence from the wing at high angles of attack. First flight took place on 24 May 1952 but early flight testing showed that the I-360 could not exceed the speed of sound in level flight on the power of its unreheated AM-5s, although Mach 1.19 was achieved in a shallow dive. The answer was to increase power and production MiG-19s were fitted with improved AM-9 (later designated RD-9) engines of 7,164 lb thrust in reheat. With these engines the MiG-19 was capable of a top speed of around 900 mph at 33,000 feet, or Mach 1.35. The basic MiG-19 was later developed as the -19S with a powered slab tail to improve longitudinal handling characteristics and a number took part in various research programmes including the MiG-19SU (SM-50) which was powered by RD-9BM engines of 7,275 lb thrust and a belly pack of U-19 rocket motors offering a total of 8,000 lb thrust at altitude. During trials with this aircraft it was flown to a speed of 1,118 mph (Mach 1.695).

Mikoyan's next creation was the ubiquitous MiG-21 which evolved from experience in the Korean War in the same way that the Lockheed F-104 Starfighter did in the USA. The development sequence was similar to that at Sukhoi in that both swept and delta wings were tried. The first to appear was the swept wing Ye-2 which, like the MiG-19, had leading edge sweep of 57 degrees, however, thickness/chord ratio was only 6 per cent (average t/c ratio on the MiG-19 was just over 8 per cent). The engine chosen was the AM-9B of 7,165 lb thrust in reheat, although the aircraft was capable of accommodating the more powerful AM-11. Flight testing commenced on 14 February 1955 and despite the relatively low power of the AM-9B, the performance envelope was extended up to a maximum of Mach 1.8. In the meantime the delta-winged version, the Ye-4, was under construction and this aircraft was flown for the first time on 16 June 1955. Compared with the Ye-2, the delta wing of the Ye-4 offered lower structure weight and improved manoeuvrability but the top speed proved to be disappointing due to excessive drag at the rear end and this ultimately led to the premature retirement of the aircraft. It was succeeded by the Ye-5 powered by a single Tumanskiy-designed AM-11 of 11,245 lb thrust in reheat (following the fall from favour of A.A. Mikulin in 1956 this engine was initially re-designated RD-11 and then R-11). With a redesigned rear fuselage to reduce drag, the top speed of the Ye-5 was much improved and the aircraft soon reached a speed of Mach 1.85 which was sufficiently impressive for it to be chosen for the Soviet Air Force. Production MiG-21s were powered by an R-11F-300 which gave 12,655 lb thrust in reheat and this engine endowed the aircraft with true Mach 2.0 performance. The MiG-21 was to be built in greater numbers than any other jet fighter and eventually around 13,500 were built, including those manufactured under licence.

Although it had received much help along the way from various sources, the Soviet aerospace industry quickly came of age and moved on from merely copying western designs so that by the end of the 1950s it was a potential world leader in performance aircraft. This was underlined when the awesome-looking, delta-wing Mikoyan Ye 152/1, powered by a Tumanskiy R15B-300 of 22,510 lb thrust in reheat, took the world speed record on 7 June 1962 at a speed of 1,666 mph (Mach 2.52). Having started virtually from scratch at the end of the Second World War, the Soviet Union had ascended to a position second only to the USA, a rapid rise that was matched by the French who were determined to reclaim their position as one of the premier aircraft-producing nations.

Of all the world's major aircraft-producing countries, France was in the most difficult position at the end of the Second World War as its aeronautical industry lay in ruins with its design teams long since split up. Progress in the field of aeronautics was set to accelerate significantly, it appeared that France was about to be left behind. However, not only did France catch up with its competitors, but in just eleven years it had designed and built the prototype Mirage III which was to be one of the world's most successful combat aircraft.

Like Britain, the USA and the Soviet Union, France benefited from German wartime research into high speed flight and when this was added to the wealth of talent that existed in the French aviation industry, highly advanced projects were not long in coming. In marked contrast to what was to follow, France's first jet-powered design, the SO.6000 Triton, was purely conventional and featured a deep section fuselage with a mid-set, straight wing. This aircraft was designed by Lucien Servanty of Sud-Ouest and actually dated back to 1943. The major problem in the immediate post-war years was a lack of suitable jet engines and the little Triton was first flown on 11 November 1946 with a Junkers 004B of only 1,980 lb thrust. This was barely enough power for sustained flight but the aircraft's capacious fuselage allowed plenty of room for larger engines to be fitted and in March 1949 it was flown with a Rolls-Royce Nene of 4,850 lb thrust built under licence by Hispano-Suiza. With this engine the Triton eventually achieved a speed of 593 mph but it was beset by stability problems and was also prone to severe vibration. Five examples of the Triton were built, the last flight being made in November 1950.

Although France had been a late starter as regards jet-powered aircraft, designers in that country did at least have the advantage of being able to start with a clean sheet of paper and original shapes tended to follow rather than the conservative designs favoured by several British aircraft companies who adopted a step-by-step approach. France's first post-war jet fighter was the SO.6020 Espadon, again designed by Lucien Servanty, which first took to the air on 12 November 1948. It was also powered by a Nene jet engine, however, the third prototype was modified to incorporate an SEPR 251 liquid-fuel rocket motor in a long ventral duct under the fuselage to become the SO.6025. The second Espadon was also rocket powered in its later life and on 15 December 1953 it exceeded Mach 1.0 during flight tests from Istres. By this time the amount of power being generated by the latest jet engines was beginning to make the use of supplementary rocket motors unnecessary and no further development work on the Espadon was undertaken.

A requirement for a shipboard jet fighter produced the VG-90 from Arsenal de l'Aeronautique, based on the previous VG-70 which was of wooden construction and powered by a Jumo 004B. Of extremely slender proportions, the VG-90 had a shoulder mounted wing with moderate sweepback, under which were the side fuselage inlets for a Nene jet engine. The first prototype VG-90 was completed in 1949 and was flown on 27 September but was lost in a fatal crash the following year. It was not replaced until June 1951 when a second machine was flown, but this was also lost following an accident in January 1952. Before these unfortunate incidents the VG-90 had shown an excellent level of performance with a top speed of nearly 600 mph and a service ceiling of 38,000 feet. A third prototype was built of metal construction and powered by an Atar 101F, but by this time the Aeronavale had lost interest in the project and this aircraft was never flown.

By far the most successful fighter aircraft produced by France after the Second World War were the designs emanating from Dassault. Having returned to France after being incarcerated at Buchenwald concentration camp, Marcel Dassault (formerly Marcel Bloch) re-commenced aircraft design, as soon as he had got together his pre-war design team, with a view to producing a jet fighter-bomber. Opting for as simple a layout as possible, Dassault came up with the MD 450 Ouragan (Hurricane) which had a low wing of only 18 degrees sweep and a tailplane set approximately halfway up the fin. As no French-built engine was available the Ouragan was powered by a Hispano-Suiza-produced Nene of 5,070 lb thrust. It was flown for the first time on 28 February 1948 (the first prototype was initially fitted with a Rolls-Royce-built Nene) and testing showed that for a first attempt at a jet-powered aircraft, the design showed a good deal of promise.

The Ouragan was also tested by A&AEE pilots during a trial carried out at the Centre d'Essais en Vol at Bretigny in July 1950. Of particular interest was the aircraft's handling characteristics at high Mach numbers and it was taken to 36,000 feet using 12,000 rpm before being trimmed into level flight at about 0.74 M and put into a shallow dive. Slight aileron twitching became apparent at 0.77 – 0.78M at 35,000 feet and by the time that 0.785M had been reached a nose-down change of trim was occurring which increased in magnitude with increasing Mach number, as did the aileron twitching. The aircraft also tended to roll to starboard and at 0.80M a heavy stick force was required to keep the wings level and at the same time the pilot had to pull back on the control column to counteract the nose-down tendency. By 0.81M the aileron buffet had reached unpleasant proportions and there was a distinct possibility that either wing could drop. At this point the airbrakes were fully deployed causing a nose-up trim change which opposed the nose-down tendency due to compressibility. Throughout the dive, directional trim was steady and no snaking was experienced.

A dive was also made from an altitude of 18,500 feet with similar characteristics being displayed although these tended to become restric-tive at a slightly lower Mach number than previously. One difference was noted in that at high altitude the aileron buffet commenced before the nose-down trim change, but at lower altitudes the reverse was the case. For a fighter, it was considered that the Ouragan's limiting maximum Mach number of 0.81 was rather low, but in service its maximum operating speed was likely to be even lower as aileron buffet would have limited accurate gun aiming to around 0.77 – 0.78M. In addition the controls were quite heavy, particularly the elevator, which tended to detract from manoeuvrability.

Unlike some other French designers Dassault preferred to adapt his creations which avoided unnecessary risk taking and ensured that each aircraft in turn stood the best chance of being a success. His next design, the Mystere II, was virtually an Ouragan with wings and tail swept 30 degrees and a more powerful engine. Although the first few aircraft were fitted with a version of the Rolls-Royce Tay built by Hispano-Suiza, the days of the centrifugal jet were numbered and later machines were powered by a SNECMA Atar 101 axial jet engine. This engine was produced by a group of former German technicians led by Hermann Oestrich and had been developed from the BMW 109-003 which had powered the Heinkel He 162 *Volksjager* (People's Fighter). As the team was called Atelier Aeronautique de Rickenbach, the initials provided the name Atar.

The speed with which France had caught up with the rest of the world was made apparent on 28 October 1952 when a visiting USAF Captain exceeded Mach 1.0 during a dive in a Mystere IIB. By this time, however, Dassault had been working on a successor for over a year which was to emerge as the Mystere IV. The trend towards wings of greater sweep angle and more powerful engines was repeated, but the transonic capabilities of the aircraft were improved still further by the use of a wing of 7½ per cent thickness/chord ratio instead of 9 per cent as on the Mystere II. Paradoxically, the new aircraft saw a return to a centrifugal jet with use of the Hispano-Suiza HS 350 Verdon of 7,716 lb thrust (the first fifty machines were powered by an HS 250 which was derived from the Tay). With a wing sweep angle of 38 degrees and more power, the Mystere IV's top speed of 696 mph at sea level was 50 mph faster than its predecessor. Ordered for the Armee de l'Air, the Mystere IVA had a long service life which included action during the Suez crisis in 1956.

The ultimate development in this particular design stream was the Super Mystere B2, often referred to as the SMB 2, which was to have the distinction of being the first western European fighter to exceed Mach 1.0 in level flight. The Super Mystere was similar in many respects to the F-100 Super Sabre, the most notable difference being the positioning of the tailplane which was located on the fin as on previous Mysteres, instead of low down on the fuselage as on the F-100. The wings were swept at an angle of 45 degrees and had a thickness/chord ratio of only 6 per cent. Power came from a single SNECMA Atar 101G which developed 9,833 lb of thrust in reheat. Maximum level speed performance was 645 mph at sea level and 740 mph (Mach 1.12) at 40,000 feet. Development delays meant that the first production aircraft did not fly until 26 February 1957 but this was still three years before the first supersonic aircraft (the English Electric Lightning) was delivered to the Royal Air Force.

In marked contrast to what was going on at Dassault, other French designers were to produce some of the most radical experimental prototypes ever seen in their quest for maximum performance. As in Britain, the concept of the mixed-power fighter, with both rocket and jet engines, held a particular fascination as developments of the rocket technology pioneered in Germany during the Second World War promised unprecedented levels of performance. Another form of propulsion, the ramjet as used in the Fieseler Fi 103 flying bomb (V-1) was also seen as a way of overcoming the modest power levels of the first jet turbine engines and led to the extraordinary designs of Rene Leduc.

Leduc had, in fact, been experimenting with ramjets since 1929 and his first design was almost complete at the time of the German *Blitzkrieg* in May 1940. Although damaged during air raids, the remains were hidden away and formed the basis for continued experiments at the war's end. These resulted in the Leduc 010, the fuselage of which comprised the ramjet duct, the pilot being accommodated in a capsule within the forward section of the duct. The straight wings were mid-set and featured slotted flaps and ailerons. As a ramjet requires a flow of air through the duct for combustion to begin, the 010 required air-launching and this was achieved by converting an SE.161 Languedoc airliner with a fixing cradle above the fuselage. The first free flight was made by Jean Gonord on 21 October 1947 although on this occasion the ramjet was not lit and the aircraft performed as a glider.

Following testing of the ramjet with the 010 still attached to the Languedoc, the first attempt at powered flight took place on 21 April 1949. Even on less than full power a speed of 450 mph was achieved and the type was eventually tested to its limiting speed of Mach 0.84. The original Leduc 010-01 was eventually joined by 010-02 but both aircraft were involved in accidents. On 27 November 1951 010-02 experienced engine failure and pilot Jean Sarrail suffered serious back injuries in the subsequent forced landing in which the cockpit pod detached from the fuselage. Another setback occurred on 25 July 1952 when 010-01 hit the carrier aircraft as they parted company. The pilot on this occasion was Yvan Littolf who also injured his back on landing. A third machine, designated 016, was intended to have two Turbomeca Marbore 1 jet engines mounted one on each wing tip but this idea was eventually abandoned and the aircraft was flown in 010 configuration. Despite the accidents, the prototypes had shown a good deal of promise and encouraged Leduc to proceed towards his goal of producing a supersonic ramjet fighter.

Having proved the concept with the 010, Leduc designed the 021 which was bigger, with a more powerful ramjet for propulsion, and this aircraft was flown for the first time on the back of its Languedoc carrier in March 1953. It was intended to be the immediate precursor of an operational fighter prototype capable of supersonic speeds. Although it was of similar configuration to the previous aircraft, the pilot was accommodated in semi-reclined fashion in a nose cone ahead of the annular intake. The nose cone could be jettisoned in an emergency. The first 021 featured a Turbomeca Artouste I jet engine behind the nose cone to ignite the ramjet and power fuel pumps and generators and this was replaced by a Marbore II in the second, and last, aircraft to fly. Although it had a limiting Mach number of 0.85, the Leduc 021 had phenomenal climb performance with an initial rate of climb of 39,000 ft/min. Even at 49,000 feet pilots were still recording a rate of climb of 2,900 ft/min. The highest altitude recorded with the 021 was 66,000 feet. The only drawback for the ramjet fighter was its need for aerial launch, but other than this, flight testing showed it to be a practical concept and both 021s were displayed at the Paris Air Show in 1955 where speeds of up to 600 mph were achieved.

The last ramjet design by Leduc was the 022 which was bigger still with a fuselage length of 59 ft 6 in (the 011 was only 33 ft 7 in long) and at 13,200 lb it was around double the weight. Of all his creations the 022 was by far the most futuristic in appearance with a sharply pointed nose cone ahead of an almost constant section tube-like fuselage with wings swept 30 degrees. To enable it to take off under its own power the 022 was fitted with a SNECMA Atar turbojet engine. It was flown for the first time on 26 December 1956 and testing soon showed that it had the potential to become the ultimate point defence fighter, but with an endurance of only 10 minutes if flown to its theoretical maximum speed of Mach 2.4. It would also have had the ability to climb to 82,000 feet in only 4 minutes. In its first year of trials the 022 was flown 141 times and achieved supersonic flight on 21 December 1957 when it was taken to Mach 1.15. Although it had performed well enough in terms of outright performance, the need for this type of interceptor fighter was called into question and the project was cancelled by the French government before the 022 could show what it really could do. It was not the only ramjet-powered aircraft to emerge from France during this period as an equally jaw-dropping design was to emerge.

Following on from its VG-90, the team at Arsenal (shortly to be merged with Nord) next came up with a small delta-wing design known as the Gerfaut. This aircraft was powered by an Atar turbojet and despite its hump-backed appearance it was the first French aircraft to go supersonic in level flight on 3 August 1954. This achievement was even more impressive as it thus became the first western European aircraft to fly in excess of Mach 1.0 without recourse to reheat. Having gained experience with a delta wing configuration the next step was to build a larger aircraft and the lure of the ramjet was again to prove irresistible. This resulted in the Griffon which in its initial form was powered only by an Atar 101F turbojet and was flown for the first time by Andre Turcat on 20 September 1955. On conversion as the definitive Griffon II it featured a much larger nose air-intake for the ramjet engine (the Atar was retained as on the Leduc 022) and it was flown in this configuration on 23 January 1957.

The design philosophy used on the Griffon was rather different to the Leduc series of ramjet-powered aircraft as the pilot sat in a more conventional cockpit positioned above the large air intake which operated rather more efficiently than the annular intake of the Leduc. A delta wing was retained and control was assisted by canard foreplanes. Right from the start of the flight testing programme confidence in the Griffon was high as its transonic handling characteristics were extremely good with little to trouble the pilot. Within a month the Griffon had been taken to Mach 1.5 and it was obvious that there was much more still to come. By October 1957 it had achieved Mach 2.05 and the following year it reached Mach 2.19. In addition it set a number of time-to-height records and was taken to 15,000 m (49,200 feet) in 3 minutes 35 seconds from a standing start. Although it was to rewrite the record books, the Griffon eventually went the same way as the designs of Rene Leduc, the French military preferring instead the multi-role capability of the Mirage III.

As well as investigating the possibilities of ramjet-powered interceptors, France also looked at the use of rocket motors as a means of bringing about a significant increase in performance. This led to the mixed power (turbojet and rocket) concept which also found favour in Britain for a time and resulted in the experimental Hawker P.1072, a development of the P.1040, which was powered by an Armstrong Siddeley Snarler rocket motor in addition to a Rolls-Royce Nene turbojet. The much more advanced delta-wing Saunders Roe SR.53 took the idea one stage further, but delays in its development meant that it did not fly until May 1957. Its prime power source was a de Havilland Spectre rocket motor of 7,000 lb thrust, but it was also fitted with an Armstrong Siddeley Viper turbojet of 1,640 lb thrust. The SR.53 was capable of supersonic speeds and was to have led to the SR.177 interceptor which had a design speed of Mach 2.35 and was powered by a Spectre 5A of 10,000 lb thrust and a de Havilland Gyron Junior turbojet of 14,000 lb thrust. This project was cancelled in 1957 following the infamous Defence White Paper of Defence Minister Duncan Sandys which stipulated that all manned fighters were soon to be a thing of the past and would be replaced by missile systems. In France the mixed-power fighter fared slightly better but ultimately shared the same fate.

In keeping with its reputation for design innovation the rocket-powered fighter prototype that France produced was unique in its layout. Known as the SO.9000 Trident I, it was designed by Lucien Servanty of Sud-Ouest and featured a long cylindrical fuselage to accommodate the fuel tanks for a three-chamber rocket motor. In defiance of contemporary thinking the wings were straight and of low aspect ratio, and at each tip was a pod for a jet engine which in the first of the series housed two Turbomeca Marbore IIs. For its time the horizontal stabiliser was quite radical as it featured anhedral and was of slab design. The Trident I was flown for the first time on 2 March 1953 on jet power alone and it was not until 4 September 1954 that the first ignition of the SEPR.481 rocket motor took place. Not long after the Marbore II jet engines were replaced with licence-built Armstrong Siddeley Vipers to provide adequate take-off performance, the rocket motor then being used to accelerate the aircraft to high speed. The Trident flew in excess of Mach 1.0 for the first time on 30 April 1955 and the aircraft was eventually taken to a speed of Mach 1.55 before it was taken out of service in December 1956.

The Trident I was replaced by the SO.9050 Trident II which was modified in several respects as the forerunner of a future operational variant. These included an ejector seat to replace the pressurised cockpit, reduced structure weight and revised undercarriage to allow the carriage of an air-to-air missile under the fuselage. The rocket was now a two-chamber SEPR.63 of 6,600 lb thrust. The maiden flight of the Trident II took place on 19 July 1955 and the potential of the aircraft was demonstrated when it went supersonic in a dive on jet power alone, the rocket motor not being tested in the air until the following December. The original SO.9050-01 was eventually joined by two other prototypes (-02 was soon written off in a take off accident) but having achieved Mach 1.93 in -03, the first aircraft was lost on 21 May 1957 when it blew up in the air killing test pilot Charles Goujon. No definitive cause could be established although it appeared that somehow there had been contact between the highly volatile rocket fuels (furaline and nitric acid).

Just when it seemed that the Trident was finally going to be accepted as a viable concept, the unexplained accident to -01 changed everything and the programme gradually fell out of favour, an order for ten improved versions being cut to just three. These were designated Trident II SE which featured more powerful Turbomeca Gabizo jet engines of 2,425 lb thrust. Before the Trident was cancelled in May 1958, ostensibly because of financial pressures, it was flown to a number of time-to-height records to emphasize its incredible performance. On 19 April 1958 a height of 59,000 feet was reached only 3 minutes 16 seconds after Jacques Guignard commenced his take-off run and on 2 May R. Carpentier claimed a new world height record when he climbed to an altitude of 79,453 feet. The last Trident II flight occurred on 6 October 1958. The pilot on this occasion was Jean-Pierre Rozier who was determined that the aircraft should go out in style and he succeeded in attaining an altitude of 85,000 feet in a ballistic climb.

The demise of France's advanced programme of ramjet and rocket-powered interceptors left the way open for the Dassault Mirage III to become the dominant fighter in the 1960s. The history of the Mirage III goes back to the early 1950s when a requirement for a lightweight fighter was formulated by the Armee de l'Air. Initially a swept wing was proposed along the lines of the Mystere but when it was realised that the wing would have to be only 4 inches thick to bring about the required thickness/chord ratio, Dassault began to look at the delta configuration (this layout was also chosen for the competing Sud-Est SE.212 Durandal which was first flown in April 1956 and went on to achieve Mach 1.6 in level flight before the programme was cancelled). The delta-winged aircraft that emerged from Dassault was designated MD.550 and was later given the name Mirage I. The official requirement had stated that the aircraft be powered by two relatively simple jet engines but as suitable French designed engines were still not ready, the MD.550 was fitted with Armstrong Siddeley Vipers and was first flown on 25 June 1955. Transonic handling proved to be excellent and despite a combined thrust of only 3,280 lb, Mach 1.15 was recorded in a 20 degree dive.

By this time Dassault was becoming increasingly frustrated by the restricted nature of the lightweight fighter concept and began pressing for the adoption of a single, large turbojet in an airframe of increased dimensions. This coincided with a change in NATO strategy to one of massive nuclear retaliation in the event of an attack by Soviet forces and the requirement for large numbers of relatively simple fighter aircraft was discarded in favour of a more advanced machine capable of autonomous operations. This resulted in the Mirage III which, although similar to the Mirage I in overall configuration, was completely re-engineered, including a wing of only 4.5 per cent thickness/chord ratio at the root, making it the thinnest wing of any European fighter at that time. Powered by a SNECMA Atar 9B of 13,225 lb thrust in reheat, the Mirage IIIA was flown for the first time on 12 May 1958 and on 24 October it was taken past Mach 2.0. Although its gestation period had been anything but straightforward, the Mirage III was to be the progenitor of a whole family of warplanes, the descendents of which remain in service with the air forces of the world.

Considering that France had to start from scratch in 1945, it was an incredible achievement to build and develop state-of-the-art aircraft capable of flying at twice the speed of sound in just fifteen years. In the same timescale Britain had initially given up on high speed flight research and in doing so had surrendered its position as one of the pre-eminent aircraft manufacturers in the world. There was no such vacillation on the part of the French aviation industry which had the expertise and the vision to move into the position recently vacated by the British. There was also a willingness to embrace advanced technology which resulted in some of the most outlandish designs that ever took to the skies. All were a technical success and were to make a significant contribution to the knowledge of transonic and supersonic flight. Although France was quickly able to make up ground on the British, the world leader was still the USA where the pioneering Bell XS-1 was the first of a whole series of research aircraft that in the space of ten years were to raise speed to 2,000 mph.

CHAPTER THIRTEEN

The USA Forges Ahead

While the US Army Air Force went ahead with the XS-1 high speed aircraft, the US Navy carried out its own transonic research programme with aircraft designed by Douglas Aircraft. There had been disagreement between the USAAF, NACA and the US Navy over certain aspects of design with NACA favouring a more conservative approach with the use of a turbojet engine in place of rocket power and a conventional take-off instead of air launching. The Navy tended to go along with this point of view and the resultant Douglas D-558-1 Skystreak was powered by a General Electric TG-180 jet engine (later designated J35) and had a tricycle undercarriage.

Proportionally the Skystreak looked a little odd as it was 35 ft 8½ in long but had a wing span of only 25 feet. The wing was straight, with a thickness/chord ratio of 10 per cent, and the horizontal stabiliser was mounted just below mid-way on the fin in a similar position to the XS-1 to keep it clear of wing turbulence. Flying controls were operated manually although the horizontal tail had variable incidence which could be activated electrically via a switch on the control wheel in the cockpit. The internal fuel capacity of 230 gallons could be augmented with two 50-gallon wing-tip tanks if required. The first Skystreak (Bu Aer No 37970) was flown for the first time by Douglas test pilot Gene May on 15 April 1947 at Muroc but the flight had to be aborted shortly after lift-off due to a drop in fuel pressure. This problem also occurred on the second flight and was followed by a number of malfunctions of the landing gear which refused to retract. These snags took some time to eradicate but by the summer of 1947 the test schedule was proceeding well.

By early August 1947 the Skystreak had been taken to 0.85M and the US Navy began to look at the possibility of an attempt on the world air speed record which was currently held by Colonel Al Boyd of the USAAF at a speed of 623.61 mph in the Lockheed P-80R Shooting Star. A course was laid out over the lake bed at Muroc and on 20 August Commander Turner Caldwell USN took the record with a speed of 640.60 mph. This achievement only lasted for five days as Major Marion Carl USMC flew the Skystreak to 650.78 mph on 25 August. Having seized the record back from the air force, the test programme was continued with speed being extended in small incremental stages. During this part of the test programme a certain amount of lateral instability was encountered at 0.86M and above, together with a tendency for the port wing to drop. By 0.94M longitudinal instability was being experienced with a distinct nose down pitch, however, the highest speed attained by the Skystreak occurred during a flight on 29 September 1948 in which Gene May reached Mach 1.0 in a 35 degree dive.

By now NACA were conducting their own tests at Muroc on the second Skystreak (Bu Aer No 37971) but on 3 May 1948 test pilot Howard Lilly was killed when he crashed shortly after take-off due to an explosive failure of the compressor in the J35 engine. At a height of only 150 feet the aircraft rolled sharply to the left and dived into the ground. Lilly had also been involved with the Bell XS-1 test programme and had been the third man to exceed the speed of sound on 31 March 1948. With the complete loss of the aircraft, the test programme was taken over by the third, and last, Skystreak (Bu Aer No 37972) and this continued until 1953 when Scott Crossfield made the last flight on 10 June. During its six-year lifetime the Skystreak produced a vast amount of transonic data which more than paid for the original investment, however it was only the first phase of the US Navy's investigation into high speed flight and it was replaced by a much more advanced aircraft, the Douglas D-558-2 Skyrocket, which was to be the first aircraft to reach Mach 2.0.

The acquisition of German data on swept wings at the end of the Second World War led to a rapidly evolving situation which affected the nature of the US Navy's research programme into high speed flight. Originally it had been the intention to build six examples of the D-558-1, however, the last three were cancelled in favour of a new swept wing design. The requirement for a normal take-off was maintained but the primary power source was a rocket motor similar to that used in the XS-1 with a Westinghouse J34 turbojet of 3,000 lb thrust also being installed for take-off and recovery to base. The D-558-2 Skyrocket was an elegant machine with a classically streamlined fuselage and mid-mounted, 35-degree swept wings. The horizontal tail was mounted mid-way up the fin and was swept at 40 degrees so that it was always slightly behind the wing in terms of shock wave development which, it was hoped, would ensure that longitudinal control was maintained at all times.

The first Skyrocket (Bu Aer No 37973) was taken on its maiden flight on 4 February 1948 by Douglas test pilot Johnny Martin on the power of the J35 (at this stage the rocket motor had not been delivered). This showed that performance was marginal on jet power alone and at 5,000 yards, the take-off run was exceedingly long. The problem was addressed by the later use of rocket-assisted take-off gear, the expended bottles being jettisoned by the pilot shortly after take-off. Early testing also showed that the Skyrocket was subject to Dutch roll and this led to the fin being modified with an extension of approximately 18 inches. It was not until early 1949 that the rocket motor was cleared for flight and the first air firing took place on 25 February when Gene May flew the third Skyrocket (Bu Aer No 37975). By the summer of 1949 all three Skyrockets were at Muroc (later to be renamed as Edwards Air Force Base) but it was becoming increasingly apparent that the programme was likely to fall well short of the speed requirements if conventional take-offs were to be continued. The only realistic alternative was to adopt an air-launching system like the XS-1 which would not only allow the deletion of the J34 turbojet, together with its associated fuel tanks, but would also allow more rocket fuel to be carried. This conversion was undertaken on Skyrocket number two (Bu Aer No 37974) and thereafter all flights were from a B-29 mother ship (US Navy designation P2B-1S).

The pilot entrusted with exploring the upper reaches of the Skyrocket's performance was Bill Bridgeman, a Douglas production test pilot who had previously flown with the US Navy. His first air launch was carried out on 8 September 1950 using the third Skyrocket but it was not until the return of the fully modified aircraft (37974) that any significant progress could be made. This was flown for the first time as a pure rocket-powered machine on 26 January 1951 which was just over a year since it had last been in free flight. The test schedule had recently been blighted by a series of aborted missions due to technical problems and at a very late stage on this flight another snag cropped up. Unfortunately the abort call was not heard by the mother ship pilot who continued his count down as normal. This put Bridgeman in an extremely difficult position as he had just a few seconds to reactivate the aircraft's systems before he was released.

The Skyrocket fell away cleanly and each of the four rocket chambers were fired in turn but Bridgeman was not expecting them to last long as his dials showed a low pressure reading. Contrary to expectations the rocket motor continued to operate and a 45-degree climb was maintained to hold the Mach number at 0.85. At the point where the indicated airspeed had dropped to the stalling speed (230 mph IAS) a push-over was commenced to maintain that speed (whilst allowing the Mach number to increase) but it soon became clear that the elevators were completely ineffective as the control wheel could be moved backwards and forwards without having any influence on the aircraft's attitude. This just left the variable-incidence tail for longitudinal control and as

Bridgeman activated the switch he could feel the force on his body relax as he approached a condition of zero 'g'. At this point in the flight the primary instrument was the accelerometer because in order to extract the maximum performance before the fuel ran out it was necessary to control the loadings on the aircraft within very fine limits. As he descended, Bridgeman watched as the indicator of the Machmeter slowly moved round the dial to 1.4 before the chambers of the rocket motor cut in sequence, the effect being as if the aircraft had suddenly run into a brick wall. A mere 14 minutes after being launched the Skyrocket was back on the ground.

Over the coming months the speed envelope was extended further until by 23 June 1951 Mach 1.85 had been reached, although lateral instability that had been apparent at a Mach number as low as 1.4 was by now becoming critical. To obtain higher speeds more altitude was required and the piloting technique was changed so that the transition from climb to descent was made much more quickly so that increased fuel would be available at the most critical part of the flight. Bridgeman began to initiate his descent at 64,000 feet and pegged the accelerometer at 0.25g but had to fight to control the aircraft laterally. The rolling oscillation was extremely violent and was enough to throw him from one side of the cockpit to the other. When it became apparent that it could not be controlled Bridgeman switched off the rocket motor, but such was his speed that even the sudden deceleration was insufficient to stop the unpleasant rolling motion. Only by pulling back on the wheel and climbing could he slow the aircraft down to the point where it came out of the speed range in which it was affected by the lateral instability. The highest speed achieved by Bill Bridgeman was 1.88M achieved on 7 August 1951, the aircraft then being turned over to NACA in whose stewardship the Skyrocket was eventually flown to 2.005M on 20 November 1953 by Scott Crossfield.

Following the success of the original XS-1, the USAF issued a contract to Bell Aircraft for an advanced version to extend the speed range up to and beyond Mach 2.0. Four aircraft were to be built, but in the event only three were to emerge, the X-1A, X-1B and X-1D (the X-1C was to have explored the use of armament and fire control systems at high speed but was abandoned). Compared with the XS-1 the second generation X-1 was a much more refined machine with a completely redesigned fuselage to house increased quantities of rocket fuel. The first aircraft to arrive at Edwards AFB was the X-1D in July 1951 but it was lost on only its second sortie following an attempt by Major Frank Everest to jettison the rocket fuel whilst still attached to the EB-50 carrier. An explosion occurred and shortly after Everest scrambled back into the mother ship the X-1D was released to crash on the lake bed 7,000 feet below. This was the first of four similar accidents that included the third XS-1 (see Chapter Ten) and the cause of the explosions was later put down to the use of Ulmer leather gaskets in the rocket motor.

The X-1A joined the test programme in January 1953 and made its first powered flight on 20 February. It was then returned to the manufacturers for modifications before returning to Edwards to commence high Mach number trials in October. During this period it was flown by Chuck Yeager and on 8 December he took the X-1A to a speed of 1,254 mph (Mach 1.9). Four days later an attempt was made to exceed Mach 2.0 which, although successful, nearly led to Yeager losing his life. Having been launched from the carrier aircraft, Yeager lit three of the rocket chambers and was thrust back into his seat as the X-1A accelerated rapidly. The fourth and last chamber was fired in the climb as the aircraft passed 40,000 feet, and then compressibility buffet announced that the aircraft was about to go super-sonic, even though it was being held in a 55-degree climb. This angle of climb was rather more than the recommended 45 degrees and was caused by strong sunlight preventing Yeager from reading his attitude indicator. As a result the X-1A shot up to an altitude of 80,000 feet before it was levelled off and despite the fact that the rocket motor expired shortly afterwards, the aircraft continued to accelerate as it commenced its descent and was soon above Mach 2.0. This was completely uncharted territory as no one had flown at these speeds before, but as the aircraft hit Mach 2.4 it began to yaw and roll uncontrollably to the left. This was the first instance of 'inertia coupling', a new phenomenon that would lead to a number of accidents before it was fully understood.

Inertia coupling had in fact been predicted by NACA who had warned that the X-1A was likely to go out of control at speeds of Mach 2.4 and above. It generally happened at the extremes of aircraft per-formance and was caused by the trend towards designing longer and heavier fuselages with relatively small wings and tail surfaces in an attempt to improve streamlining and reduce drag. A long, heavy fuse-lage not only places considerable mass in front of and behind the centre of gravity, but increases its lever arm so that a considerable force can be applied, one that aerodynamic surfaces of reduced size may not be able to counteract. The coupling was due to any interaction between pitch, roll and yaw. In Chuck Yeager's case yaw to the left was followed by roll in the same direction, and then complete loss of control. The X-1A had suddenly become divergent on all three control axes and the aircraft tumbled out of the sky with its pilot a helpless passenger. Even though he was tightly strapped in, he was tossed around like a rag doll and his helmet hit the canopy with sufficient force so as to crack the hood. The aircraft was out of control for nearly a minute in which time it fell 50,000 feet. But for its immensely strong airframe which was stressed to

18g, it would undoubtedly have broken up. By the time that it descended through 30,000 feet it was in an upright spin from which Yeager was able to recover to make a normal landing on the lake bed.

Following this incident no further ultra-high-speed flights were made with the X-1A which was limited thereafter to Mach 2.0. It survived until 8 August 1955 when another gasket-related explosion occurred as it was being taken aloft under an EB-29 mother ship. NACA pilot Joseph Walker was fortunate to escape but, like the X-1D, the aircraft eventually had to be released over the Edwards AFB bombing range. Testing was continued with the X-1B until January 1958 but the highest speed achieved by this aircraft was Mach 1.8. The last straight-winged Bell X-Plane was the X-1E which was a rebuild of 46-063, the second XS-1. It featured a completely revised cockpit with ejector seat and a low pressure turbopump for the fuel, but its most significant feature was a wing of only 4 per cent thickness/chord ratio produced by the Stanley Aviation Corporation of Denver run by Robert Stanley who had first flown the Bell XP-59A Airacomet back in 1942. The X-1E proved that such a thin wing was not only technically feasible, but was also adequate from the point of view of stability and control. The highest speed that the X-1E achieved was 1,487 mph (Mach 2.22) on 8 October 1957.

The successor to the straight-winged X-1 series was the swept-wing X-2 which was to have a chequered history. It was designed to explore the region between Mach 2.0 and Mach 3.5, an area in which one of the main problems would be excessive heat build-up due to skin friction. To combat this, the fuselage was constructed largely of K-monal alloy and the wings and tail surfaces were of stainless steel. The rocket motor was a Curtiss-Wright XLR25 which offered variable thrust up to 15,000 lb. This was delivered via two chambers, the upper chamber being capable of delivering 5,000 lb of thrust and the lower 10,000 lb. Although the inception of the X-2 was shortly after the end of the Second World War, the first aircraft was not completed until November 1950 and its first glide flight did not occur until 27 June 1952 when it was flown by Jean Ziegler at Edwards AFB. Further delays were caused by development problems with the XLR-25 rocket motor and the first flight-cleared engine was only delivered in early 1953. The first step towards full flight clearance was a series of flights under an EB-50 mother ship but during a test of the rocket fuel dump system on 12 May 1953 an explosion occurred which killed Ziegler and an observer from the EB-50. The remains of the X-2 fell into Lake Ontario and although badly damaged, the carrier aircraft was able to return to base. This was yet another case of an explosion being caused by the use of Ulmer gaskets at the joints of fuel lines in the rocket motor, although this was only established some time later.

This was a major setback for the X-2 programme which was already over two years behind schedule. By July 1954 the second X-2 was ready to be transported to Edwards AFB for initial testing and the first glide flight was made by Frank Everest on 15 August. Further delays were incurred due to instability on landing which required modifications and the first powered flight did not take place until 11 November 1955. By the summer of 1956 the X-2 was finally beginning to show its potential and on 23 July Everest flew it to a speed of 1,900 mph (2.87M). The flight was not without incident and Everest reported a worrying sensitivity as regards longitudinal control which led to a certain amount of over-controlling. Following an altitude record of 126,000 feet set by Captain Iven Kincheloe on 7 September, the X-2 was next flown by Captain Milburn Apt on 27 September on what would be the aircraft's thirteenth powered flight. The delays to the programme had caused a major headache for the USAF as it was due to hand the aircraft over to NACA shortly and it wanted to get the most from the X-2 before it did so. Consequently there was significant pressure to get the X-2 above Mach 3.0, but when this was added to Apt's relative inexperience (he had not flown any of the previous rocket-powered research aircraft) a potentially serious situation was beginning to develop.

The X-2 was released at an altitude of 31,800 feet and was soon supersonic in the climb to 72,000 feet. Despite his inexperience the flight profile adopted by Apt was close to ideal which meant that the aircraft's performance was as good as it could possibly be. This was continued as he pushed over to begin a brief powered descent at which point the aircraft achieved its maximum speed of 2,094 mph (3.2M). By now the X-2 was rapidly heading for the edge of the range and the rocket motor cut as the last of the fuel was used up. Apt attempted a turn to the left but lost control and the aircraft then became subject to inertia coupling with significant yaw being experienced as well as roll. There was no structural break-up but as the X-2 was still out of control at 40,000 feet, Apt activated the emergency escape system which involved the nose section being detached from the rest of the airframe. This was then slowed by a parachute to allow the pilot to make his escape at lower altitude by using his own parachute. Although the system appeared to have functioned correctly Apt was later found dead lying alongside the wrecked nose section. The canopy had been released and the seat belt removed, but it appeared that this had been done at very low altitude which suggested that Apt had been incapacitated for part of the descent. The accident brought the troubled X-2 programme to a close but its legacy, bought so dearly, was a greater understanding of thermal stresses at high speeds and the problems caused by inertia coupling.

The next aircraft in number sequence (if not in chronology) was the X-3 produced by Douglas. It was designed to explore sustained flight at speeds of Mach 2.0 but in that respect it was to be an abject failure. Various power sources and combinations were evaluated, including turbojet, rocket and ramjet, before the finalised design emerged as a twin-jet. The proposed powerplant was a new engine from Westinghouse, the 24C-10 (later designated J46) of 4,200 lb thrust, or 6,600 lb in reheat, but this hit severe development problems so that the X-3 had to be fitted with the lower powered J34. Of all the early X-Planes, the X-3 looked the most futuristic as it possessed a fuselage of extreme fineness ratio with straight wings of exceptionally low aspect-ratio. It also pioneered the use of titanium as a structural element as this material was lighter than conventional alloys and had excellent heat resistance. The X-3 was flown for the first time by Bill Bridgeman on 20 October 1952 from Edwards AFB but it was immediately apparent that it was hopelessly underpowered. It eventually went supersonic but this was only possible in a dive and the highest speed that it achieved was 811 mph (1.21M).

After its assessment by the USAF the X-3 was handed over to NACA. Its extreme length (66 ft 9 in) and low span (22 ft 8 in) meant that the X-3 was a prime candidate for inertia coupling and this was particularly apparent during a flight on 27 October 1954 that was made by Joseph Walker. A roll to the left produced a sudden nose-up pitch (20 degrees angle of attack) together with a 16 degree sideslip. For a short period the aircraft took over completely but Walker managed to regain control after a few seconds. A second attempt produced an identical reaction which prompted Walker to quit while he was still in one piece and make a quick return to base. The X-3 continued to fly until May 1956 and although it failed to meet the original requirement due to lack of thrust, it performed a useful role in the development of new generation fighter aircraft, in particular the Lockheed F-104 Starfighter.

The X-Plane programme also investigated two designs to come out of Germany at the end of the Second World War and this led to the swept wing, tailless X-4 which was similar in concept to the Me 163 and DH.108, and the variable sweep X-5 which was based on the Messerschmitt P.1101. The X-4 was built by Northrop who had considerable experience with tailless aircraft having been responsible for the all-wing B-35 bomber prototype. It was powered by two Westinghouse J30 turbojets of 1,600 lb thrust and had a wing incorporating 40 degrees sweep at the leading edge with a thickness/chord ratio of 10 per cent. The X-4 was designed to explore the transonic region up to Mach 0.9 or just above and to determine any advantages that a tailless design might have. Two aircraft were built and the first of these was taken on its maiden flight on 16 December 1948. Subsequent testing showed that the aircraft had similar characteristics to the DH.108 in that it was subject to pitching oscillations that commenced at around 0.87M, together with instability in the rolling and yawing planes. Inserts to the split flaps and blocks attached to the elevons to make a blunt trailing edge tended to raise the speed at which the porpoising motion set in to 0.91M and the highest speed achieved by the X-4 was 0.94M.

The X-5 was based on the Messerschmitt P.1101, but whereas the wing of the latter was ground-adjustable between 35–45 degrees, the wing of the X-5 could be altered in flight between 20–60 degrees. Although its basic layout was the same as the P.1101, it was somewhat larger, its fuselage length at 33 ft 4 in being 3 feet longer than the German aircraft. Power came from a single Allison J35 turbojet which gave 4,900 lb thrust. The X-5 was flown for the first time on 20 June 1951 by Jean Ziegler and was joined by a second aircraft the following December. Although it went on to prove the concept of variable wing sweep, the X-5 added little to the knowledge of high speed flight and was only ever flown to a speed of 637 mph (0.95M). It was not the easiest aircraft to fly and was particularly dangerous at the stall where it exhibited instability about all three axes. This led to the second machine (50–1839) being lost in a stall/spin accident on 14 October 1953 which claimed the life of Major Raymond Popson.

In the first ten years of the X-Plane programme speeds had risen from 600 mph to over 2,000 mph and this had a profound effect on the development of combat aircraft for the USAF. Having produced the incomparable F-86 Sabre, North American was keen to build on its success and was soon designing a supersonic replacement. The result was the F-100 Super Sabre which was to hit serious trouble and was to cause a crisis situation for the Air Force. The F-100 had a low-set 45-degree swept wing, together with a low, slab tail and was powered by a Pratt and Whitney J57 of 10,000 lb thrust dry and 14,000 lb (later 16,000 lb) thrust in reheat. It was developed as a matter of priority during the Korean War and the prototype YF-100 was first flown on 25 May 1953 by George Welch who showed his confidence in the aircraft by taking it above Mach 1.0 straight away. The first examples of the F-100A soon followed but compared with the YF, production aircraft were fitted with a fin of reduced height to save weight and reduce drag and a number of aircraft were lost in mysterious circumstances. These included a crash which killed Air Commodore Geoffrey Stephenson who at the time was O.C. of the RAF's Central Fighter Establishment at West Raynham.

One common aspect of all the accidents was that they occurred during high speed flight and on 12 October 1954 George Welch was killed when his aircraft broke up during diving trials. Welch had been working his way up to the very corner of the flight envelope and was attempting a 7½g recovery from a dive at maximum IAS when disaster struck. With

the Super Sabre already in service, and in full production it was impera-
tive that the cause of the accidents be established, and quickly. It was soon
discovered that the aircraft had been lost to the new phenomenon of
inertia coupling and in Welch's case the violent pull-out manoeuvre had
been followed by a sudden yaw to the right which had overstressed the
airframe. The cure was to increase wing span by 2 feet to 38 ft 9 in and to
increase the height of the fin but the disruption led to serious delays
which allowed the MiG-19 to catch up with its American counterpart.

The Super Sabre was not the only USAF fighter programme to have
major problems in the early 1950s as the delta-winged Convair YF-102
was digging its heels in and stubbornly refusing to exceed the speed of
sound in level flight, even though it had the benefit of the most powerful
engine of the day, the Pratt and Whitney J57. Convair had been impressed
by the work of Alexander Lippisch in Germany, in particular his DM-1
glider which was to have led to a ramjet-powered interceptor, the LP-13A
with a 60-degree delta wing and a large triangular fin. The delta shape
offered several advantages over a swept wing as the extended root chord
allowed the wing to be built thicker whilst keeping thickness/chord ratio
acceptably low. It also allowed the wing to be built lighter and reduced
any tendency towards aileron reversal due to wing twist when high loadings were imposed. As this type of wing was entirely new a research
aircraft (the XF-92A) was built and this was first flown on 9 June 1948.
Leading edge sweep was 60 degrees and thickness/chord ratio was 6.5
per cent. It was powered by an Allison J33 centrifugal jet engine and was
used to evaluate the aerodynamic properties of the delta wing at subsonic
speeds.

The definitive interceptor based on the XF-92A was the F-102 which
was to be ordered straight from the drawing board without the normal
testing of prototypes. This proved to be the aircraft's undoing as the first
YF-102 (52-7994) ran into heavy buffet at around 0.93M and could only
be made to fly at supersonic speeds in a full-power dive. Various modifications were attempted which improved the aircraft's handling
characteristics at high subsonic speeds but failed to make it go any faster.
Fortunately for the whole F-102 programme in December 1953 Richard T.
Whitcomb of NACA came up with his area rule theory. This stated that
to avoid excessive wave drag a graph showing the cross-sectional area of
the fuselage, wings and tail assembly should change in a smooth curve
from nose to tail without any sudden variations. In the case of the YF-102
the fuselage was relatively short and the aircraft's cross-section was
anything but smooth in several places, especially at the front end where
the cockpit and air intakes were located.

In view of Whitcomb's new theory it was clear that the F-102 needed
a fair amount of redesigning if it was to meet the performance require-

ments of the USAF. The major alteration was to increase the aircraft's length by 16 feet and streamlined bulges were also added to each side of the rear fuselage next to the jet efflux. With these modifications the F-102 was transformed and it was soon taken to 1.2M in level flight. Although the lengthened fuselage solved one problem it created another as its increased fineness ratio meant that there was a distinct possibility of inertia coupling being experienced during extreme manoeuvring. To guard against this the aircraft's fin area was increased and in view of its rework, which involved nearly 200 modifications, it was referred to thereafter as the F-102A.

Republic Aviation was another noted US fighter manufacturer which was quick to embrace the new technology offered by the jet engine. The straight-winged F-84 Thunderjet was a workhorse for the USAF in Korea but had a limiting Mach number of 0.82 and was quickly followed by a swept wing derivative. This was the F-84F Thunderstreak which was powered by an Armstrong Siddeley Sapphire-derived Wright J65 that produced 7,200 lb thrust. It was flown for the first time on 14 February 1951 but was subsonic in level flight, reaching a speed of 658 mph (0.94M) at 20,000 feet. It was followed by the photo-reconnaissance version, the RF-84F Thunderflash which had marginally inferior performance.

Republic also produced the XF-91 Thunderceptor which became the first combat prototype to exceed the speed of sound in level flight in December 1952. The XF-91 was one of the most radical aircraft of the early 1950s as it possessed an inverse taper wing whereby the chord of the wing-tips was greater than that of the wing roots. The reasoning behind this was to ensure that the wing roots stalled first at high angles of attack so that lateral control was retained and pitch up was avoided. The wing was also extremely advanced in that it had variable-incidence which could be controlled from the cockpit. The engine chosen was a single J47 of 5,200 lb thrust but this was backed up by a four-chamber XLR-11 rocket motor. With all power units operating the XF-91 was capable of a top speed of 1,126 mph (1.7M) at 50,000 feet. Republic went on to design the Mach 2.0-capable F-105 Thunderchief, but mention should be made at this point of another of its projects, the XF-103, if only to prove that American designs could be cancelled as well as British ones!

The XF-103 was the most ambitious fighter programme of the 1950s anywhere in the world as its projected maximum speed was a staggering 2,450 mph (3.7M). It was designed around a novel propulsion system devised by Curtiss-Wright which combined a J67 (Olympus) turbojet with an XJR55 ramjet. Take-off was to have been made using the turbojet with the ramjet taking over later in the flight profile. As the powerplant was 39 feet in length, the fuselage was exceptionally long at 82 feet and comprised a structure of stainless steel and titanium. The wing was a small mid-mounted 60-degree delta and the XF-103 had a low-mounted tail, also of delta configuration. Although a mock up was completed in March 1953, continued development problems with the turbojet/ramjet led to the XF-103 being cancelled in August 1957.

Having produced the first successful American jet fighter, the F-80 Shooting Star, Lockheed went on to produce the F-94 derivative before embarking on the F-104 Starfighter. The design of this aircraft was heavily influenced by the experiences of F-86 Sabre pilots in Korea who were fed up with being bounced from above by MiG-15s with their superior altitude capability. Lockheed allowed no compromises in its quest for maximum performance and built the minimum airframe around the most powerful engine they could find, the General Electric J79 which was rated at 14,800 lb thrust in reheat (the prototype XF-104 was powered by a Wright J65). The F-104's long, slender fuselage had to house virtually everything as a low aspect-ratio straight-wing had been chosen which was made incredibly thin to fly at supersonic speeds. Thickness/chord ratio was 3.36 per cent so that actual wing thickness at the root was a little over 4 inches. The wing also had marked anhedral and the horizontal stabiliser was placed at the top of the fin. Although the J79-powered Starfighter easily met its performance requirements and was capable of speeds in excess of Mach 2.0, the aircraft had a troubled gestation and a number of aircraft (and their pilots) were lost. Several accidents were engine related but the aircraft also showed a tendency to 'deep stall' in which the T-tail was blanketed by the wing at high angles of attack making recovery impossible. In the event the F-104 was not taken up by the USAF but was sold to a number of foreign air forces as a strike fighter with secondary air defence capability.

Like their air force counterparts, the US Navy soon came to rely on jet-powered fighters and attack aircraft. Of the established manufacturers of naval aircraft, Grumman produced the straight-winged F9F-2 Panther and the swept-wing F9F-6 Cougar before coming up with the F11F-1 Tiger which was capable of Mach 1.34 at altitude. McDonnell started off with the XFD-1 (later FH-1) Phantom which was powered by two Westinghouse J30 turbojets, producing a modest 1,600 lb thrust. With a top speed of just under 500 mph the FH-1 showed no improvement over the latest piston-engined fighters and it was quickly followed by the F2H Banshee which was broadly similar in design but was powered by two Westinghouse J34s rated at 3,000 lb thrust. McDonnell's first swept wing aircraft was the F3H Demon but as the design preceded Whitcomb's theory of area rule it was strictly subsonic in level flight. Its successor, the F-4 Phantom II, was to be developed into the West's most important combat aircraft with over 5,000 being built. Powered by two General Electric J79 turbojets with a combined thrust of 34,000 lb in reheat, the F-4 went on to claim a whole host of speed and altitude records including a world speed record of 1,606.51 mph (Mach 2.59) set on 22 November 1961.

Two US Navy fighters that are occasionally overlooked are the Douglas F4D Skyray and the Vought F-8 Crusader, both of which were extremely advanced designs. Ed Heinemann, the Chief Engineer at Douglas, was another to be influenced by the work of Alexander Lippisch, though in the case of the F4D the basic delta shape was subsequently adapted so that it became more of a swept wing with very low aspect ratio and broad chord at the root. The F4D was designed around the Westinghouse J40 but the severe development problems that afflicted this engine led to the prototype being flown with an Allison J35. Any hope of exceeding Mach 1.0 was delayed until the arrival of the J40 with the result that this feat was only achieved in August 1953 at Edwards AFB. Despite its problems the J40 held together long enough to propel an F4D to a new world speed record on 3 October 1953 when Lieutenant Commander James B. Verdin achieved 752.78 mph, but this engine was eventually discarded in favour of the Pratt and Whitney J57 which was capable of delivering a maximum of 16,000 lb. With such power the F4D had remarkable climb performance and on one occasion a Skyray reached 40,000 feet in a little less than 2 minutes. It entered service with the US Navy in April 1956 and the last aircraft were replaced in 1964. But for its engine difficulties the F4D could have beaten both the F-100 and the MiG-19 to become the first supersonic interceptor, in which case it would be much better known today than it is. It was followed by the F5D Skylancer which was a larger and more refined development of the Skyray. This was powered by an uprated J57 of 18,000 lb thrust in reheat and was flown to Mach 1.35, however, it was cancelled in 1956.

Had the F5D been developed it could have rivalled the F-8 Crusader which was first flown on 25 March 1955. Vought had already produced the F7U Cutlass which was built in relatively small numbers for the US Navy. It was a tailless design with a 38-degree swept wing, but with vertical surfaces positioned towards the trailing edge of the wings at their mid point. Power came from two J34 turbojets and the Cutlass was just supersonic in a dive. The F-8 Crusader was conceived in 1953 and was timed to perfection as Vought's designers were able to take advantage of the new area rule theory, in addition to using the J57 engine from the outset instead of the troubled J40. Design innovation abounded on the F-8, in particular the wing which was set high on the fuselage and was of 35 degrees sweep with 5 degrees of anhedral and 5 per cent thickness/chord ratio. Its most ambitious feature, however, was its variable incidence whereby the fuselage remained in a level attitude on landing, thus allowing a good view ahead for the pilot. The F-8 was taken to 1.2M on its first flight and the ultimate variant (the F-8D powered by a

J57-P-20 of 18,000 lb thrust in reheat) was capable of a speed of 1,227 mph (1.86M). Although nearly everything about the F-8 was right from the start, an advanced version, the XF8U-3 Crusader III, was flown on 2 June 1958. With a Pratt and Whitney J75 offering 28,800 lb thrust and various airframe modifications including twin ventral fins to increase directional stability, the XF8U-3 had exceptional performance and could reach (and sustain) a speed of Mach 2.3, but when it came to production orders for the US Navy it lost out to the F-4 Phantom II.

CHAPTER FOURTEEN

Britain Lags Behind

Having given up on the radical Miles M.52 the responsibility for the development of British aircraft capable of transonic flight was returned to the established fighter manufacturers. Perhaps with the possible exception of de Havilland, none of these companies showed the same drive and imagination of their counterparts in the USA and with no real stimulus coming from the customer to match the achievements on the other side of the Atlantic, it would be several years before products of the British aircraft industry could match what the Americans had already done. Although much research data had been secured from Germany, the very diversity of the material obtained, which showed varying configurations and power source (rocket and jet), led to confused thinking, with the result that a number of blind alleys were followed which were both time consuming and expensive. This chapter looks at aircraft that did actually make it into the air, their performance and handling characteristics at the upper end of the speed range and some of the trials and tribulations that afflicted the various programmes.

HAWKER AIRCRAFT

The Hawker company was one of the principal suppliers of fighter aircraft to the RAF, so in view of this fact it might seem surprising that Sydney Camm, its Chief Designer, was rather slow to appreciate the possibilities of the jet engine. Only when it became clear that power levels would soon exceed the latest piston engines did he begin to take a real interest in the new method of propulsion. This conservative attitude was consistent with his previous work, however, as Hawker was not renowned for radical and innovative solutions, rather for a gradual progression of types along a particular design stream. When it became apparent that the jet engine was a practical proposition Camm initially looked at a jet powered version of his latest piston-engined fighter, the Fury. This resulted in the P.1035 powered by a Rolls-Royce B.41 (later Nene) but this was quickly dropped in favour of a completely new design, the P.1040 which was developed into the Sea Hawk for the Royal Navy.

The order for three prototypes was given on 28 May 1946 (six months after the swept wing version of the P-86 was given the go ahead) but the P.1040 was to remain a straight-winged aircraft. It had been difficult enough for certain factions in the Navy to accept a jet-powered fighter in the first place, one with swept wings as well would clearly have been going too far! The first P.1040 (VP401) was flown for the first time on 2 September 1947 but was afflicted initially by severe airframe vibration at certain speeds. The aircraft was powered by a Nene turbojet derated to 4,500 lb thrust, the engine being fed through air intakes on each wing root with the efflux exiting via bi-furcated jet-pipes at the trailing edge where the wing root met the fuselage. After adverse comment from Hawker test pilot Bill Humble, Lieutenant Commander Eric 'Winkle' Brown was asked to assess the P.1040:

There were several marked peculiarities in the behaviour of this aircraft under normal flight conditions, all of which were closely allied to engine handling. Firstly, any increase in RPM set up a resonant vibration in the vertical plane throughout the airframe, and this was accompanied by a peculiar sound effect i.e. a swishing noise alternating with short periods of complete silence. Careful attention to the latter feature suggested that it emanated from well behind the pilot.

These vibrations were all of a fairly mild order and experienced at speeds from 250–300 knots, increasing very slightly in severity the higher the RPM were taken. Conversely, closing the throttle set up directional snaking which increased markedly the larger the drop in RPM. The indicated airspeeds at which these throttle movements were initiated were only over the range 200–300 knots and the resultant vibration and snaking seemed to die out spontaneously when the revs settled down to the new setting chosen, although the rev counter showed they were slow to do this. Further yawing oscillations were felt in medium turns when the aircraft goes round in a series of jerks, as if it tended to skid out of the turn, then nose back into it again. All these characteristics were checked and rechecked and repeated themselves without fail.

The aircraft was climbed to 12,000 feet and with the engine revs at 11,000, pushed gently into a 10 degree dive. All was smooth up to 315 knots when a violent vertical shaking set in which was so severe that all the instruments on the blind flying panel became completely blurred at 325 knots, and fearing structural failure I eased gently out of the dive and all became smooth again very quickly. During the heavy shaking the top of the stick was vibrating rapidly to and fro, but no corresponding motion was being translated to the elevators and I noticed that the bottom of the stick was quite steady. This stick movement was the only sign of a fore-and-aft vibration, everything else seemed visually, and by feel, to be shaking vertically. In case this might be an isolated freak condition I repeated the dive exactly and got identical results. Next I set the revs at 9,500 and from the same height as before nosed into a 20 degree dive, reaching 350 knots perfectly smoothly. A further 30 degree dive was made to 350 knots at 8,000 rpm and again all was perfectly smooth.

The vibration problems were quickly overcome by redesigning the jet efflux to a 'pen-nib' shape in place of the rectangular fairings used previously and at the same time an acorn fairing was fitted to smooth the airflow over the fin/tailplane intersection. The first P.1040 was a very basic aircraft as it featured a manual flight-control system, no airbrake or pressurisation and no aileron trimmer. The later Sea Hawk (WF143, the first production aircraft was taken into the air for its maiden flight on 14 November 1951) was a much more sophisticated aircraft, which also featured a Martin Baker ejection seat in place of the Malcolm type used on the P.1040, a larger tailplane and a wing span extended by 30 inches. For a straight-winged design its high Mach characteristics were relatively good and VP413, the first Sea Hawk prototype, was delivered to Boscombe Down in August 1949 for an intensive series of trials which included an investigation into its behaviour during high speed dives.

It was discovered that compressibility effects first became apparent at 0.79 IMN, a nose-down trim change being noted. The pull force required on the control column varied with increasing Mach number reaching a maximum of 10 lb at 0.84 IMN at which point there was a sudden reversal of trim so that at 0.85 IMN a push force of 20 lb was needed to maintain the desired attitude and prevent speed from decreasing. Varying levels of buffet were experienced during the dives commencing with slight rudder buffet at 0.82 IMN which increased to a maximum at 0.83 IMN when the rudder bar oscillated with an amplitude of about ½ inch, however, this was not considered to be a serious adverse feature. Of more concern was the fact that the ailerons appeared to vibrate as speed was increased to 0.84 IMN. At 0.85 IMN both ailerons were upfloating appreciably and there was severe aileron vibration at a very high frequency so that the trailing edge was blurred. On some occasions the amplitude of this vibration and the amount of upfloat was estimated to be as much as 2–3 inches. The wing tips appeared to the pilot to be twisting and bending vertically and there was considerable airframe buffet. In some dives, however, no aileron vibration occurred up to 0.86 IMN.

At 0.85 IMN the port wing started to drop but could be held up by the application of opposite aileron. By the time that 0.86 IMN had been reached (the maximum Mach number attained) the wing drop had become violent and uncontrollable. On some flights the airframe buffet faded out above 0.85 IMN but usually it persisted and increased in tendency until at 0.86 IMN it was very severe indeed. The increase in positive 'g' brought about during the dive recovery tended to increase buffet levels still further. After the initial investigation of these character-istics it was decided for reasons of safety to discontinue tests above 0.83 IMN as it was thought possible that further flying under these con-ditions of severe buffeting might cause structural damage or even failure.

The ultimate limitation in terms of Mach number for VP413 was thus 0.86 IMN, the point at which uncontrollable wing dropping occurred. Due to the severe aileron vibration which set in at 0.84 IMN it was recom-mended that the aircraft be limited to 0.83 IMN at which speed it was still considered to be a satisfactory gun platform. Although the aileron vibration was largely cured on production Sea Hawks, pilots found it difficult to exceed 0.85 IMN due to the strong nose-up trim change which could not be held, even with full forward stick movement. Below 30,000 feet the compressibility effects were similar to those at higher levels except that at high IAS, the initial nose down trim change was usually less powerful and was offset by the natural nose up trim change of the aircraft as IAS increased. For this reason the later nose up trim change of compressibility was more powerful and could not be held above 0.83 IMN. The Sea Hawk eventually entered Fleet Air Arm service in March 1953 when No.806 Squadron at Brawdy began to re-equip and it was to continue in the fighter/ground attack roles until December 1960.

In keeping with his step-by-step approach, Sydney Camm's next design was the P.1052 to Specification E.38/46. The fuselage and tail unit were virtually identical to the P.1040 but the wing was swept by 35 degrees at the quarter-chord point and thickness/chord ratio was 10 per cent. In fact Hawker had proposed a swept wing design to the Air Ministry and Ministry of Supply in late 1945 but such was the lack of urgency in official circles that E.38/46 was not issued until November 1946. A further six months were then taken up in the submission and acceptance of a tender so that the contract for two prototypes was not received by Hawker until May 1947. In a similar timescale North American had designed and built the XP-86 Sabre and were virtually ready to commence flight testing! The first P.1052 (VX272) was flown for the first time by Squadron Leader T.S. 'Wimpy' Wade at Boscombe Down on 19 November 1948 and was followed into the air by the second prototype (VX279) on 13 April 1949.

VX279 was delivered to A&AEE at Boscombe Down in July 1949 for handling trials in which an assessment was also made of its merits as a fighter. It was considered to be pleasant to fly with high performance and a high useable Mach number of 0.90 which allowed greater freedom of manoeuvre. It was, however, prone to Dutch rolling, although to an extent this could be damped out by the pilot. The P.1052 was flown in mock combat with a Meteor F.4 and although it had a substantial speed advantage, it was to exhibit qualities that were to dog British fighter design for several years to come. As soon as combat was joined it became clear that the elevator control was far too heavy and was lacking in response and effectiveness. Very large fore-and-aft stick movements were required to manoeuvre the aircraft and in steep turns at 4g and above the control column was too far back for ease of control. This, plus the heavy nature of the elevator, made it extremely tiring to hold sustained turns. Little assistance was to be gained by using the elevator trimmer to offset the pilot's effort when manoeuvring as the gearing of the trimmer was too low. This was in complete contrast with the F-86A Sabre which had excellent longitudinal control, a feature that was improved even further with the introduction of the F-86E in July 1950 with its all-flying tail in which the tailplane was the primary control with the elevators being linked so that they moved with the main surface. Overall, A&AEE pilots felt that if the P.1052 had been fitted with a lighter and more responsive elevator it had the makings of a good fighter, although gun aiming was likely to be adversely affected by its directional oscillation.

Interest in the P.1052 had been shown by the Australian Government which was in the market for a swept-wing fighter for the RAAF. In response Hawker proposed a reworked aircraft with all its flying surfaces swept and powered by a Rolls-Royce Tay jet engine of 8,750 lb thrust. As the Tay had been designed to accept reheat a new straight-through jet pipe was incorporated. The new aircraft was designated P.1081 and VX279 was converted as the prototype, making its first flight as such on 19 June 1950. Due to development delays with the Tay, however, it had to be fitted with a Nene for its initial flight trials. It has often been said that a Tay-engined P.1081 could have been in service with the RAF up to two years before the Hunter, however, during testing carried out by the manufacturers a number of undesirable handling characteristics at transonic speeds were noted which would have taken some time to sort out. Some of the P.1081's foibles are illustrated in the following flight report written by 'Wimpy' Wade after a sortie on 20 June 1950:

The aircraft was climbed at 12,000 rpm, 350 kts IAS, with the tailplane set at 3 degrees positive. At this speed there was a push force which produced an acceleration of 2g on releasing the stick. At 275 kts IAS the aircraft was in trim. The push force gradually decreased as fuel was drawn from the rear tank which holds some 25 gallons more than the front tank. At 30,000 feet the aircraft was levelled and at 0.77 IMN there was a slight push force which decreased until the aircraft was in trim at 0.80 IMN. At 0.83 IMN a slight nose-down trim change was experienced, accompanied by the onset of slight compressibility buffet, which increased proportionally until at 0.88 IMN it had assumed moderate proportions.

At between 0.84 – 0.85 IMN a form of Dutch rolling and 'snaking' started, becoming marked at 0.86 and severe at 0.88. This characteristic was considered to be unpleasant and appeared to produce not only a yawing effect, with the characteristic rolling component, but also a longitudinal pitching component, resulting in a general impression being gained of the aircraft being 'balanced on a pin head'. During a brief control assessment at 30,000 feet (0.86 IMN) the ailerons were light and effective up to the highest IMN obtained. The rudder was similarly pleasant, bearing in mind its ineffectiveness at low IAS. The elevator was not in harmony being slightly heavier and not as responsive, there being a lag between applying either positive or negative stick force and obtaining a pitching moment.

A similar run was made at 22,000 feet when a maximum of 0.88 IMN (395 kts IAS) was obtained. There was a similar build up as at 30,000 feet which started at 0.84 IMN. Its characteristics, however, were thought to be somewhat harsher. At 7,000 feet with the tailplane set at 3 degrees positive as previously, speed was gradually increased. The 'snaking' started at 460 kts IAS and developed until at 490 kts IAS (0.84 IMN) it had assumed somewhat vicious characteristics. It was noted that a Rate 1 turn was registered on the turn and bank indicator approximately every two seconds. There appeared to be no high speed buffet similar to that experienced on the P.1052 under similar conditions, but underlying compressibility buffet was felt. At 3,000 feet speed was gradually increased to 500 kts IAS (0.80 IMN) without incident. There was a moderately strong stick force.

Flight testing continued with the P.1081 over the next few months but there was no improvement in the difficulties being experienced by the Tay and the engine was cancelled altogether in November 1950. This proved to be the death knell for the P.1081 as the Australian's were only interested in an aircraft powered by the up-rated Tay and the RAF were extremely indifferent to the project, preferring instead the P.1067 (later

Hunter) which was powered by their preferred engine, the Rolls-Royce Avon. VX279 was delivered to Farnborough in early 1951 to participate in the Royal Aircraft Establishment's programme of transonic research but it was written off in an accident on 3 April 1951 which claimed the life of 'Wimpy' Wade. The subsequent investigation could find no definite cause for the crash although it has been suggested that Wade was carrying out a high speed dive when he got into difficulties and ejected too late. His body was found still strapped to his seat and the aircraft itself crash landed in open country with relatively little damage, the change in CG on the pilot's departure having been sufficient for it to pull out of the dive without any control input.

Although the P.1081 could have been developed into a useful second-generation jet fighter, its ultimate demise was not as damaging to Hawker Aircraft as would have been the case if an alternative had not been at hand. In October 1947 Sydney Camm had proposed the P.1067 to be powered by either a Rolls-Royce AJ.65 (Avon) or Metropolitan-Vickers F.9 (Sapphire). At the time, Specification F.43/46 for a new single-seat day fighter was being circulated but its requirements showed a lack of understanding on the part of the Air Staff as to what was needed and what was technically possible. The arrival of Camm's new design clarified the situation superbly and resulted in a revised Specification (F.3/48) being written around it. Although a nose-mounted air intake and a T-tail (both straight and semi-delta shape) were considered at first, the air intakes were soon moved to the wing roots as had been the case with all previous Hawker jet aircraft, and the high-set tail was abandoned in favour of swept surfaces attached to the fin. The wing had a sweep angle of 40 degrees, a thickness/chord ratio of 8.5 per cent and an aspect ratio of 3.33.

After completion, the prototype P.1067 (WB188) was dismantled at Kingston before being trucked to Boscombe Down where it was flown for the first time on 20 July 1951 by Neville Duke. Early test flying was highly encouraging although a high frequency vibration noted at the rear of the aircraft was eventually traced to the fin/tailplane junction which was soon cured by fitting an acorn-type fairing to smooth the airflow in this region. The second P.1067 (WB195) was first flown on 5 May 1952 by which time the name Hunter had been chosen for the new fighter. The first two prototypes were both fitted with Avon engines and they were joined by the Sapphire-powered WB202 which joined the test programme following its first flight from Dunsfold on 30 November 1952. As the Hunter had been awarded 'super-priority' status as a result of tension created by the Korean War, there was a desire to get the aircraft into RAF service as quickly as possible and consequently a comprehensive series of handling and performance trials were carried out at various test establishments. Before this, Neville Duke took WB188 to a speed in excess of Mach 1.0 on 24 June 1952. This milestone was achieved in a shallow dive from 30,000 feet with recovery by 15,000 feet.

Of all the fighter prototypes and research aircraft produced by Britain in the period immediately after the Second World War the Hunter had the least trouble in the transonic region, although it was not above criticism. During a preliminary handling assessment at Boscombe Down, WB195 was flown to high Mach numbers in both level and diving flight. Level flight tests were carried out at 44,000 feet and the highest speed attained was 0.93 IMN (275 kts IAS). With the aircraft in trim at 0.80 IMN, it was accelerated by increasing engine power and remained in trim until reaching 0.90 IMN when a nose-down trim change was noted which became stronger up to 0.93 IMN. An undamped lateral rocking was experienced which was almost impossible to stop by use of ailerons or rudder and this was occasionally accompanied by a longitudinal pitching motion at 0.91 IMN.

Tests were made to higher Mach numbers by diving at full engine thrust and the highest value attained was a little in excess of 1.0. Dives commenced at 45,000 feet and the peak IMN was reached at about 30,000 feet. The nose-down trim change that had been apparent during the level speed runs was experienced once again but with increase in speed the pull force that was needed to counteract this had to be lessened until at 0.94 IMN the aircraft was in trim again. By about 0.96 IMN a full single-handed push was needed if the Mach number was to be maintained. This led to a technique of trimming into the dive to achieve higher Mach numbers by selecting +2 degrees of tailplane trim and increasing the dive angle from 10–15 degrees to 30 degrees. Acceleration up to 0.98 IMN was fairly rapid and the application of full nose-down tailplane trim (+2½ degrees), together with a moderate push force on the control column, caused the Machmeter to work its way round to 1.0. By increasing the push force the angle of dive was steepened slightly and the indicated Mach number rose to 1.01. Recovery was made by reducing the push force and trimming back during the pull out, whilst at the same time throttling back. On most occasions the aircraft was flying level again on reaching 21,000 ft at about 0.91 IMN.

In a break from the day-to-day job of getting the Hunter ready for the RAF it was decided in 1953 to make an attempt on the World Absolute Speed Record which at the time was currently held by the Americans with a speed of 715.75 mph set by an F-86D Sabre. By this time WB188 (now designated as the Mark 3) had been fitted with a reheated Avon RA.7R offering 9,600 lb of thrust via a two-position fixed nozzle and the aircraft had also been modified with a pointed nose cone. It was finished off in a high-gloss red paint scheme. The course was the same as used by the RAF High Speed Flight's Meteors in 1946 (see Chapter Eight) and the pilot was Neville Duke who once again operated out of Tangmere. The compressibility problems that had plagued Duke's first attempt at the speed record were no longer apparent, although he did have a major fright on 1 September when approaching the timed section at a speed of nearly 700 mph at low level. The port undercarriage leg suddenly extended with a loud bang and the aircraft lurched violently over on to its side producing an acceleration of +6g. Duke managed to regain control and reduce speed, climbing to 10,000 feet to carry out low-speed handling checks and to burn off fuel. On landing the port undercarriage collapsed, however, the damage sustained was not serious and the aircraft was ready for another attempt on the record a week later. This went without a hitch and the record was taken with a speed of 727.63 mph.

Shortly before the Hunter F.1 entered service it was tested by the Central Fighter Establishment (CFE) at West Raynham who found that there was a marked absence of any form of compressibility effects on the wing in the transonic speed range. Unlike a number of other aircraft of the period there was no hint of wing drop at these speeds. It was noted, however, that there was a 1–1½ inch forward movement of the control column at approximately 0.97 IMN with no accompanying change of attitude or trim. A speed of Mach 1.0 could be reached in a very shallow dive using full power but care had to be taken with the elevator control as stick forces were very high above 0.96 IMN and longitudinal control had to be maintained by use of the trimmer. In marked contrast to fore-and-aft control, the ailerons remained light and effective throughout the speed range.

When recovering from a dive care had to be taken with the use of nose-up trim owing to the strong trim reversal which occurred as speed decreased. For a transonic dive it was recommended that the pilot trim the aircraft 1½ degrees nose down either just before, or when rolling into the dive. During recovery it was best to trim the tailplane to zero and use maximum stick force for the remainder of the pull out. Finally, as the aircraft passed through the line of the horizon it was suggested that the aircraft be trimmed from zero to 1½ degrees nose down to counteract the trim reversal as the aircraft left the sonic speed range. If this change of trim was delayed, considerable forward stick had to be applied to counteract a strong noseup tendency which could lead to excessive accelerations. Although the Hunter is generally regarded as a classic, many pilots of the early Marks were critical of the rate of application of the variable incidence tail trimmer and during comparative trials with an F-86 Sabre, the American aircraft's superior longitudinal control as a result of its all-flying tail meant that it was able to retain the initiative over the Hunter in practice interceptions. The Hunter was also prone to pitch up during tight turns at high altitude, although this characteristic was not as severe as that which afflicted the Supermarine Swift.

SUPERMARINE AIRCRAFT

Although it was responsible for the classic Spitfire, Supermarine found it something of a struggle to produce a successful transonic jet fighter to match those being produced by the USA and the Soviet Union. The Type 541 Swift, after a long wait and much perseverance on the part of the RAF, proved to be a dismal failure in its intended role as an interceptor. The evolutionary process at Supermarine was similar to that at Hawker and like that company's P.1040, the first jet-powered aircraft to emerge from the design office at Hursley Park was a straight-winged design powered by a Rolls-Royce Nene for which Specification E.10/44 was formulated. This was to be developed into the Attacker which entered service with No.800 Squadron of the Fleet Air Arm at RNAS Ford on 22 August 1951. It employed the laminar flow wing of the piston-engined Spiteful mated to a new fuselage employing side-mounted air intakes adjacent to the cockpit and a straight-through jet pipe with the efflux well aft of the tailplane. Despite the trend towards tricycle undercarriage, the Attacker incorporated a retractable twin tailwheel arrangement with the wide-track main gear folding inwards into the wings.

The first prototype E.10/44 (TS409) was flown for the first time by Jeffrey Quill from Boscombe Down on 27 July 1946. The Nene engine initially fitted to this aircraft was restricted to 12,000 rpm which produced a thrust of 4,300 lb, but this was soon replaced by a production standard engine in which maximum rpm was 12,440 producing a thrust of 5,000 lb and a top speed of 580 mph at sea level. The next machine off the line was TS413 which was first taken into the air on 17 June 1947 by Mike Lithgow and was fully 'navalised' as the Attacker F.1. Over a two month period commencing in April 1948 TS413 was tested at Boscombe Down, the trial including dives to high Mach numbers. The aircraft was trimmed at 0.70 IMN at 20,000 feet (325 kts IAS and 11,850 rpm) and dived to 17,500 feet by which time it had accelerated to 0.80 IMN. The Attacker exhibited classic transonic characteristics with a small push force being required on the stick to maintain the angle of dive, however, by the time that 0.75 IMN had been reached this had changed to a pull force which had to be increased progressively until at 0.80 IMN a pull of 50–55 lb was needed to hold the aircraft steady. No vibration or porpoising was experienced at high Mach numbers which had the effect of giving no warning of the onset of compressibility during straight dives from altitude. Considerable buffeting was apparent, however, on a number of pull outs at high 'g' at 0.80 IMN. A serious criticism of the Attacker was that the elevator control was extremely heavy at low airspeeds and at high Mach numbers, and the Mach number limitation was considered to be relatively low for a new type of fighter.

The large variation in fore-and-aft stick forces required at transonic speeds was still apparent in early 1950 when TS409 was delivered to Boscombe Down for trials with a 250-gallon ventral fuel tank. The severe nose-down trim change that occurred at high Mach numbers was 'most undesirable' and at 0.81M the pull force was estimated to be 60–65 lb. On recovering without use of the air brakes, very high pull forces were necessary but as speed fell-off the pull quickly disappeared to be replaced by a push force of around 30 lb. This handling deficiency was exacerbated by the heavy elevators, an aspect of the aircraft that was particularly disliked by A&AEE test pilots who, on occasion, were required to move the stick smartly forwards to prevent excessive 'g' forces developing during recoveries. The first production aircraft (WA469) was tested in August 1950 but check handling-trials showed that the elevator heaviness was at least 25 per cent worse than that previously noted with the proto-types. As a result a service limit of 0.78 IMN had to be imposed. The eventual use of a 'flat-sided' elevator brought about some improvement, but the control was still considered to be too heavy when it was tested on TS409 in April 1951. The Attacker went on to give valuable jet experience with the Fleet Air Arm but its time in first-line service was short and it had been replaced by Sea Hawks and Sea Venoms by 1954. In addition it was used by several RNVR squadrons; however, these were disbanded due to defence cuts in 1957.

Following on from the Attacker, Supermarine's next venture into jet-powered flight was rather more adventurous although it was based on a standard Attacker fuselage. The emergence of the radical MiG-15 in the Soviet Union and the F-86 Sabre in the USA caused considerable conster-nation within the Air Ministry in Britain and led to the issue of two specifications (E.38/46 to Hawker and E.41/46 to Supermarine) for single-engined, swept-wing designs. The latter was given the Type number 510, but despite clear evidence that the pace of aircraft develop-ment was beginning to escalate with more powerful engines and advances in aerodynamics, it was to be a full two years before Mike Lithgow first flew the Type 510 (VV106) on 29 December 1948 at Boscombe Down. This was less than two months before the Sabre entered USAF squadron service and one wonders how long it would have taken if the manufacturers had been required to design and build a completely new fuselage as well.

The downside of using an Attacker fuselage was that the tailwheel installation was retained which looked somewhat incongruous in comparison with similar aircraft of the period. In the air at least the Type 510 was impressive enough, having a 40 degree swept symmetrical section wing of 10 per cent thickness/chord ratio and swept horizontal tail surfaces, the first British aircraft to have both features. For most of the initial testing the Type 510 was fitted with a rounded, short nose but it was later fitted with an elongated and pointed nose with nose-mounted pitot head for high speed trials. At the same time that the nose was changed, the aircraft was painted. Within a short period the aircraft had been flown to Mach 0.93, the first time that a Supermarine-built machine had been taken to these speeds since the trials carried out at RAE with a Spitfire XI in 1943/44! It was exhibited at the 1949 SBAC Display at Farnborough before being delivered to A&AEE for a series of handling trials by which time it was being referred to as the Swift.

As had been the case with the Attacker, the elevators were criticised for being too heavy for a potential fighter design. While the control was light enough for small movements, the amount of effort required for larger stick displacements was excessive and became 'tiringly heavy'. The response of the aircraft to elevator movement was sluggish through the speed range and large control movements were required when manoeuvring. In contrast the ailerons were very light at all speeds so that the overall harmonisation was poor. Apart from this major disadvantage, the Type 510 was considered to be fairly easy to fly and was free from some of the troubles that were supposed to inflict aircraft with large angles of sweep-back. In many ways the Type 510 handled better in the transonic region than the Hawker P.1081 as it did not show any tendency towards snaking or Dutch rolling and its delightfully light and crisp ailerons gave it an excellent rate of roll. It did tend to drop a wing uncontrollably on the approach, particularly when landing with a crosswind and the touchdown was not always easy, the tailwheel layout being disliked on a swept-wing aircraft.

During dives to high Mach numbers from 36,000 feet the Type 510 exhibited excellent flying characteristics and, although the trim changes were similar to the Attacker, the amount of effort required on the part of the pilot to hold the desired attitude was much less. The aircraft was trimmed at 0.83 IMN using 12,000 rpm (the elevator trimmer being set slightly nose up). On gaining speed a slight nose-down change of trim occurred at 0.86 IMN and the out of trim pull force increased progressively with Mach number, being 9 lb at 0.89 IMN. By the time that 35,000 feet had been reached in a shallow dive, a pull force of 16 lb was needed to prevent the aircraft from nosing down and at 0.92 IMN the aircraft began to roll to port although this could easily be countered by use of starboard aileron. Although the pull force peaked at 19 lb, on increasing speed to 0.93 IMN this had reduced to only 14 lb. The rolling tendency, however, continued to strengthen with increase in speed so that when 0.94 IMN was reached it could not be checked, even with full opposite aileron. No buffeting was experienced and the recovery was effected by throttling back and pulling up from the dive, the stick force per 'g' being high.

Dive characteristics were also tested at 15,000 feet and 20,000 feet with similar results, although the pull force needed to maintain a steady angle of dive reached a maximum of 28 lb at 0.92 IMN at 15,000 feet. During the latter dive, oscillation and airframe buffet were present but were subsequently traced to a loose door over part of the anti-spin parachute installation. After securing this door no vibration or buffet was noted during subsequent dives. Handling characteristics were also carried out up to the maximum permitted airspeed of 570 kts IAS at low altitude (1,000 feet). This was attempted by commencing a 20 degree dive from 12,000 feet and 350 kts IAS (0.65 IMN) using 11,800 rpm. The aircraft gained speed rather slowly and 540 kts IAS (0.845 IMN) had been reached at 2,500 feet where the nose-down trim change became apparent. Control was fairly comfortable at this speed, though there was a slight tendency for the aircraft to snake, however, it was free from buffet. A heavy stick force was necessary to recover from the dive and it was considered that elevator response was poor, with considerable stick movement per 'g'.

As far as Boscombe Down was concerned the maximum controllable Mach number of the Type 510 was considered to be 'outstanding' and a considerable step forward from the aircraft currently in service with the RAF (Meteor and Vampire). It was, however, handicapped by its wing dropping tendencies which precluded any further advancement until this particular handling problem could be eradicated. The point was made by A&AEE that this appeared to be a universal problem on high subsonic speed aircraft of the period and serious consideration to methods of overcoming it had to be found. It was also felt that the lack of airbrakes on the Type 510, even considering that it was a research aircraft, was regrettable. Although it appeared that Supermarine were on the right lines with the Type 510, the subsequent developments based on this aircraft led to a whole catalogue of problems and the eventual cancellation of the entire Swift programme.

The second aircraft produced to Specification E.41/46 (VV119) was known as the Type 528 and was flown for the first time on 27 March 1950. Not long after it was grounded for three-and-a-half months for extensive modifications which included a completely new nose section, a tricycle undercarriage and a revised rear fuselage to allow the use of reheat. A new wing with increased chord over the inner section and ailerons of reduced span was also incorporated. In its new form VV119 became the Type 535 and it was first flown as such on 23 August 1950. By now the

Korean War was under way and the Type 535 was given 'super-priority' status. Unfortunately this belated action only served to highlight the lethargy of the previous five years brought about by the UK Government's naïve assumption that there would be no more wars for ten years following the end of hostilities in Europe in 1945. Development of the Type 535 was seen as an insurance policy for the Hawker Hunter which was still around four years from squadron service.

The final steps that led to the Swift F.1 were the construction of two production prototypes (WJ960 and WJ965) fitted with a Rolls-Royce Avon turbojet of 7,500 lb thrust which gave 50 per cent more power than the Nene of the Type 535. Even at this late stage these aircraft were not representative of full production machines and their modification state showed how far Britain was behind the USA in terms of the controllability of high speed aircraft. By the end of 1952 both aircraft had yet to be fitted with a variable-incidence tail (this was first flown the following year on VV106 which had become the Type 117) and lateral control was by antiquated spring-tab ailerons, the much more effective geared-tab surfaces still being several months away. Supermarine's Chief Test Pilot Mike Lithgow summed it up in his autobiography *Mach One* (Allan Wingate)as follows: 'Now we are beginning to find that the problems associated with supersonic flight are not so great after all. The right shape, the right controls, and we're there.' Unfortunately the rest of the world had done it all five years before and had already moved on.

WJ965 did at least achieve the distinction of being the first Supermarine-built aircraft to exceed Mach 1.0 in a dive on 26 February 1953 when the assembled workers at Chilbolton were treated to a sonic boom. Although the type was clearly supersonic it was not long before serious handling deficiencies were discovered when two Swift F.1s from the first production batch (WK201 and WK202) were tested by A&AEE at Boscombe Down in early 1954. These aircraft were flown up to 0.99 IMN (>1.00 TMN) in moderately steep dives between 25,000 and 40,000 feet using full throttle. In general the behaviour of the Swift at high Mach numbers was considered to be good, particularly as the trim changes due to Mach number were small and there was very little buffeting. There were, however, three aspects of the aircraft's handling that impaired its capabilities at the upper end of the speed range, these being of such a nature that its operational effectiveness was likely to be severely limited.

A marked reduction in elevator control was noted above 0.90 IMN so that restrictions would have to be imposed for service use on the minimum height needed to pull out from steep dives to avoid flying into the ground or into the tops of cloud layers. It was discovered that at 40,000 feet at 0.90 IMN when the pilot applied full practicable backward stick, only 6–7 degrees of up elevator was available even though the control had 28 degrees of up travel available. There was also serious longitudinal instability above 0.80 IMN prior to the stall, resulting in tightening in turns and pull outs. This was most marked in the region 0.85-0.90 IMN and tended not to occur above this speed only because of the lack of elevator control already noted which meant that the pilot was so limited in the amount of 'g' he could apply that the aircraft did not reach the pitch-up stage. Likewise, below 25,000 feet the 'g' required to reach the point where pitch-up occurred could not be attained due to high stick forces.

The other main handling criticism was very strong wing drop between 0.92-0.94 IMN which required almost full opposite aileron to hold. This was most noticeable when recovering from high Mach number dives when the slow reduction in Mach number between 0.94 and 0.92 IMN as a result of poor elevator control, made the period of wing dropping appear comparatively long. In addition there was a marked wing drop above 0.94 IMN when the airbrakes were extended, the engine was liable to surge at any time and turning performance at altitude was limited to a low value by the onset of buffet. If that were not enough, the Swift also showed a distinct inclination to depart into a spin during fully developed stalls.

During a tactical trial carried out in early 1954 by the Air Fighting Development Squadron, which was part of the CFE at West Raynham, the Swift was assessed as follows:

The Swift Mark 1 accelerates rapidly in a dive from 40,000 feet. At an angle of 30 degrees it quickly reaches 0.96 IMN which is a true Mach number of 1.00. As speed increases, the control column moves progressively aft of the central position and the elevator control becomes less and less effective. Response to the elevator is extremely slow as 0.92 IMN is approached. At speeds above 0.92 IMN the elevator is tactically useless, since with the stick fully back the nose will rise only gradually and the pilot must sit and wait for the response. The elevator effectiveness decreases with increasing altitude as well as with increasing speed.

If the airbrakes are operated above about 0.93 IMN during a dive, a nose down pitch is produced and the dive angle may be increased by 15 to 20 degrees with no trim change. Slight buffeting is felt. At above 0.93 IMN it is doubtful whether the airbrakes are effective. It is felt that under these circumstances their use will not help during the dive recovery phase and is liable to aggravate the situation.

Throughout the dive little trim change is felt and the stick forces are so light that little use need be made of the trimmer. As 1.00 TMN is reached there is a slight tremor on the elevator which might be accompanied by the stick moving slightly fore-and-aft. For recovery the throttle should be closed and the stick held firmly back until the denser air is reached when the elevator feel begins to return. A slight push force may then be necessary in order to prevent the aircraft tightening up of its own accord and stalling from excessive 'g' during the pull out.

In a dive from 40,000 feet during which 1.00 TMN is reached, the aircraft will regain level flight at approximately 25,000 feet. This loss of 15,000 feet is tactically unacceptable. The highest Mach number achieved with a vertical dive at full throttle from 40,000 feet was 1.13 TMN. The aircraft was rolled on its back at 0.80 IMN and pulled through to a vertical dive with full throttle. 1.00 TMN was immediately exceeded. At 25,000 feet with an IAS of 440 knots, the throttle was closed and the pull out was achieved at 17,000 feet. The mean air temperature was -35 degrees C.

Another of the Swift's most serious deficiencies was a basic lack of manoeuvrability above 35,000 feet. In a later trial carried out by the Central Fighter Establishment a Swift FR.5 (which was close to the definitive F.4 interceptor and was powered by a reheated Avon RA.7R) was tested against a Hunter F.6. With the Swift on the Hunter's tail, the latter was able to reverse this situation within one turn, the actual turn radius of the Swift at 0.90 IMN and 40,000 feet being over five miles. It also had an inadequate operational ceiling, a lack of stall warning and poor rearwards visibility. Doubts remained about the aircraft's stall/spin characteristics (two aircraft failed to recovery from intentional spins and one pilot was killed) and there was a serious problem with the powered ailerons which were liable to revert to 'manual' without warning or become locked solid. This led to a fatal accident on 13 May 1954 when Flying Officer Neil Thornton of 56 Squadron was killed when his aircraft (WK208) dived into the ground shortly after take-off from Waterbeach. The RAF persevered with the Swift for twelve months after it entered service with 56 Squadron but the problems proved to be insurmountable and it was withdrawn from use as a fighter in March 1955.

Although there was very little to brighten the gloom at Supermarine the Swift did at least manage to reclaim the World Absolute Speed Record for Britain on 26 September 1953 with a speed of 735.7 mph. The record attempt was made in Libya where high air temperatures could be guaranteed to raise the speed of sound at low level so that compressibility effects could be kept in check. The aircraft used was WK198 and the course that was selected lay adjacent to the Azziza road; some 50 miles to the south-west of Tripoli which was dead straight and represented an excellent course marker in an otherwise featureless desert. Piloted by

Mike Lithgow, WK198 made four runs over the 3 km course at a height of only 100 feet. This was despite the failure of the cockpit cooling system so that Lithgow had to endure intense heat in the cockpit which was a combination of an outside air temperature of 40 degrees C and heat generated as a result of skin friction at high speed. Unfortunately the record was only to last for a few days as it was retaken by the US Navy on 3 October when Lieutenant Commander J.B. Verdin took a Douglas F4D-1 Skyray to a speed of 752.78 mph at Salton Sea, California.

Like several other British fighters which had been designed as high altitude interceptors, the Swift turned out to be rather more at home at low level where its speed was eventually put to good use for tactical photo-reconnaissance, a role in which the aircraft's lack of manoeuvrability was not an issue. If the Swift had been more fortunate it may have had a successor as Supermarine had begun to work on a supersonic development known as the Type 545. With a compound-sweep wing of relatively thin section (8 per cent thickness/chord ratio at the root reducing to 6 per cent at the tips) the Type 545 was powered by a Rolls-Royce Avon RA.14 with 14,500 lb thrust in reheat and the estimated top speed was Mach 1.3. With the Swift in deep trouble, however, and with the world being deemed a slightly safer place following the end of the Korean War, it was no great surprise when the Type 545 was cancelled in 1955, shortly before completion of the first prototype, in an attempt to save money.

GLOSTER AIRCRAFT

Having been one of the jet pioneers with the E.28/39 and the Meteor, Gloster next produced a straight-wing, single-engined design to Specification E.1/44. This aircraft had first been proposed in 1942 with a de Havilland H.1 or H.2 jet engine for which Specification E.5/42 had been drawn up, but continual changes to the requirements and the emergence of the new Rolls-Royce Nene engine led to a somewhat protracted development. It was not until 9 March 1948 that the prototype ((TX145) was flown at Boscombe Down by which time its straight-wing was beginning to look rather archaic compared to the swept wing designs coming out of Hawker and Supermarine. Despite the fact that it showed a fair turn of speed with a maximum of 620 mph at sea level, the design was not proceeded with and the prototypes ended their days as targets on the gunnery ranges at Shoeburyness.

With the Meteor in full scale production, Gloster began to look at a possible replacement and its next major design, the GA.5 (later to be named Javelin), evolved through Specifications F.44/46 and F.4/48 for a two-seat night/all-weather fighter. The configuration that was finally chosen was a pure delta which was heavily influenced by the work of

Lippisch in Germany. The prototype GA.5 (WD804) was flown for the first time on 26 November 1951 and the test programme continued until 29 June 1952 when Chief Test Pilot Bill Waterton experienced a severe case of elevator flutter at high speed:

> The Javelin was to be shown off together with all other new fighter prototypes at CFE, West Raynham, so on the Sunday afternoon before it was due to go I took off from Moreton Valence, the Company's aerodrome just south of Gloucester to check it over. I went towards Oxford, then turned west near Brize Norton to return to base at 3,000 feet. As I was still accelerating past 560 knots IAS there occurred a small, sharp bump followed by extreme, medium amplitude up-and-down vibration, blurred sight, this being accompanied by a buzzing noise like an angry bumble bee. Shortly afterwards (about 2½ seconds) there was a loud crack followed by another which brought a complete cessation of vibration and noise. Both elevators had broken off at the hinges. The corrected speed of the aircraft when this happened was just beyond 680 mph.
>
> I advanced the throttles fully and the nose came up into a slight climb during which time I found that there was slow trim by tailplane movement via the trim wheel and screw jack. I was then able to throttle back and climb to 10,000 feet thinking to bale out over the Bristol Channel where the aircraft would not strike land and cause any damage. I then had second thoughts as the Gloster boffins would never believe me when I reported what had happened, assuming I was still around to be able to tell them. I found I could fly it down to 160 knots without flaps which would have pitched it upwards, perhaps beyond the trim-out capacity. The long east-west runway at Boscombe Down with a clear approach was a good choice. I made a good touchdown at 160 knots, but gusts of wind and runway irregularities tossed the aircraft up (people said it would have cleared a hangar in height) and after 2–3 of these gigantic bounces the port undercarriage leg was driven up from the spar and through the port fuel tank which exploded. The aircraft then pivoted round the port wing tip, skidded off the runway and stopped in a heap, the starboard undercarriage leg having also now collapsed.
>
> So far, not so good, but I was still alive, although jarred and bruised. At least the aircraft had stopped upright, although by now there was some 300 gallons of fuel going up in flames and the port side of the canopy was melting. I had to get out but the canopy appeared to be jammed and the electrics had gone. I was then aware of an explosion as the starboard wing tank went up in flames. Two

young RAF officers had been running towards my blazing wreck but when the starboard tank pooped off they turned about and all I could see were two arses pumping up and down and rapidly disappearing behind the watch tower. I heard myself saying aloud "You poor pair of pricks – you're leaving me here to cook."

As I was trapped I shut off the oxygen, thinking not to encourage fires then realised the future didn't appear too rosy. The Martin Baker ejection seat was propelled by the shell of a 3 inch artillery piece and the heat could cook it off like an overheated breech of a rifle could set off a round. Also at that time Martin Baker seats had no perspex cutters atop them like the later models did. I pushed and bashed away at the canopy overhead; it opened enough to get my fingers into the gap and with much effort the gap became large enough for me to extract myself from the aeroplane. The flames on the starboard side were now much reduced and I was able to get at the recorder panel ahead of the cockpit and retrieve the 'black box'. The next day I flew a Dragon Rapide to West Raynham to see the prototype Swift, Hunter and DH.110 but the Sabre was the most impressive of the lot in flight. Later, a farmer near Witney in Oxfordshire found the elevators from the Javelin – the RAE said that it was flutter at the highest rate ever recorded at 22 cycles per second.

In recognition of his bravery in saving his aircraft and rescuing the data recorder, Bill Waterton was later awarded the George Medal. This was yet another incident which highlighted the perils of flying at high indicated airspeeds at low level but at least on this occasion the outcome was a happy one.

Having been conceived in the late 1940s the Javelin finally made it into service in February 1956 when 46 Squadron received its first aircraft at Odiham. Although the Javelin had been designed as a heavy all-weather fighter it was still capable (just) of achieving supersonic speed, although the early FAW.1 was limited in service to Mach 0.93 above 20,000 feet. Pilots had to be warned that this speed was easily exceeded, however, as a nose-down trim change commenced at about 0.88M which increased until 0.98M had been reached. This nose-down pitch was particularly marked at 0.93–0.94M and if the angle of dive was greater than 10 degrees it was virtually impossible to prevent the speed from increasing to 0.98M. Extending the airbrakes did not help too much, at least not at first, as this also resulted in a small nose-down pitch.

Above 0.95M there was a serious loss of elevator effectiveness and a large increase in elevator forces so that even when using maximum pull force the recovery was slow. On pulling out of the dive as speed dropped below 0.95M the elevator regained its effectiveness and the stick force

· lightened off so that there could be a sharp increase in 'g' if the pull force was not relaxed quickly enough. Slight wing drop was also experienced at about 0.94M although the speed at which this occurred tended to vary from aircraft to aircraft. Airframe buffet normally set in at about 0.92M assuming that the aircraft was not subject to any positive 'g' loadings. In service the Javelin acquired the nickname 'Dragmaster' as any manoeuvre which increased the 'g' loading was likely to induce considerable buffet with a resultant loss of speed. Pilots thus had to 'fine tune' their handling techniques as any reduction in speed could only be regained by picking up speed in a dive.

Later versions of the Javelin featured an 'all-flying' tail which allowed pilots 'legally' to fly at higher speeds. The FAW.4 when flown in the clean configuration had a limit speed of 1.04M above 35,000 feet which was reached in a dive from 45,000 feet. The nose-down trim change was less violent in the FAW.4 than the FAW.1 and tended to set in at higher Mach number (0.95 compared to 0.93) but this became nose-up above 0.98M so that the pilot had to apply a push force if he was to go supersonic. Stick forces were fairly high but the aircraft handled well going into and coming out of the dive. The stick force lightening that became apparent when decelerating through 0.96M could lead to porpoising if the recovery was too rapid. Although the FAW.4 could be pushed further in the dive without infringing flight limitations, its maximum level speed put it firmly in the subsonic bracket as only 0.93M was possible at 40,000 feet.

Throughout its lengthy development period the Javelin had caused some to question its speed potential due to its size and weight. This criticism had already been answered in emphatic fashion by Gloster test pilot Wing Commander R.F. 'Dicky' Martin DFC AFC who 'inadvertently' planted a sonic boom on London during the evening of 4 July 1953. The incident led to questions being asked in the House of Commons and the explanation given was that the pilot's oxygen system had failed while flying at high level so that in the ensuing dive the aircraft had accidentally exceeded Mach 1. Everyone who was 'in the know', however, was of the opinion that it had been done deliberately. Throughout its service career the Javelin continued to raise a few eyebrows when pilots were first introduced to it, one USAF exchange officer being heard to say – 'That airplane is supersonic? Gee it sure says a lot for thrust!'

DE HAVILLAND AIRCRAFT

Following its successful introduction to jet-powered flight with the diminutive Vampire, de Havilland then came up with the Venom which was of similar configuration.

The Goblin engine of the Vampire was quickly superseded by the Ghost which produced around 5,000 lbs thrust thanks to an impellor of increased diameter that allowed a 50 per cent increase in mass flow. Due to the relatively low compressibility threshold of the Vampire, its speed tended to be limited by aerodynamic considerations and so there was little point in a changeover to the more powerful engine. It was clear that for the potential of the Ghost to be fully realised a new aircraft was required and this resulted in the Venom. Although similar in layout to the Vampire, the Venom had very little in common with its predecessor and featured a completely new wing of 10 per cent thickness/chord ratio and 17 degrees 6 minutes sweep on the leading edge which moved the wing's centre of pressure rearwards in response to the Ghost's increased weight. The prototype Venom FB.1 (VV612) was flown for the first time on 2 September 1949 and the type went on to become the RAF's principal fighter-bomber in 2nd Tactical Air Force in Germany.

Initial testing of the Venom showed that progress with engines and airframes had to be matched in other areas as well, particularly operation of the control surfaces. With the higher speeds now regularly being attained, flutter of the ailerons or elevators was becoming an ever more serious problem. Flutter was a type of high frequency vibration which could occur with frightening rapidity and was a product of the flexibility of the cables and rods in the control circuit and inadequate balancing of the surface. In the most severe cases it could develop to such levels that it also affected the main aircraft structure, in which case there was a high risk of failure. In the case of the Venom aileron flutter was experienced at high speed which caused great concern for test pilots John Derry and John Wilson whose job it was to take the aircraft to its limit to discover exactly what was happening. Eventually the problem was eased by careful re-profiling of the ailerons themselves, however this was far from being a complete cure. This would have necessitated the use of fully powered controls which were less prone to flutter as the hydraulic actuating rams provided a virtually inelastic linkage. Derry was one of the first test pilots to speak out on this subject and the Venom FB.4, which was flown for the first time on 29 December 1953, featured hydraulically operated ailerons with artificial feel for improved control at high Mach numbers.

The first trials with the Venom also showed that its critical Mach number was around 0.84 which was a big improvement on the Vampire and was also slightly better than the later Meteors. Although the new wing delayed the onset of compressibility effects, it was still easy for pilots to get into trouble and the Venom was to develop something of a reputation which led to terminal velocity dives being approached with a certain amount of trepidation. To many RAF pilots this became known as the 'death dive'. The term was rather an overstatement as control was invariably regained at lower levels, however, it does convey the fact that the dive was not exactly a pleasant experience. Chris Golds discovered how frightening a high speed dive in the Venom could be during a pairs sortie with his Flight Commander which occurred early in his first tour with No.11 Squadron at Wunstorf in Germany

> I was suddenly called into close battle position and heard the shout for "Buster", i.e. full power and climbing. Gerry [F/L Gerry Eades] had spotted a dogfight to the west of us and was itching to join in. We climbed well above the top of the fight which seemed to have dozens of aeroplanes wheeling round and round and zooming up and down. Gerry took us up to about 45,000 feet to look down and judge his entry dive to a nicety. At last he was satisfied, called "Black section rolling left – Go" and peeled of quickly into his dive. I followed him but had to pull hard to keep up. Too hard in fact and I flicked rapidly to the right. That was something the Venom really could do well – flick! Eventually I sorted myself out at about 40,000 feet by which time I was most definitely on my own.
>
> I looked down and spotted another Venom, about 15,000 feet below me. As I rolled gently over into a dive I could see numerous other aircraft all in a fur-ball well below my quarry. I pulled down my goggles and peered through my gunsight to search for my singleton. I was not conscious of how fast I was going downhill, but a glance at the Mach meter would have shown about 0.86 or 0.87 just as my aircraft rolled uncommanded to the right and the nose tucked under despite my heroic pulling on the stick. She was out of control and nothing I did would affect the plunge.
>
> I throttled to idle and popped the airbrakes but still she plunged earthwards. I had of course exceeded the limiting Mach number for the aeroplane and this was quite plainly stated in Pilot's Notes which I ought to have read! My target whirled up towards me and passed above in a flash. Next I speared through a circling punch-up and as I glanced at my altimeter I saw about 25,000 feet in an unwinding blur. By now I was feeling distinctly un-brave and beginning to think of using the Mk.1 bang seat to escape this death ride [Golds' aircraft was an FB.4 which had an ejector seat unlike the earlier FB.1]. At last as I got down below about 20,000 feet the stick began to have some effect and I pulled out, sweating with fear, at about 12,000 feet, once more entirely on my own. With quite a lot showing on the also brand new g-meter, I decided to go home to await my fate.

On landing back at base Chris Golds had to endure the wrath of his flight commander for leaving him without a wingman and for endangering his aircraft, however, he learned a lesson that he never forgot as the sortie was an object lesson as to what was likely to happen if an aircraft was pushed beyond its limits.

Having proved the swept wing on the DH.108 research aircraft, de Havilland were well placed to respond to RAF and Royal Navy require-ments for a twin-jet, all-weather fighter. This resulted in the DH.110, the design of which was first submitted in March 1947 for consideration in respect of Specification F.44/46 for an RAF night-fighter. In the event RAF interest in de Havilland's proposal began to wane with the rival Gloster GA.5 being favoured instead. The Navy also backed out for a time but luckily the RAF had funded the building of two prototypes in case the GA.5 ran into trouble so that when naval interest was revived the aircraft was still around to be developed into the Sea Vixen which eventually entered Fleet Air Arm squadron service in 1958.

The DH.110 was a big, purposeful-looking aircraft which utilised design features from both the Vampire and DH.108. The horizontal tail unit was housed on twin booms, although in the case of the DH.110 it was mounted on top of upswept vertical fins. The wing was swept 40 degrees at the quarter-chord line and incorporated wing fences on the outer sections to disrupt the spanwise flow of air at high angles of attack. Power was provided by two Rolls-Royce Avon turbojets, the first prototype (WG236) having 6,500 lb thrust RA.3s, whereas the second machine (WG240) was fitted with RA.7s of 7,500 lb thrust. The DH.110 was flown for the first time by de Havilland Chief Test Pilot John Cunningham on 26 September 1951 and was soon into a hectic test schedule that was designed to extend the flight boundaries as quickly as possible. Initial manufacturer's trials showed that the rapid fore-and-aft pitching oscilla-tion of the DH.108 was absent and the aircraft was much more pleasant to fly at high speeds. There was a slight nose-down pitch at high Mach numbers but of more concern was a snaking motion at high speeds which was eventually traced to aeroelasticity or flexing in the twin booms. This was cured in the crudest of ways by riveting reinforcing strips on the exterior surface of each boom to provide extra stiffness (WG240 did not need this draconian measure as the alloy used on its tail booms was of thicker gauge).

On 9 April WG236 was flown to a speed in excess of Mach 1.0 by John Derry to become the first twin-jet aircraft in the world to break the sound barrier, but by the summer the inadequacies of its cable-operated control system was beginning to be noticed with cable stretch restricting full movement of the ailerons at high Mach numbers. It was also found that the servodyne power boosters tended to stall at high speeds. Having been solely responsible for all test flying over the last ten months, WG236 was at last joined by the second prototype (WG240) which was flown for the first time on 25 July. Painted in an all-black colour scheme as befitting its intended role as a night/all-weather fighter, WG240 looked very futuristic and as it had better performance than WG236, being lighter and having more powerful Avon engines, it was selected for the 1952 SBAC display at Farnborough to be held in the first week of September. During a high speed dive in this aircraft on the 5th a loud bang was felt when the airbrakes were deployed and Derry loosened his straps to look back to carry out a visual inspection of the wings. To his horror he saw that they were in flutter which was the first that he knew of the condition as it was not being transmitted through the control column.

By the time of the second public day on Saturday 6 September an increasingly troublesome starboard engine on WG240, which had been running hot for some time, could not be started up and so Derry and his flight observer Anthony Richards were forced to switch to WG236 if they were not to lose their display slot. The sequence of events that followed led to one of the worst disasters at an air display and came to epitomise the dangers that had to be faced by test pilots on a day-to-day basis as it was witnessed by thousands of spectators.

The Farnborough show was the highlight of the year for Britain's aircraft manufacturers who were keen to show off their products to best advantage. The need to secure vital Government contracts from rival firms and obtain orders from foreign air forces put a huge strain on the test pilots who were required to fly their aircraft to the limits of their performance capabilities at low level. There was additional pressure from the spectators themselves who by 1952 had been gripped by lurid newspaper headlines of daring pilots breaking the sound barrier and the Farnborough show of that year was the first real opportunity for the general public to experience the phenomenon of a sonic bang. The feature film *The Sound Barrier*, directed by David Lean and starring Ralph Richardson, Nigel Patrick, John Justin and Ann Todd had just been released and had also been a factor in elevating the real-life test pilots of the day to a status that is the preserve of Formula 1 drivers today. John Derry was a member of a small, elite band of experimental test pilots and had risen to the very top of his profession as a result of his consummate skill as a pilot and his patient, analytical approach to test flying. Although his abilities are undisputed, some have suggested that the occasion might have led to him pushing his aircraft that little bit too far in an endeavour to impress the onlookers on the ground.

With WG240 having gone unserviceable, Derry and Richards had to fly back to Hatfield in the company Dove to prepare WG236 for flight. The air of tension that had inevitably arisen was not helped by the late arrival of the engine starting gear which had been delayed in traffic on its way back from Farnborough. The DH.110 finally got airborne from

Hatfield at 1515 hrs and within a few minutes Derry was positioning the aircraft over Farnborough at 40,000 feet prior to commencing his dive to supersonic speeds. The aiming of a sonic boom at a particular point on the ground is no easy matter as the boom is only heard within a relatively small area of around 2 miles diameter, indeed Derry had missed Farnborough entirely earlier in the week, the bang arriving a few miles away at Blackbushe instead. On this occasion, however, there was to be no mistake and the spectators got what they had come for, a loud triple bang which had its epicentre directly on the airfield. Shortly after, the DH.110 appeared from the direction of Laffan's Plain at a speed of over 700 mph to sweep past the crowd before commencing a long, sweeping left-hand turn to bring the aircraft back over the airfield to begin its display. What happened next has gone down as one of the defining images of the 20th century.

When the DH.110 was in the latter stages of its turn and heading towards the airfield once again spectators were horrified to see several pieces detach from the aircraft before it suddenly reared up and broke apart. Most of the airframe structure fell on the airfield itself, the largest portion, comprising the centre section, inner wings and booms, gliding down to hit the ground at low speed near the boundary. Although Derry had reduced speed after his high speed flypast, he was still flying at around 450 mph at the time the aircraft broke up and this was sufficient to propel the engines in an arc high over Farnborough. One fell in open ground outside the airfield, but the other fell onto a hillside area packed with spectators killing twenty-eight and seriously injuring a further sixty. The cockpit section had been one of the first parts of the aircraft to break away from the main structure and impacted with the ground close to a public enclosure leaving no hope that Derry and Richards could have survived.

As part of the crash investigation numerous witness statements were taken, the majority coming from members of the public which proved to be of little value. However, as Farnborough was the shop window for the British aircraft industry, the crash was also seen by many highly qualified witnesses. Some were to provide extremely accurate assessments of what had happened despite the fact that the break up had occurred in a little over a second. One of those was Wing Commander P.J.H. 'Bull' Halahan, a civil defence officer who had formerly been a pilot in the RAF and had led No.1 Squadron during the Battle of France in May 1940:

> Shortly after it had been announced that the 110 was starting its dive I noticed two white puffs in the sky and focusing my binoculars there I picked up the aircraft. Almost as I did so the aircraft started very gently to come out of the dive, I followed it round with my

glasses as it crossed over the stands and went into a left-hand turn. I followed it through the left-hand circuit and watched it as it increased its rate of turn to the left almost opposite the 10/- enclosure. At that time the aircraft was doing a shallow left-hand diving turn. I saw the aircraft straighten out pointing a little to the left of the 10/- enclosure, the nose rose to the straight and level position and it was at that instant that I saw a stream of bits and pieces flying past the tail boom below it, and to the starboard side of it and also directly underneath it. These bits and pieces were of two colours, black and a lighter colour, they were quite small but there was a considerable number.

I saw at this time a vibration on the wings and the wings themselves, particularly at the trailing edges and near the fuselage, becoming jagged. At this time the sun was shining on the top wing and shades appeared that were not there a second or two before. I estimate that the condition when bits and pieces were leaving the aircraft was a matter of perhaps two seconds. I then saw a puff of smoke at the starboard wing root, the aircraft instantly decelerated and the impression was that a giant had put up a hand and taken a firm hold of the fuselage, this impression of deceleration from a reasonably high speed to a stop was most noticeable.

At the same time I saw three large pieces leave the front of the aircraft, further pieces broke off and the airframe flicked over on to its back. At this point the tail plane, elevators and fins disappeared and the airframe came down like a lift on its back and I noticed three large gaping black holes at the front end. At that point I removed my binoculars and followed the course of the three larger bits which had left the front of the aircraft. One of these was black and looked like a large waste paper basket, this was turning over and over, the middle one I recognised as the cockpit of the aircraft and as I watched it I noticed something breakaway and fall out. The third bit was proceeding in a straight line like a shell, I saw a white ring round the front end of it.

Halahan went on to express his deepest sympathy with those who suffered as a result of the tragic accident, in particular the loss of John Derry who had done so much to ensure the survival of Britain in the event of war. Another high ranking RAF officer to witness the accident was Group Captain G.J. Christopher Paul DFC an extremely experienced pilot who was to become the Managing Editor of *Air Pictorial* magazine:

The DH.110 was first seen as a flash of silver almost simultaneously with the appearance of the three flak-like vapour bursts in the sky which marked its arrival. It was then lost sight of until spotted for a second time still fairly high after passing over the airfield in a southerly direction towards Farnham. Except when out of sight behind trees and buildings it was then continuously in view until breaking up. It appeared at all times to be flying normally. The aircraft was seen turning towards the airfield in a left-hand turn banked at between 45–60 degrees. It was neither gaining nor losing height. It then levelled off abruptly as if to make a run over the airfield from north to south at about 1,000 feet and at that instant broke up. At the point of break up it seemed to be in straight and level unbanked flight, it had not begun to climb. No parts were observed to fall off before that moment.

Those parts which broke away appeared to begin their individual trajectories in the direction in which the aircraft had been moving at the instant of break up, i.e. in level flight; in addition, it was noted that one engine seemed to continue with its fore-and-aft axis still horizontal and initially with an almost flat trajectory. This was the engine which travelled furthest. Simultaneously the mainplane, together with the tailbooms and tail unit appeared to turn violently through 90 degrees so that these parts were presented in planform at right angles to what had been the line of flight with the tail pointing vertically downwards. With the exception of the gap left by those parts of the fuselage which continued in the original direction, the plan silhouette thus presented showed no gaps in the outline of either wing or tail plane. The wing and tail structure although turned violently through 90 degrees did not appear to be thrown upward very much, if at all. No signs of explosion or fire were seen, no unusual noise was heard. At the time of the accident no shock condensation vapour was visible around the aircraft.

Another factor which affected the accuracy of witness statements was the particular vantage point from which the break up was seen. Mr J.W. Newby, who was a member of the Royal Observer Corps from York, was viewing the display from the south side of the airfield and watched through binoculars as the DH.110 flew directly towards him. He was absolutely certain that the starboard wing broke up first, followed by the port wing and then the nacelle. The twin booms and the tailplane were still intact at this point but his attention was quickly drawn to the two engines that were heading in his direction, one of which came down only 30 yards away from where he was standing. The letter that Newby wrote to the accident investigation team, which is preserved in a file at the National Archives along with many others, has had the words 'an accurate report' written along the bottom.

Many other witnesses were, however, of the opinion that the accident was caused by a failure of the tailplane which did detach during the break up, but was not the primary cause. The external strengthening that had been required on the booms of WG236 was a known factor and several onlookers were of the view that the horizontal stabiliser had been flexing during Derry's high speed flypast. The investigation into the crash was to prove once and for all that the initial failure had occurred in the starboard wing and was backed up by a piece of cine film taken by a spectator. At the time Derry was in a 30 degree bank to port and was just beginning to raise the nose for an upward roll. On the film the failure is seen as a distinct blurring of the wing outboard of the boom, but at this stage the tail is clearly still intact. With a significant loss of lift on the right-hand side, the aircraft rolled sharply to starboard, at which point the corresponding section of the port wing also disintegrated. The loss of both outer wing sections meant that the centre of pressure suddenly moved forwards which pitched the nose violently upwards such as to break off the forward fuselage. Only at this stage in the film is the tail section seen to begin to break up as it is hit by debris. The sudden nose-up pitch was so extreme that the centre section was presented to the relative airflow at an angle of 90 degrees, the stresses being so great as to break both engines from their mountings and fling them forwards through a distance of around half a mile. Although many images were taken of the aircraft as it flew back towards the display line, it was only from a piece of cine film that a true understanding of the break-up sequence could be made as the disintegration happened so quickly.

The question as to what caused the wing to fail was to take some time to establish, especially as the wreckage had been spread over a large area. What was left of the DH.110 was collected in a hangar at Farnborough where the accident investigation team sifted through the shattered remains looking for clues. Initial suggestions of flutter were soon discounted and the breakthrough came when compression damage was found on the starboard wing leading edge between ribs 8 and 9. This pointed to a weakness in the wing structure which under a combination of loads that had not been imposed during previous test flights had resulted in a catastrophic break-up of the aircraft. At the time that the wing failed Derry had been initiating a pull up, whilst at the same time banking the aircraft so that both pitch and roll were present. This meant that the wing had been subjected to bending and twisting forces at the same time. As part of the investigation into the crash a wing from a DH.110 was given a structural test at de Havilland to discover its ultimate strength. When subjected to bending loads, as would be applied in a straight pull-up, the wing performed satisfactorily, however, when twisting loads were introduced, as would be the case when the aircraft would be rolling and banking at the same time, it failed at around 4½g, an application of 8½ degrees of up aileron and a speed of 650 knots.

The wing of the DH.110, the main structural element of which comprised a main spar and a reinforced D-nose leading edge, had been built along similar lines to the Vampire and Venom and although it was adequate for these subsonic types, there was a gradual realisation that it was not strong enough to withstand the additional stresses that were imposed at the speeds that the 110 was capable of. It should be emphasised that the wing complied fully with the Air Ministry requirements of the day, but such was the rate of progress in aviation at the time, it was, perhaps, inevitable that a new aircraft, whose construction techniques were based on experience gained with less advanced types, would run into trouble at some point in its development. One thing that did become clear as the investigation progressed was that John Derry was entirely blameless in the tragedy that had occurred as the wing structure was weaker than had been thought, and the fact that the aircraft was being placed in danger during its last rolling pull-up could not have been foreseen by the crew.

In the aftermath of the accident valuable lessons as regards aircraft structures were learnt, but this process was painfully slow as with each advance in performance, a whole new set of problems had to be overcome. As regards the DH.110, the remaining prototype had its wings reinforced including the fitment of a front spar web and thicker wing ribs. It also was to receive an 'all-flying' tail in early 1954, the first British aircraft to be so equipped, and was to play an important role in the development of the Sea Vixen which was used in the interceptor/strike role by the Fleet Air Arm until 1972. Although this aircraft retained the overall configuration of the DH.110, internally it was completely different and was much liked by its crews for its handling qualities and superb reserve of power.

Although it had sponsored the first two prototypes, the RAF had rejected the DH.110 in its quest for a new all-weather fighter even before the Farnborough crash, despite the fact that the favoured GA.5 (Javelin) was also beset by difficulties. A few months later the Gloster aircraft began to exhibit an entirely new phenomenon as a result of its T-tail configuration. This was the deep stall, whereby the tail surfaces were blanketed by the wing at high angles of attack, rendering them ineffective and incapable of effecting a recovery. This led to the death of Peter Lawrence, the deputy Chief Test Pilot at Glosters, who was killed when his aircraft entered a deep stall from which he was unable to recover. Even disregarding this particular shortcoming, which was to lead to the Javelin being restricted in terms of manoeuvres in the vertical plane, had the two aircraft gone head-to-head in a comparative trial, there is little doubt that a fully developed DH.110 would have been the more capable machine.

In terms of technical development Britain was beginning to catch up with the rest of the world by the mid 1950s. The superb Hawker Hunter was just beginning to enter RAF service while Bomber Command was introducing the Vickers Valiant and was eagerly looking forward to the arrival of the Avro Vulcan and Handley Page Victor V-bombers which were capable of cruising at transonic speeds over long distances to deliver conventional or nuclear weapons. The intervening period had been an extremely difficult one, mainly as a result of official reluctance to accept that the world in the immediate post-war years was far from being a safe place. This attitude had led to a mixture of complacency and indecision in equal measure, the latter brought about by the plethora of ideas that had come out of Germany at the end of the Second World War. Among all the confusion, however, there were some individuals deep within the Ministry of Supply who were to sow the seeds that would bring about a reawakening of interest in supersonic flight in Britain and lead to two outstanding designs that were to prove that flight at speeds above Mach 1.0 was not as difficult, or as dangerous, as others had stated.

CHAPTER FIFTEEN

Better Late Than Never

Although Britain had opted out of supersonic research in February 1946, at least there was still dialogue on the subject between the aircraft manufacturers and the Ministry of Supply (MoS) which was ultimately to lead to a complete reversal of policy. A deteriorating political situation in eastern Europe, together with the rapid advances that were being made elsewhere in aircraft performance, especially in terms of speed, brought the sudden realisation that Britain had no choice but to join the new technology race. By the time that the penny dropped, however, eighteen months had been lost and it would be another seven years before Britain was able to produce aircraft that were even remotely comparable in performance terms with the latest products of the USA and the Soviet Union.

The deliberations that took place between the Ministry of Supply and the British aircraft industry resulted in the issue of Experimental Requirement No.103 towards the end of 1947. Orders were eventually placed with Fairey and English Electric for prototype aircraft that were to be capable of supersonic speeds, the main aim being to explore the transonic region of flight. Fairey were well placed to take this work on as they were already involved in an advanced project to develop a vertical take off (VTO) point defence fighter which had as its inspiration the wartime Bachem Ba.349 Natter. This resulted in the FD.1, an extremely compact delta wing design which was intended mainly for Fleet defence. In keeping with the British way of thinking at the time, the principle was at first evaluated by the use of models and it was not until 12 March 1951 that a full-scale aircraft was flown, although by this time interest in VTO had evaporated. The FD.1 was only flown as a conventional aircraft with a wheeled undercarriage and under the power of a Rolls-Royce Derwent jet engine (additional booster rockets had been planned for VTO operation but were never fitted). Its original role having been rejected, the sole FD.1 (VX350) ended its days as an experimental machine investigating delta wing handling characteristics and continued to fly until 6 February 1956 when it was damaged in a landing accident.

The first intimation that Fairey might be about to be involved in high speed flight research came when they were asked by the MoS whether the models they were developing in connection with the VTO project would be able to fly at transonic speeds. The company responded that it would be pointless to conduct experiments on this basis unless it was to provide information for a future supersonic aircraft. This viewpoint struck a chord at the Ministry who presumably now thought that it was quite acceptable for test pilots to risk their lives in the quest to achieve supersonic speeds. Having been suitably encouraged by their discussions with officialdom, Fairey began a design study which would ultimately lead to the FD.2.

At first the shape that was devised by Chief Designer Herbert E. 'Charlie' Chaplin was remarkably similar to that of W.E.W. Petter, his opposite number at English Electric, in that the design possessed a wing of pronounced sweepback with a conventional tail, with thrust coming from two engines fed by a nose intake. This did not find favour with the MoS (perhaps because it mirrored the English Electric design too closely) and Chaplin was informed that a single engine would be preferred. It was a case of back to the drawing board but by this time (1949) Fairey were much more experienced as regards differing configurations and eventually came up with a tailless delta, similar to, but not inspired by that of the FD.1. By the end of the year the design was largely fixed, the airframe being the smallest that could be fitted around the Rolls-Royce RA.5 jet engine, with much effort having been expended in keeping frontal and wetted areas to a minimum to reduce drag. The reduction of weight to the lowest value possible was another design priority and fuel capacity was also limited to the bare essentials.

Now that the MoS were of the opinion that full-scale flight research at transonic speeds was actually necessary, it did not mean that any extra money was likely to be released to make it happen. A contract for two prototype aircraft and a third airframe for static tests was not received by Fairey until October 1950 by which time the Korean War had started. Short term expediency, which manifested itself in Britain with the setting up of the 'super-priority' scheme, resulted in Fairey having to put all its effort into developing the Gannet anti-submarine aircraft so that detail design of the FD.2 did not begin until mid-1952. Even then the FD.2 was not given priority status so it was a creditable performance on the part of the manufacturers to have the first aircraft (WG774) ready for flight testing towards the end of 1954.

Considering the period in which it was conceived the FD.2 was of radical appearance with a delta wing of 60 degrees leading edge sweep and a thickness/chord ratio of only 4 per cent. Fuel was carried in the wings in integral tanks and was of a capacity of 320 gallons. Duplicated power controls were fitted to work the control surfaces on the trailing edge of the wing which comprised inboard elevators and outboard ailerons, together with a conventional fin-mounted rudder. Mass balance weights were not fitted, a first for a British aircraft intended to fly at transonic speeds. By the time of first flight the engine was an RA.14R offering 12,000 lb thrust in reheat and the air intakes were located at the wing roots. The main fuselage aft of the sharply pointed nose was cylindrical and was of the smallest diameter to fit around the RA.14R with a mere 5 inches between the engine and the external surface of the fuse-lage. As the aircraft had a streamlined canopy to reduce drag and would have a relatively high angle of attack on landing, an ingenious scheme was devised to provide an adequate view for the pilot whereby the nose section, including the cockpit, could be lowered hydraulically through 10 degrees.

The FD.2 was flown for the first time on 6 October 1954 from Boscombe Down by Fairey deputy chief test pilot Peter Twiss. Initial impressions were favourable, however, concern had been expressed at the possibility of control flutter which would be particularly hazardous as the powered controls would prevent it being felt by the pilot through the control system. As a result the progression up the Mach scale was taken in increments of around Mach 0.01 so that any flutter that occurred would be picked up by accelerometers fitted to the aircraft, the results of which were assessed at the end of each sortie. By Flight No.14 on 17 November speed had been increased to Mach 0.9 when fuel starvation caused the engine to lose power and Twiss was fortunate to make a forced landing back at Boscombe Down. Due to the fact that it had only been possible to lower the nosewheel, the aircraft was extensively damaged on landing and the test programme was delayed by about nine months. For his courageous decision to risk a forced landing, Twiss later received the Queen's Commendation for Valuable Service in the Air.

During its rebuild, WG774 was fitted with the wings of the structural test airframe and finally took to the air again in August 1955. It was taken to Mach 1.1 in dry thrust on 28 October, the maximum that it could achieve without reheat, although flutter clearance was extended up to Mach 1.2 in a shallow dive. The FD.2 was able to fly to supersonic speeds in level flight with relative ease as it fortunately complied with area rule theory, unlike the Convair YF-102 for which the term 'sound barrier' really did apply. The eventual use of reheat did not allow the luxury of being able to increase speed in small stages, however, no flutter problems were experienced and by November 1955 the FD.2 had reached a speed in excess of 1,000 mph (Mach 1.56). At the time the world speed record was held by the USA in the shape of an F-100C Super Sabre which had been flown to 822.09 mph by Colonel H.A. Hanes on 20 August 1955. With more performance still to come it was clear that the FD.2 would obliterate this particular mark and preparations were begun for an all out assault on the record.

Despite the favourable publicity that would come from a successful attempt, the MoS provided little encouragement or assistance to Fairey. Even Rolls-Royce was lukewarm to the idea as the Avon engine had not been designed to operate at such speeds. It was thus left to the manufacturers themselves to organise (and pay) for the record attempt and this took place on 10 March 1956. By now the rules had been amended by the FAI so that flights could be made at high level and Peter Twiss flew two opposite runs over the same course at 36,000 fet to record an average of 1,132 mph or Mach 1.73. During the timed sections the FD.2 had continued to accelerate but it was limited by its small fuel capacity. Had it possessed more fuel it is quite possible that it would have been able to fly at twice the speed of sound. Having raised the record by the biggest margin ever, Fairey retained it until 12 December 1957 when Major Adrian Drew of the USAF achieved 1,207.34 mph in a McDonnell F-101A Voodoo.

The RAF managed to get its hands on the FD.2 when WG774 was delivered to A&AEE at Boscombe Down in June 1956. It was at this time that the FD.2 was flown by Wing Commander Harold Bird-Wilson AFC DSO DFC who was a former O.C. of the Air Fighting Development Squadron at the Central Fighter Establishment. He was most impressed with the aircraft and described its transonic handling as follows:

I carried out general handling at 36,000 feet. Accelerating without afterburner, the transonic characteristics proved mild. No trim change was noticeable until 0.96M was reached, when a slight nose-down tendency appeared, easily trimmed out. As Mach number increased through 1.0 the nose-down continued, but no extra trim seemed necessary. Without afterburner Mach 1.05 can be reached in level flight. I then selected the afterburner fuel cock switch, then the master switch, and moved the throttle forward past the gate. I felt a thump, and acceleration was outstanding. On Flight 2 I cut in the afterburner at about 0.88M, and in 140 seconds was at Mach 1.57. At an indicated Mach 1.0 at 30,000 feet it was possible to pull 3.5g with only trivial buffet, and at about 0.95M at 37,000 feet over 2g was possible. When decelerating, a significant pitch-up was felt at 0.96M, but with experience this was trimmed out almost automatically. The airbrakes were extended at Mach 1.0 at 30,000 feet, and at 300 kts at 10,000 feet with no noticeable trim change. Lateral control proved crisp and effective throughout.

On 11 October 1956 WG774 was flown to Cazaux near Bordeaux in south-west France for further supersonic testing, as the region offered enough sparsely populated areas so that sonic bangs could be made without causing too much offence. In Britain regulations had recently been introduced whereby flight at supersonic speeds was prohibited over populated areas below 30,000 feet. By the time that it returned to Britain on 15 November WG774 had flown forty-seven supersonic sorties from 30,000 feet down to a height of only 2,500 feet. It was at Cazaux that Marcel Dassault was able to have a close look at the FD.2 for the first time. There had been contact between Dassualt and Fairey during the development of the delta-winged Mirage I lightweight fighter but the choice of a single powerful turbojet for the FD.2 was to have a considerable influence on the French company which went on to produce the highly successful Mirage III series of fighters powered by the SNECMA Atar, the French equivalent of the British Avon.

The outward flight from Bedford to Cazaux was via Bretigny and was made at a cruising speed of Mach 0.93 but it proved to be quite tiring for Peter Twiss as continual lateral corrections were needed to prevent the aircraft from rolling. This was due to a characteristic of the spring feel system in the powered controls which meant that it was virtually impossible to fly the aircraft accurately. Once established in France the weather conditions and the terrain were found to be ideal and the first test flight was carried out on 15 October. A particular transonic characteristic of the FD.2 was noticed during the testing period from Cazaux. This was a continuous oscillation that felt to the pilot as though it was general buffet. It was most marked on the fin accelerometer pick up and had amplitude of about 16 cycles per second. It was also very critical to Mach number and appeared at an IMN of 0.96, but was not present at 0.01 IMN above or below this particular value. The amplitude became more marked with increasing indicated airspeed as altitude was reduced below 20,000 feet. Although it was not serious enough to be a major concern, a technique was evolved in which the aircraft was accelerated past 0.96 IMN with the minimum of delay. It was considered that this condition had probably been present during the test flying carried out in the UK, but that it had been put down to the effects of slight turbulence. The conditions over France were much smoother so that it could be seen for what it really was.

The fact that the FD.2 was able to be flown supersonically at much lower altitudes than had been possible in Britain highlighted some differences in its transonic handling characteristics. As indicated airspeed was increased the longitudinal trim change that occurred at approximately 0.95M became much more marked. During a rapid acceleration with reheat the nose-down pitch was severe and the resulting negative 'g' was sufficient to starve momentarily the fuel supply to the reheat system. This resulted in an immediate cancellation of reheat. Where the acceleration was made more slowly, the change of trim could be held and trimmed out. When decelerating below 0.97M, if no correcting action was taken, a nose-up trim change of up to +4g was experienced. This was most uncomfortable from the pilot's point of view and any attempt at correction could easily lead to a pilot induced oscillation. On several occasions a quite noticeable nose-up pitch occurred before the trim change noted above and occurred at 0.95 to 0.96M. This characteristic was more noticeable at high EAS. The main nose-up trim change was considered to be the FD.2's most unpleasant handling feature. Should the trim change occur when the aircraft was in a turn, or if 'g' was applied when decelerating below 0.97M, the increase in 'g' was sufficient for it to be momentarily overstressed.

Prior to the test flights carried out at Cazaux, the elevator and aileron gear change mechanism had been separated, which made it possible for the pilot to vary either throughout its entire range. In respect of the elevator gearing it was found that the optimum setting was 1¼ : 1 for take-off and landing, 3½ : 1 when subsonic above 300 kts, and 1½ : 1 when supersonic up to 45,000 feet. During low altitude manoeuvring at high EAS, an elevator gearing of 3½ to 4 : 1 was best when flying at indicated airspeeds above 500 knots and turns of up to 4g were made at 0.9M at 2–3,000 feet. There was, however, still a tendency for a pilot induced oscillation to commence during small corrective stick movements. This was only stopped by releasing the control column. The oscillation was most apparent when correcting for the transonic trim change at high EAS, particularly when a rapid acceleration was made.

Manoeuvring at supersonic speeds was limited throughout by elevator jack stalling. The maximum 'g' which could be applied reduced from around 3g at 20,000 feet and 1.3M to 0.75g at 3,500 feet and 1.05M. No buffet or instability was experienced during these supersonic manoeuvres. Rapid stick deflections were made to produce a pitch of 0.75 to 1g at various supersonic Mach numbers however the damping proved to be very positive with steady flight being resumed in a maximum of three cycles. Rolling performance was good up to the highest EAS/Mach number combination attempted. A few 360 degree rolls were made to obtain an accurate assessment of the rates of roll at both subsonic and supersonic speeds. A rate of 250 degrees per second was attained during some high subsonic rolls and it was noticed that the rates of roll per degree of aileron available at high subsonic speeds were noticeably higher than at an equivalent EAS supersonically. Although to the pilot there appeared to be no evidence of yaw developing during these rolls, the auto observer showed a rapid build up in the rate of yaw, particularly in the region around 0.9M.

During the trial the opportunity was taken to investigate an apparent instability which had been seen during examination of the trim curves. In theory, when accelerating from a condition of low Mach number/EAS to one of high Mach number/EAS a pull force would be needed on the control column to prevent the dive from steepening. An attempt was made to simulate this condition which was ultimately unsuccessful. The aircraft was trimmed at 1.1M at 40,000 feet and then put into a 20–25 degree dive with reheat selected. This was maintained until a Mach number of 1.45 had been reached at an altitude of 25,000 feet but this particular flight profile was insufficient to cause any change in the normal handling characteristics. One thing that was noticeable however, was the lack of available elevator jack effort to apply the 'g' that was needed to pull out of the dive.

The flying technique adopted during the Cazaux trials was to climb the aircraft northwards towards the south of the Gironde. The medium altitude runs (20,000 feet and above) required an acceleration distance of some thirty miles which was well out of reliable radar range. At the lower altitudes it was possible to remain within radar cover during the whole flight. Speed was stabilised as soon as possible at the predetermined Mach number. At the lower Mach numbers this involved short bursts of reheat followed by a period of coasting. The ability to select reheat at intermediate rpm was of great benefit. Supersonic runs were made from 30,000 feet down to 15,000 feet at 5,000 feet intervals, and from 15,000 feet down to 3,500 feet at intervals of 2,500 feet. An assessment was made of the spread of the sonic bangs and it was found that at 25,000 feet (1.5M) the bang was heard distinctly, if not loudly, over a wide area. As height was reduced the spread became less and at 5,000 feet (1.125M) the bang varied in intensity, but in some areas was not heard at all. Those who did experience the bang reported that it could be felt as well as heard.

Although the FD.2 was very much a research machine the delta wing layout had the potential to be developed into a formidable fighter. Fairey then proposed the ER.103/C which was a development of the ER.103/B, that was, in turn, a modification of the FD.2. The ER.103/C would have had wings of 50 per cent greater area for better turning performance, a single de Havilland Gyron engine and increased fuel capacity. Top speed would have been around Mach 2.26. In the event this proposal was overtaken by a more advanced two-seat design which was intended to conform with Specification F.155T. This would have resulted in a much larger aircraft with an all-up weight of around 30,000 lb and powered by a reheated Gyron and two Spectre Junior rocket motors. Performance calculations predicted a maximum speed of Mach 2.5 at 60,000 feet and with both rocket motors in use the F.155T should have been able to reach an altitude of 90,000 feet. All of this development work was to come to nothing with the publication of the Sandys White Paper in April 1957 so that the only real beneficiary of the FD.2 was Marcel Dassault. A comparison of the planforms of the Mirage III and the FD.2 shows how similar the two aircraft were and the fact that the Mirage went on to be one of the world's best selling warplanes, and was to spawn a whole series of derivatives, shows what damage was caused to the UK aviation industry by the deluded thinking of certain politicians, aided and abetted by several high-ranking RAF officers who should have known better.

The other aircraft to be developed as a result of ER.103 did actually manage to survive to see operational use but it did so by the skin of its teeth and was not developed to anywhere near its potential due to the blinkered thinking of the time which considered that it would be the RAF's last interceptor fighter and as such there would be nothing to gain by spending any money on it. This was the Lightning, a development of the English Electric P.1A which was created by a new forward-looking design team based at Preston and headed by W.E.W. 'Teddy' Petter who had joined English Electric as Chief Engineer in July 1944. Following consultations with the MoS, Petter began to look at the ER.103 proposal in mid 1948 and he immediately decided upon a twin-engined design to provide sufficient power. Right from the beginning the two engines were arranged in the fuselage as a vertical pair but they were staggered so that frontal area was less than might otherwise be expected from this layout. Having initially considered separate air intakes positioned above and below the fuselage, a simple nose intake was soon chosen which was to remain during the design evolution. By this time the advantages of a swept wing were clearly understood and the initial schemes that were drawn up show a mid-mounted wing of 45 degrees sweep and minimal taper. The vertical tail was sharply raked, and at its top was a horizontal stabiliser of almost delta planform.

By early 1949 the design had changed to the extent that wing sweep had increased to 60 degrees and the tail had been lowered to a position at the base of the fin. At this stage the leading edge of the wing extended almost to the nose of the aircraft in a similar way to the chines of the General Dynamics F-16 of the 1970s but this was later discarded for a leading edge of constant sweep. By now the ultimate shape of the P.1A was nearly decided upon, the last major design change being the positioning of the slab tail at the bottom of the fuselage. This resulted in a serious disagreement with the RAE who favoured a high set tail as they thought that a low tail would lead to problems of pitch up during manoeuvring. It is one of the ironies of British defence procurement in the 1950s that in a period of supposed economies, sufficient funds were forthcoming to pay for the construction of the Shorts SB.5, an aircraft whose main purpose was to prove that RAE were right and English Electric were wrong.

The SB.5 looked similar to the P.1A in overall layout, but its wings could be adjusted on the ground to give sweep angles of 50, 60 and 69 degrees and its horizontal stabiliser could be moved between the high T-tail position as recommended by RAE, and the low position as chosen by English Electric. It was powered by a Rolls-Royce Derwent engine which limited it to the low speed regime but this did not matter a great deal as it had been designed solely to provide definitive answers as regards the aircraft's longitudinal handling. Unfortunately in the UK nothing happens quickly and it took nearly as long to build the SB.5 as it did the P.1A. The aircraft was only flown for the first time on 2 December 1952, by which time the design of the P.1A had been fixed and the first aircraft was under construction. It was fortunate therefore that it showed that English Electric had been right all along and that the position low down on the fuselage was the ideal location for the horizontal tail. In fairness, the SB.5 did make some contribution towards the P.1A, in particular the chord-wise notches which were developed to inhibit the flow of air towards the wing tips at high angles of attack.

Following the departure of 'Teddy' Petter to Folland Aircraft in February 1950, the detail design of the P.1A became the responsibility of F.W. Page who took over as Chief Designer. Under his guidance the P.1A took shape and was complete by May 1954. It was powered by two Armstrong Siddeley Sapphire Sa.5 turbojets of 8,100 lb thrust each. As all-up weight was around 27,000 lb, the P.1A had an excellent power to weight ratio for the period and much was expected of it. Like many other British fighter prototypes of the time, the P.1A was transported to Boscombe Down for its first flight which was successfully undertaken by Roland Beamont, English Electric's Chief Test Pilot on 4 August 1954. On only its third flight on 11 August the P.1A exceeded the speed of sound in level flight to become the first British aircraft to do so [it was not the first European aircraft to achieve this mark as it was beaten by the tiny French Gerfaut which had been flown supersonically eight days before].

Manufacturers' testing continued back at Warton and by March 1955 the P.1A was returned to Boscombe Down for a preview assessment by A&AEE test pilots. At the time that it was received it had flown 49½ hours in 76 sorties but was still subject to fairly severe limitations as the maximum Mach number was restricted to 1.15 TMN and airspeed to 480 kts IAS. Even so a useful evaluation was possible, the performance potential being extremely impressive with an altitude of 40,000 feet being reached only 4 minutes after brake release. Transonic handling was extremely good and a level speed of 1.00 TMN was easily attainable at the same altitude. Like the FD.2, the shape of the P.1A more-or-less conformed to area rule theory even though its design had already been decided about four years before Whitcomb's findings were released.

A more comprehensive test was carried out by A&AEE on the P.1A in November 1955 by which time the test speed limits had risen to 1.3 TMN and 600 kts IAS. The aircraft was found to be easy to trim and very pleasant to fly throughout the whole of the speed range. As speed was increased to 0.97M there was a slight nose-down trim change until 1.0M was reached. Thereafter the trim change returned to normal and there was a progressive nose-up trim change with increasing speed up to the limit of 1.3M. Recovery from high speeds was smooth but there was a slight pitch up at 0.97M, although the normal acceleration recorded was no more than ½g. There was no sensation whatsoever of exceeding the speed of sound and because of this it was considered that 'inadvertent' sonic bangs would be commonplace with the P.1A and its descendants. The full assessment of the P.1A's transonic handling was as follows:

Up to 0.94M the handling was normal, the ailerons were responsive and very effective, the tailplane was effective but had a lower than expected response, the rudder was sufficiently responsive and effective although only small amounts of sideslip could be applied due to the heavy foot forces. Between 0.94-0.97M the lateral control remained satisfactory but the longitudinal control was somewhat touchy. This characteristic was noticeable when small amounts of 'g' were applied or when re-trimming to counteract the slight nose-down trim change which occurs during this range of Mach numbers. It was manifest as over-controlling which was of a mild degree, but might make accurate (gun) aiming difficult. Slightly heavier stick forces over this range might improve matters. A small amount of buffet was apparent on occasions around these Mach numbers but it was not consistent and its magnitude was small enough to be disregarded. Above 0.97M the longitudinal sensitivity decreased and control became much more pleasant and accurate flying became easy once more. The nose down change of trim required about 1 degree of tailplane to trim out, but the stick forces were light and the trim setting was not critical.

Flight at supersonic Mach numbers was restricted to gentle manoeuvres using not more than one third aileron and a maximum 'g' of 3. The maximum Mach number achieved was 1.28 indicated in an estimated 30 degree dive at full throttle from 40,000 feet, the maximum IMN being reached between 25,000 and 30,000 feet. The aircraft was very pleasant to fly up to the permitted limits, the ailerons being responsive and effective and giving an adequate rate of roll for the amount of aileron angle used. The tailplane response was as usual i.e. a little sluggish but adequate and there was ample effectiveness for 3g. The rudder forces were very heavy, permitting only a small amount of pedal movement and having negligible effect on the aircraft. The stick forces were satisfactory up to 3g but it is thought that they may be rather heavy for higher values of 'g'. It remains to be seen just what 'g' will eventually be attainable and also what the drag penalties will be. It may be found inadvisable to use 'g' much in excess of 3, in which case the present stick forces would be satisfactory.

The limiting IAS of 600 kts was reached at various Mach numbers and altitudes. The handling at supersonic Mach numbers was as above. At subsonic Mach numbers 600 kts was reached with about 8,000 rpm. Acceleration to this figure was rapid and once reached was slow to reduce, even when throttled well back. The ailerons were responsive and very effective without being over sensitive. The tailplane response was less sluggish than at lower speeds but could still not be described as crisp, although this was not found to be any disadvantage. The tailplane was very effective and the control forces were pleasantly light. The 'g' restriction of 3 over 500 kts was reached with light stick forces and could easily be exceeded but it was considered unlikely that heavier stick forces will be necessary bearing in mind that the design limitation is 7g. The foot forces were heavy and the small amount of rudder available produced an equally small amount of sideslip. At 400 kts IAS at 2,000 feet a slight buffet commenced at 4g and a distinct feeling of lightening was apparent. There was no actual pitch up but some degree of stick force lightening was definitely felt.

An attempt was made to investigate the buffet and manoeuvre boundaries as far as the limits would allow in the usual manner, that is by increasing the rate of turn while keeping the Mach number constant. Due to the rapid and considerable drag rise associated with 'g' no satisfactory results were obtained as it was not found possible to steepen the spiral sufficiently rapidly to maintain the Mach number. It was noticed, however, that the low buffet boundary which was a previous feature of the aircraft had been much improved [this was due to the fact that the width of the leading edge notches had been reduced in size since the first preview]. No buffet could be appreciated above the normal engine vibration at 1.00 IMN and 4g, and no buffet was experienced in 3g turns in excess of 1.00 IMN.

The conclusions drawn by A&AEE pilots on the P.1A were extremely favourable which augured well for the production Lightning. The aircraft's transonic handling was particularly praised and they thought it commendable that the 'peculiarities' associated with compressibility had been confined to a relatively narrow band of flight speeds. To extend the speed range further a rudimentary fixed-nozzle reheat system was employed which raised the thrust of each engine to around 9,200 lb. This was first tested in January 1956 and the Mach number was soon increased up to a maximum of 1.53M by which time directional stability was becoming marginal due to inadequate fin area.

With the P.1A having reached the limit of its performance, the remainder of the flight envelope was investigated by the P.1B which looked much more like the definitive Lightning with a circular nose intake and fixed centrebody, together with a large bubble canopy that blended into a fuselage spine that was used to house various ancillaries. The major advance, however, was the replacement of the Sapphire engines with two Rolls-Royce Avon RA24Rs with a combined thrust in reheat of nearly 30,000 lb, together with revised jet pipes and reheat nozzles. With over 50 per cent more power, the P.1B was capable of Mach 2 performance and it became the first British aircraft to fly at this speed in level flight on 25 November 1958. Its handling at these speeds was exemplary and it could even be flown at Mach 2.0 with the autostabilisers switched off which showed just how much progress the aviation industry had made since the end of the Second World War. The first production Lightning was delivered to the RAF in 1960 when No.74 Squadron began to re-equip at its base at Coltsihall near Norwich and the type was to remain in service until 1988.

With the arrival of the Lightning in Fighter Command the RAF once again possessed a state-of-the-art interceptor, which was something of a miracle considering the level of official intervention over the previous fifteen years which had only served to compound the technical problems faced by the British aviation industry in achieving supersonic flight. To restore parity with the rest of the world Britain had been forced to skip a whole generation of aircraft and jump straight from subsonic speeds to Mach 2, a hugely difficult task, and it is to the eternal credit of the industry that it was able to do this. Even then the politicians of the day still managed to do a disservice to Britain by coming to the conclusion that interceptors were about to become the dinosaurs of the aviation world and would be completely replaced by 'cheap' (that word again) missile systems. As a result the technical brilliance of the FD.2 was completely wasted (except by the French) and the Lightning was not developed to anything like its full potential. With Britain having opted out for a second time it was no great surprise when all the major orders for supersonic fighters from the air forces of the free world were won by the USA and France.

Glossary

A&AEE – Aeroplane and Armament Experimental Establishment
AFC – Air Force Cross
AFDU – Air Fighting Development Unit
AFS – Advanced Flying School
BAC – British Air Commission
CG – Centre of Gravity
CFE – Central Fighter Establishment
CTP – Chief Test Pilot
CP – Centre of Pressure
DFC – Distinguished Flying Cross
DFM – Distinguished Flying Medal
DFS – *Deutsches Forschungsinstitut fur Segelflug*
DSO – Distinguished Service Order
EAS – Equivalent Airspeed
ETPS – Empire Test Pilots School
FAW – Fighter All-Weather
FS – Fully Supercharged
IAS – Indicated Airspeed
IMN – Indicated Mach Number
kts – Knots
MB – Millibars (air pressure)
M_{crit} – Critical Mach Number
MS – Moderately Supercharged
NAA – North American Aviation
NACA – National Advisory Committee for Aeronautics
OKL – German High Command
SBAC – Society of British Aircraft Constructors
RAE – Royal Aircraft Establishment
RFC – Royal Flying Corps
RNAS – Royal Naval Air Station
RNVR – Royal Naval Volunteer Reserve
RPM – Revolutions Per Minute

TAS – True Airspeed
T/C Ratio – Thickness/Chord Ratio
TMN – True Mach Number
USAAF – US Army Air Force
VTO – Vertical Take Off

Bibliography

Barker, Ralph, *The Schneider Trophy Racers* (Airlife Publishing, 1981)

Beamont, Roland, *Testing Years* (Ian Allan, 1980)

Bridgeman, William, *The Lonely Sky* (Cassell, 1956)

Brown, D.L., *Miles Aircraft since 1925* (Putnam, 1970)

Bullen, Annie and Rivas, Brian, *John Derry* (William Kimber, 1982)

Buttler, Tony, *British Secret Projects – Jet Fighters since 1950* (Midland Counties Publishing, 2000)

Caygill, Peter, *Jet Jockeys – Flying The RAF's First Jet Fighters* (Airlife Publishing, 2002)

Caygill, Peter, *Lightning from the Cockpit* (Pen and Sword, 2004)

Duke, Neville, *Test Pilot* (Allan Wingate, 1953)

Duke, Neville and Lanchberry, Edward, *Sound Barrier* (Cassell, 1953)

Foxworth, Thomas G., *The Speed Seekers* (Haynes Publishing, 1989)

Golley, John, *Whittle, The True Story* (Airlife Publishing, 1987)

Gunston, Bill, *Faster Than Sound – The Story of Supersonic Flight* (PSL, 1992)

Gunston, Bill, *The Development of Jet and Turbine Aero Engines* (PSL, 2002)

Hallion, R.P., *Supersonic Flight – Breaking The Sound Barrier and Beyond – The Story of the Bell X-1 and the Douglas D-558* (Brassey's, 1997)

Jackson, Robert, *Combat Aircraft Prototypes since 1945* (Airlife Publishing, 1985)

Jarrett, Philip (Ed), *Faster, Further, Higher* (Putnam, 2002)

Jones, Barry, *British Experimental Turbojet Aircraft* (Crowood Press, 2003)

Libis, Scott, *Skystreak, Skyrocket and Stiletto – Douglas High-Speed X-Planes* (Speciality Press, 2005)

Lithgow, Mike, *Mach One* (Allan Wingate, 1954)

Matthews, H., *DH.108* (HSM Publications, 1996)

Miller, Jay, *The X-Planes X-1 to X-45* (Midland Publishing, 2005)

Rotundo, L., *Into The Unknown – The X-1 Story* (Smithsonian Institution Press, 1994)

Schick, Walter and Meyer, Ingolf, *Luftwaffe Secret Projects – Fighters 1939–1945* (Midland Counties Publishing, 1997)

Sweetman, Bill, *High Speed Flight* (Jane's Publishing, 1983)

Thomas, Lowell and Jablonski, Edward, *Bomber Commander – The Life of James H. Doolittle* (Sidgwick and Jackson, 1977)

Twiss, Peter, *Faster than the Sun* (Grub Street, 2000)

Waterton, W.A., *The Quick and the Dead*, (Frederick Muller, 1956)

Wood, Derek, *Project Cancelled – British Aircraft That Never Flew* (Macdonald and Jane's, 1975)

Yeager, General Chuck and Janos, Leo, *Yeager* (Century Hutchinson, 1985)

Index

Agello, Warrant Officer 19
Apt, Captain Milburn 151
Arnold, General H.H. 49, 59
Arsenal VG-90, 136
Atcherley, Flying Officer R.L.R.
  18
Atwood, John 'Lee' 108

Bachem Ba 349A Natter, 62, 189
Bad Zwischenahn, 72
Banks, F.R. 17, 19
Barnes, Florence 'Pancho' 106
Beamont, Roland 34–5, 81–2, 197
Bechereau, Louis 5, 9
Bell XP-59A Airacomet 49–51, 60,
  150
Bell XS-1, 98–101, 103–110, 120
Bell X-1 (second series), 148–150
Bell X-2, 150–1
Bell X-5, 77, 152–3
Berezniak-Isayev BI-1 62
Bettis, Lieutenant Cyrus 15
Bird-Wilson, Wing Commander
  Harold 192–3
Birkigt, Marc, 9
Bleriot, Louis 3
Boothman, Flight Lieutenant John
  18
Boscombe Down, 12, 111, 161,
  163, 165–6, 168–9, 176–7,
  191–2

Boyd, Colonel Al 105, 145
Brawdy, 162
Bridgeman, Bill 147–8
Briggs, A. 118
Bristol M.1C, 9
British Thomson Houston Co, 57
Brown, Eric 123–4, 160–1
Busemann, Adolf 24–25
Butler, Keith 99

Cactus Kitten (Curtiss), 13
Caldwell, Commander Turner
  146
Camm, Sydney 159, 162, 165
Cannon, Joseph 108
Carl, Major Marion 146
Carpentier, R. 143
Carter, George 45, 51
Cayley, Sir George 1
Cazaux, 193–5
Chanute, Octave 2
Chaplin, Herbert E. 190
Cody, S.F. 4
Coltishall, 200
Conant, Hersey 15
Constant, Hayne 59
Convair XF-92A, 154
Convair YF-102, 154–5, 191
Cox, S.E.J. 12
Cranwell, 46, 57
Crossfield, Scott 146, 148

Cuddihy, Lieutenant George 16
Cunningham, John 119, 181
Curtiss, Glenn 3
Curtiss CR-1, 13
Curtiss CR-2, 13
Curtiss R-6, 13–4
Curtiss R2C, 14
Curtiss R3C, 14–15

Dassault, Marcel 137, 193
Dassault Mirage III, 143, 193, 196
Dassauly Mystere II, 138
Dassault Mystere IV, 138
Dassault Ouragan, 137–8
Dassault Super Mystere B2, 138
Daunt, Michael 83
Davie, Squadron Leader Douglas
    46, 59
De Bernadi, Major Mario 16
De Havilland DH.108, 100,
    114–25, 152
De Havilland DH.110, 125, 181–8
De Havilland, Geoffrey 6
De Havilland, Geoffrey Jnr 115–9,
    123
De Havilland Ghost engine, 59
De Havilland H.1 Goblin engine,
    58–9
De Havilland Vampire, 53–5, 58,
    79, 187
De Havilland Venom, 179–180,
    187
Delage, Gustave, 11
Delagrange, Leon 4
Deperdussin racer 5, 7
Derry, John 100, 120–3, 179, 181–7
DFS 346
Dittmar, Heini 69–72
Donaldson, Group Captain E.M.
    81, 83–7
Doolittle, Lieutenant James H. 15
Douglas Skylancer, 157

Douglas Skyray, 157
Douglas Skyrocket, 146–8
Douglas Skystreak, 103, 145–6
Douglas X-3, 151–2
Drew, Major Adrian 192
Driffield, 55
Duke, Neville 81, 83–7, 165, 167
Dunn, Charlie 35
Dunsfold, 165
Dushkin, Leonid 62

Eades, Flight Lieutenant Gerry
    180
Edwards AFB, 147, 150–1
Ellor, Jimmy 17
English Electric, 119, 189
English Electric P.1A, 196–200
English Electric P.1B, 200
Everest, Major Frank 107, 148, 151

Fairey FD.1, 189–190
Fairey FD.2, 190–6, 201
Farman, Henry 3–4
Farnborough, 6, 46–7, 51, 59, 68,
    90, 116, 182–7
Fieseler Fi-103 (V-1), 63
Fitness, T. 117
Focke-Wulf Ta 183, 76–8
Folland, Henry 6, 11
Frost, Dick 106

Gallai, Mark 127
Garner, Dr H.M. 94, 96
Genders, Squadron Leader G.E.C.
    116
General Electric, 60
Gilkey, Major Signa 30
Gloucestershire Mars I, 11–2
Gloster E.28/39, 45–9, 57, 64–5
Gloster F.9/40 Meteor, 51–3, 59,
    65, 67, 79–88
Gloster GA.5 Javelin, 175–8, 187

Gluhareff, Michael 24
Gnome engine 4–5
Godfrey, Flight Lieutenant
    H.W.A. 117
Golds, Chris 180
Gonord, Jean 139
Goodlin, Chalmers 104–5
Gosling, Flight Lieutenant Clive
    67
Gothert, Dr 71
Goujon, Charles 142
Greenwood, Eric 79–81
Grierson, John 46
Griffith, John 108
Griffiths, Dr A.A. 59
Grinchik, Alexei 127
Grumman F9F-2 Panther, 156
Grumman F9F-6 Cougar, 156
Grumman F11F-1 Tiger, 156
Guignard, Jacques 143

Halahan, Wing Commander
    P.J.H. 183–4
Halford, Major Frank 53, 58–9
Hall, R. 117
Hanes, Colonel H.A. 192
Harbison, Flight Lieutenant
    Paddy, 111
Harrison, Flight Lieutenant N.F.
    113
Hatfield, 116, 119, 121,182
Hawker P.1035, 159
Hawker P.1040, 141, 160–2
Hawker P.1052 162–3
Hawker P.1067 (Hunter), 111,
    165–8, 174
Hawker P.1072, 141
Hawker P.1081, 163–5
Hawker Tempest, 56
Hawker Typhoon, 34–6
Heinemann, Ed 157
Heinkel, Ernst 61,68

Heinkel He 72, 68
Heinkel He 112, 68
Heinkel He 162, 75
Heinkel He 176, 69
Heinkel He 178, 64
Heinkel He 280, 65
Hendon, 12
Hibbard, Hall 29
Hillard, Bob 55
Hoover, Lieutenant R.A. 105
Horkey, Ed 108
Huffman Prairie, 3
Humble, Bill 160
Hunt, Squadron Leader D.A.C. 99

Jacobs, Eastman 24
Jenson, Jack 32
Johnson, Clarence L. 29, 32
Jones, Sir Melville 94, 96
Jones, Robert T. 25
Junkers Ju 287, 75

Kelley, Frank H. 49
Kelsey, Colonel Benjamin S. 32–3
Kennedy, H.V. 92
Kill Devil Hills, North Carolina 1
Kincheloe, Captain Iven 151
Kirkham, Charles 12
Klimov, Vladimir 130–1
Kositkov 302, 63
Kotcher, Ezra 103

Langley, S.P. 2
Langley Field, Virginia 32
Latham, Hubert 8
Lavochkin La-150, 129
Lavochkin La-152, 129
Lavochkin La-154, 129
Lavochkin La-156, 129
Lavochkin La-160, 129
Lavochkin La-168, 129
Lavochkin La-174TK, 129

Lavochkin La-176, 129
Lawrence, Peter 187
Leblon, Hubert 4
Leconte, Sadi, 11
Leduc, Rene 139
Leduc 010, 139
Leduc 021, 139–140
Leduc 022, 140
Leeming, 55
Levavasseur, Leon 3
Lewis, George W. 25
Lilienthal, Otto 1
Lilly, Howard 146
Lindner, Gerd 67
Lippisch, Alexander M. 68–70,
    154, 157, 176
Lithgow, Mike 169, 175
Littolf, Yvan 139
Lockheed P-38, 29–34
Lockheed P-80 Shooting Star, 60,
    79–80, 87, 106, 145, 156
Lockheed F-94, 156
Lockheed F-104 Starfighter, 156
Lockspeiser, Sir Ben 94–5, 97
Lucas, Philip 35

Macchi M.39 16
Macchi M.52 16
Macchi M.67 17
Macchi MC.72 18, 80
Mach, Ernst 21
Manley, Charles 2–3
March AFB, 110
Martin, Johnny 146
Martin, Wing Commander R.F.
    178
Martindale, Squadron Leader
    Tony 41–2
Maughan, Russell 14
May, Gene 145–7
McDonnell FH-1 Phantom, 60,
    156

McDonnell F2H Banshee, 156
McDonnell F3H Demon, 156
McDonnell F-4 Phantom II, 156–8
McDonnell F-101 Voodoo, 192
McKinnon Wood, R. 95
Messerschmitt Bf 109R, 70, 79
Messerschmitt Bf 110C, 70
Messerschmitt Me 163, 61, 69–75,
    126–7
Messerschmitt Me 262, 61, 65–8,
    78
Messerschmitt Me 263, 126–7
Messerschmitt P.1101, 77–8, 152–3
Metropolitan-Vickers, 59
MiG-9, 127–8
MiG-15, 78, 130–1
MiG-17, 131–2
MiG-19, 133–4
MiG-21, 134
MiG I-270, 126–7
MiG Ye 152, 135
Mikoyan, Artem 130
Miles, F.G. 92, 97
Miles, George 90
Miles 'Gillette Falcon', 92
Miles M.52, 89–102, 115, 120
Mitchell, General Billy 14
Mitchell, R.J. 17
Monti, Lieutenant Giovanni 18
Moreton Valence, 176
Motta, Captain Guiseppe 17
Mudge. F. 118
Muller-Rowland, Squadron
    Leader J.S.R. 124
Multhopp, Hans 76
Muroc, California 87, 104, 109,
    145, 147

Newby, J.W. 185
Nieuport-Delage 29, 11
Nord Gerfaut, 140
Nord Griffon, 141

North American F-100 Super
    Sabre, 109, 134, 153–4, 192
North American P-51 Mustang,
    36–8, 43–4
North American P-86 (Sabre),
    108–114, 131, 162
Northrop X-4, 152–3

Odiham, 177
Operation Neptune, 98–101
Opitz, Rudolf 72–3
Orlebar, Squadron Leader A.H.
    18
Ostertag, Wilhelm 68

Page, F.W. 197
Paul, Group Captain G.J.
    Christopher 184–5
Peenemunde, 72–3
Petter, W.E.W. 190, 196
Pilcher, Percy 2
Pinecastle Army Air Field, 104
Pixton, Howard, 8
Pohs, Oberleutnant Josef 72
Polikarpov Malyutka, 63
Popson, Major Raymond 153
Power Jets Ltd, 57–8, 90
Prevost, Maurice 5, 7–8
Pye, Dr D.R. 57

Quill, Jeffrey 168

Radlett, 116
Reed, Arthur 34
Reed, Dr S.A. 14
Republic F-84 Thunderjet, 60, 80,
    155
Republic F-84F Thunderstreak,
    155
Republic F-105 Thunderchief, 155
Republic P-47 Thunderbolt, 34, 37,
    39–41

Republic RF-84F Thunderflash,
    155
Republic XF-91 Thunderceptor,
    155
Republic XF-103, 155–6
Reynolds, J.H. McC 45
Richards, Anthony 182–3
Ridley, Captain Jack 105–6
Rittenhouse, Lieutenant David 15
Roe, Alliott Verdon 4
Rohlfs, Roland 12
Rolls-Royce, 58
Rover, 58
Rowledge, A.J. 17
Rozier, Jean-Pierre 143

Santos-Dumont, Alberto 3
Saro SR.A/1, 59
Sarrail, Jean 139
Saunders-Roe SR.53, 141
Saunders-Roe SR.177, 141
Sayer, P.E.G. 46
Schilt, Lieutenant Frank 16
Schneider, Jacques 7
S.E.4, 6
S.E.5, 9
Serby, J.E. 93
Servanty, Lucien 136,142
Seth-Smith, Ken 34
Sidgreaves, A.F. 19
Siebert, Oberleutnant Lothar 62
Skeel, Burt 14
Smelt, R. 94–5
Smith, Joe 92
SO.6000 Triton, 136
SO.6020 Espadon, 136
SO.9000/9050 Trident, 142–3
Sommer, Roger 4
Sopwith Snipe, 9
Sopwith Tabloid, 7–8
Sound Barrier (film), 182
Squire, S.M. 118

Stack, John 103
Stainforth, Flight Lieutenant G.H.
    18, 80
Stamer, Fritz 68
Stanbury, Philip 81
Stanley, Robert 150
Stephenson, Air Commodore
    Geoffrey 153
Sukhoi Su-7 (Fitter), 133
Sukhoi Su-9, 128
Sukhoi Su-9 (Fishpot), 133
Sukhoi Su-11, 128
Sukhoi Su-13, 128
Sukhoi Su-15, 129
Sukhoi Su-17, 130
Supermarine S.4, 15
Supermarine S.5, 16
Supermarine S.6/S.6B, 17–18
Supermarine Attacker, 168–170
Supermarine Spitfire, 34, 36–8,
    41–2, 44, 48, 56, 74, 91
Supermarine Swift, 172–5
Supermarine Type 510, 169–171
Supermarine Type 535, 171–2
Supermarine Type 545, 175
Symington, W. Stuart 110

Tangmere, 81–7, 116, 167
Taylor, Charles 3
Texas Wildcat (Curtiss), 12
Thornton, Flying Officer Neil, 174
Tizard, Sir Henry 58
Tobin, Squadron Leader J.R. 36
Twiss, Peter 191, 193

Udet, Ernst 70

Vedrines, Jules 5
Vessey, H.F. 95–6
Verdin, Lieutenant Commander
    James B. 157, 175
Virden, Ralph 31–32

Von Braun, Werner 68
Von Ohain, Hans Pabst 60–1, 64
Vought F7U Cutlass, 157
Vought F-8 Crusader, 157–8

Wade, Squadron Leader T.S.
    162–5
Waghorn, Flight Lieutenant H.R.
    18
Walker, Joseph 150, 152
Wallis, Barnes 95, 98
Walter, Hellmuth 61, 68, 73
Warsitz, Erich 64, 68–9
Warton, 197
Waters, S.J. 6
Waterton, W.A. 81, 83–7, 176–7
Webster, Flight Lieutenant S.N.
    16
Welch, George 109, 153–4
Wendel, Fritz 70, 79
Westinghouse, 60
West Raynham, 153, 167, 173,
    176–7
Weymann, Charles 7
Whitcomb, Richard T. 154, 156,
    198
Whitstable, 118
Whittle, Frank 45, 49, 56–60, 92–3
Williams, Al 14
Wilson, Wing Commander H.J.
    50, 79–80
Wilson, John 179
Wisley, 74
Wittering, 74
Wocke, Hans 75
Woodbridge, 115
Woolams, Jack 104
Wright, Orville 1
Wright, Wilbur 3, 7
Wright-Patterson AFB 3, 108
Wunstorf, 180

Yak-15, 127–8

Yak-17, 128

Yak-19, 128

Yak-25, 128, 132

Yak-30, 130, 132

Yak-50, 132

Yak-140, 132–3

Yeager, Captain C.E. 'Chuck'
    105–6, 109–111, 149–150

Yuganov, Viktor N. 130

Ziegler, Jean 150, 153